THE ULTIMATE ROCK GUITAR FAKE BOOK

INCLUDES TABLATURE

Two special listings and a Strumming Pattern section provide the "ultimate" in handy references and can be found on the following pages:

ALPHABETICAL LISTING — page 2

All songs are listed alphabetically with the page number on which each song can be found. The listing includes the artist who recorded the song.

ARTIST INDEX — page 6

An alphabetical listing of the major recording artists who performed the songs in this book with corresponding page numbers for the music.

STRUM PATTERNS — page 9

Shows how to play eighteen different **Strum Patterns.** Refer to this list for the numbered pattern suggested on each song.

7777 W. Bluemound Rd. P.O. Box 13819 Milwaukee, WI 53213

ISBN 0-88188-978-4

WHAT IS A FAKE BOOK?

When a musician is asked to play a song he's never played before, he "fakes" it. One of the most valuable possessions any musician can have is a **fake book** which contains the melodies, lyrics and chords for hundreds and hundreds of songs. With the access to the melody, lyrics and chords, the musician can improvise his own arrangement of a song.

In this fake book, **tablature** notation is also included for each song.

ALPHABETICAL LISTING

In the ALPHABETICAL LISTING, the song titles are listed alphabetically, followed by the name of the recording artist. The page on which each song can be found is the number to the left of the song title.

Editor's Note to Guitarists: If there is no X or O over a string in a chord diagram, the string(s) should not be played.

A

B

C

W

Y

ARTIST INDEX

STRUM PATTERNS

ABOUT THE STRUMS

The tunes in this fakebook include suggested strum patterns (Strum No. 2). These numbers refer to the numbered strumming patterns on the next two pages. Practice playing them with a flatpick and always keep your strumming wrist loose.

The strumming notation uses arrows to indicate up or down strokes; all other symbols are standard music notation (accents, ties, dotted notes, etc.) except for occasional x marks. These refer to the Chuck Berry-style extensions of barred chords, such as the following:

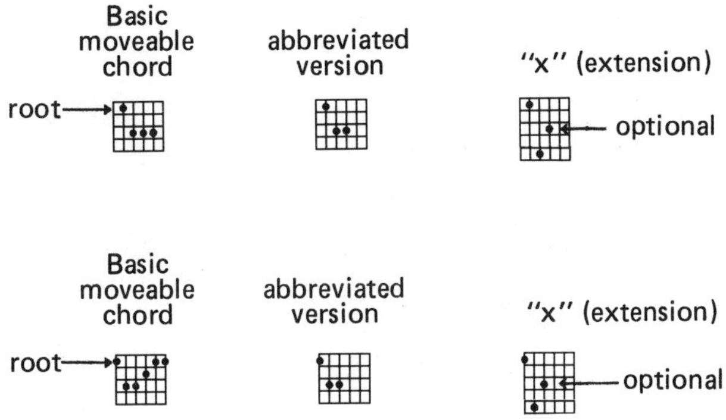

When a strum pattern has an eighth-note feel, strum eight alternating up-and-down-strokes, and do not touch the strings with your flatpick where tied notes or rests occur. This will help you strum smoothly and rhythmically. For example, on Strum Pattern No. 2:

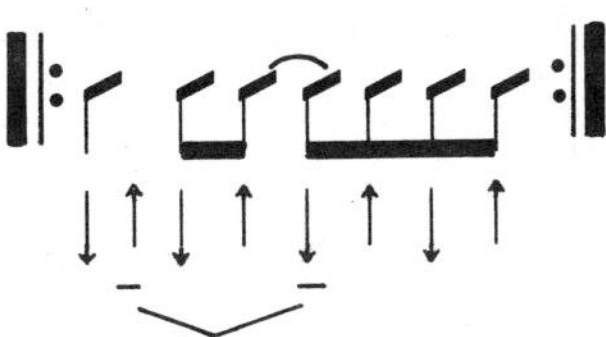

Do these strums without touching the strings.

Likewise, when a pattern has a sixteenth-note feel, do sixteen alternating up-and-down-strokes per measure and leave appropriate rests or ties by not touching strings. For example, on Strum Pattern No. 4:

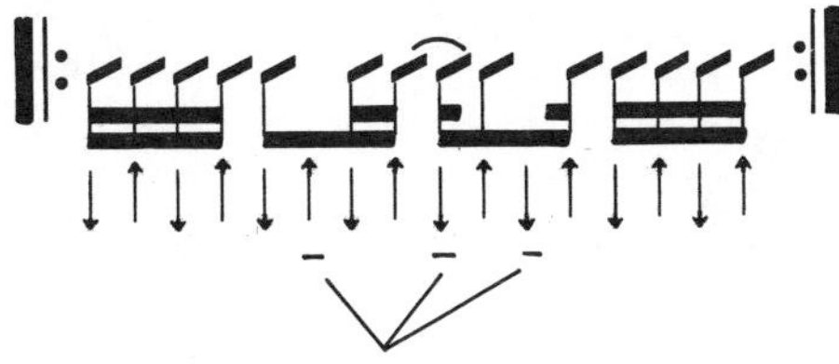

Strum, but do not touch the strings.

Notice that some shuffle beats are expressed two ways: With dotted notes, as is often done in pop and jazz notation, and with triplets, which is technically more accurate. (See Strum Pattern No. 7 for a sample.)

STRUM PATTERNS

No. 1 BASIC ROCK	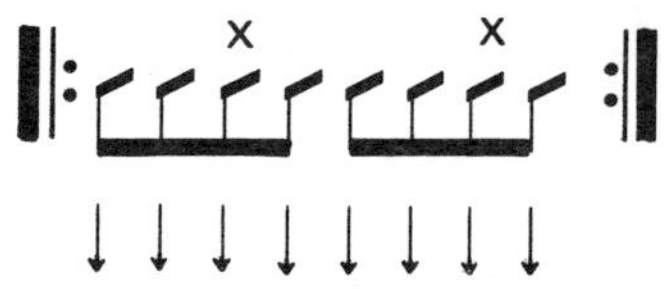 ↓ ↓ ↓ ↓ ↓ ↓ ↓ ↓	The most-often-used pattern in rock is all down-strokes. The "extensions" are optional. Examples: **DAY TRIPPER, SURFIN' U.S.A** most Chuck Berry tunes.
No. 2 BASIC ROCK	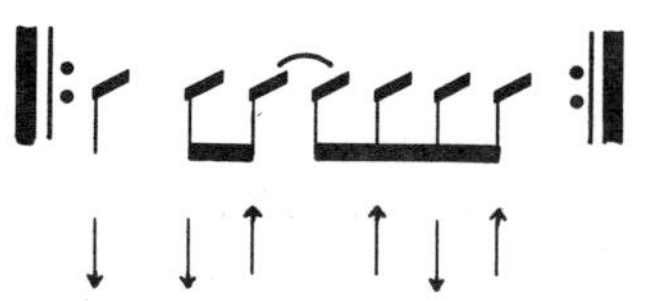 ↓ ↓ ↑ ↑ ↓ ↑	The second-most-used rock strum has a more easy-going feel than Strum Pattern No. 1 Examples: **HERE COMES THE SUN, STAN BY ME.**
No. 3 FUNK/ROCK	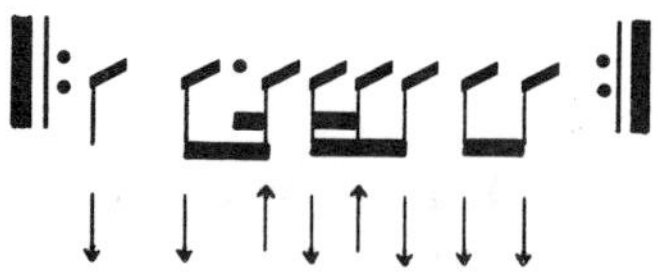 ↓ ↓ ↑ ↓ ↑ ↓ ↓ ↓	Remember to play all the sixteenth note strokes even though you only touch the strings on half of them. Examples: **WILD THING, SWEET HOME ALABAMA.**
No. 4 FUNK/DISCO	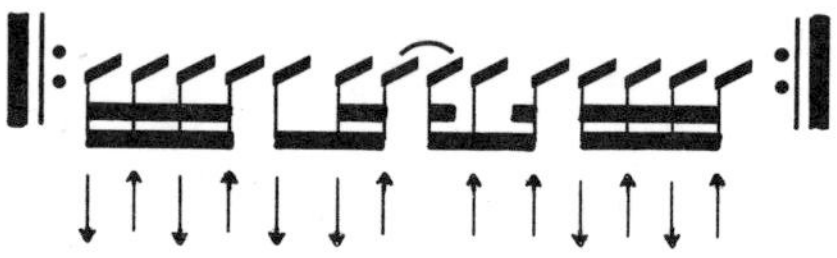 ↓ ↑ ↓ ↑ ↓ ↓ ↑ ↑ ↑ ↓ ↑ ↓ ↑	Example: **STAYIN' ALIVE**
No. 5 ROCK BALLAD	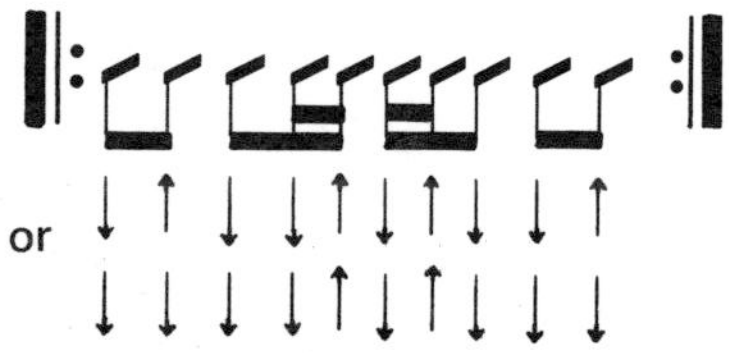 ↓ ↑ ↓ ↓ ↑ ↓ ↑ ↓ ↓ ↑ or ↓ ↓ ↓ ↓ ↑ ↓ ↑ ↓ ↓ ↓	Here are two possible up-and-down stroke patterns. Example: **HEY JUDE.** (Notice that Strum Pattern No. 5 is similar to a slowed-down Strum Pattern No. 3.
No. 6 FAST ROCK	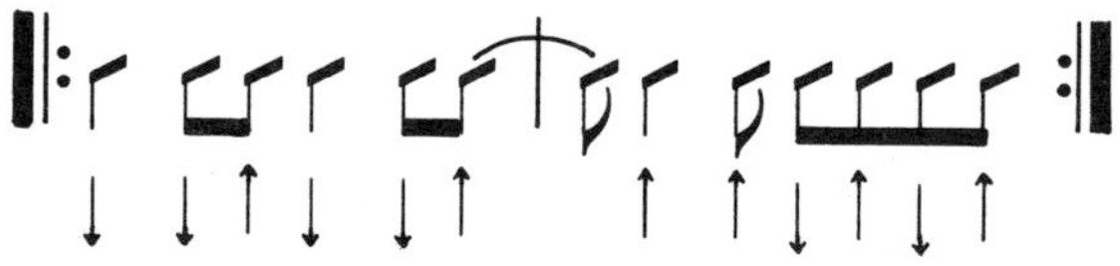 ↓ ↓ ↑ ↓ ↓ ↑ ↑ ↑ ↓ ↑ ↓ ↑	This strum pattern is two bars long. Be sure to play two bars of alternating up-and-down strokes (eight strokes per bar.) Example: **GOOD LOVIN'.**
No. 7 ROCK SHUFFLE	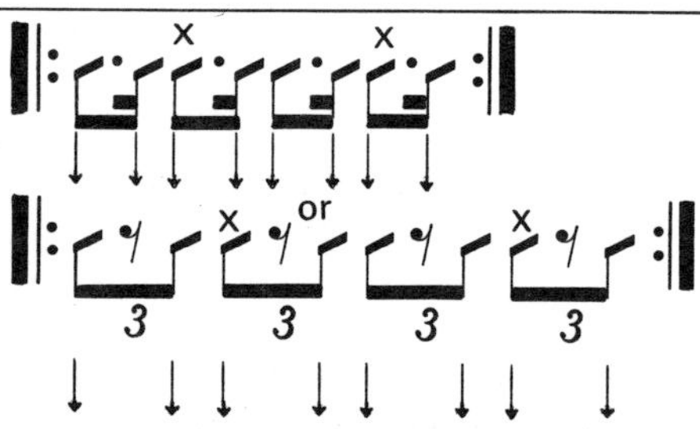 ↓ ↓ ↓ ↓ ↓ ↓ ↓ ↓ or 3 3 3 3 ↓ ↓ ↓ ↓ ↓ ↓ ↓ ↓	The extensions are optional Examples: **THAT'LL BE THE DAY, SOME KIND OF WONDERFUL, DOCTOR, MY EYES.**
No. 8 BOOGIE SHUFFLE	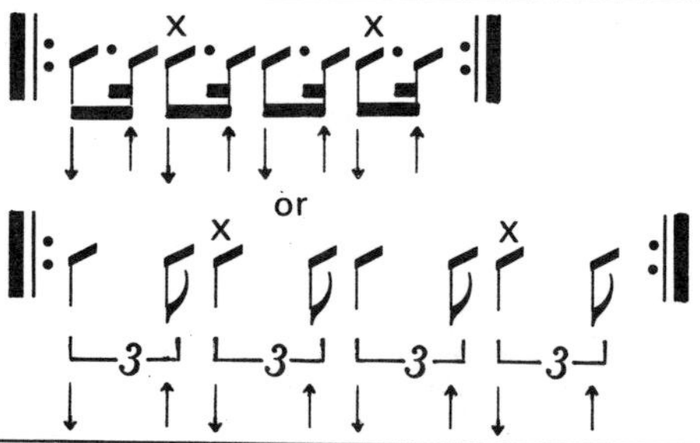 ↓ ↑ ↓ ↑ ↓ ↑ ↓ ↑ or 3 3 3 3 ↓ ↑ ↓ ↑ ↓ ↑ ↓ ↑	This is the same as Strum Pattern No. 7, but faster. The alternating up-and-down strokes allow for a speedier tempo. The extensions are optional. Examples: **BLUE SUEDE SHOES, AT THE HOP.**
No. 9 FAST COUNTRY SHUFFLE	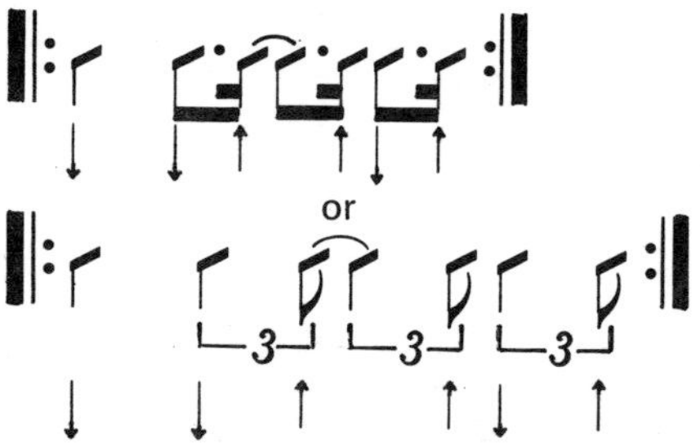 ↓ ↓ ↑ ↑ ↓ ↑ or 3 3 3 ↓ ↓ ↑ ↑ ↓ ↑	This strum pattern is like Strum Pattern No. 8, but with a little extra swing. Examples: **WAKE UP LITTLE SUSIE, CAN'T BUY ME LOVE.**

No. 10 FAST COUNTRY SHUFFLE	↓ ↓ ↑ ↓ ↓ ↑	Examples: **YAKETY YAK, WHO DO YOU LOVE**
No. 11 ROCK SHUFFLE	x x x x x ↓ ↓ ↓ ↓ ↓ ↓ ↑ ↑ ↓ ↑	Examples: **MEMPHIS TENNESSEE, HI-HEEL SNEAKERS' LAY DOWN SALLY**
No. 12 BO DIDDLEY - STYLE	↓ ↓ ↑ ↑ ↓ ↑ ↓ ↑ ↓ ↓	Examples: **BO DIDDLEY, NOT FADE AWAY**
No. 13 DISCO	↓ ↑ ↓ ↑ ↓ ↑ ↓ ↑ ↓ ↑ ↓ ↑ ↓ ↑ ↓ ↑	The accent can also fall on the *first* sixteenth note of each group of four instead of the *third* sixteenth note. Example: **JIVE TALKIN'**
No. 14 BOLERO	3 3 ↓ ↓ ↓ ↓ ↓ ↓ ↓ ↓	Example: **BECK'S BOLERO**
1 No. 15 7/4 ROCK	↓ ↓ ↑ ↓ ↓ ↓ ↓ ↑ ↓ or 3 3 ↓ ↓ ↑ ↓ ↓ ↓ ↓ ↑ ↓	Example: Pink Floyd's **MONEY**
No. 16 6/8 or 12/8 TIME	↓ ↓ ↑ ↓ ↓ ↓ ↓	Play this 6/8 figure twice in a row for one bar of 12/8 time. Examples: **SLEEP WALK, RED HOUSE**
No. 17 LATIN APACHE RHYTHM	↓ ↑ ↓ ↑ ↑ ↑	Example: **APACHE**
No. 18 WALTZ	↓ ↓ ↑ ↓ ↑	Could be used for backup on Randy Rhoad's **DEE**

Don't hesitate to experiment with all of these Strum Patterns. They can be varied in many different ways. For example, you can add sixteenth note strums to make a strum pattern more energetic and add accents to give a strum pattern a unique sound. It's a good idea to listen to records and other players to gain more ideas.

AIN'T NO WOMAN (LIKE THE ONE I'VE GOT)

Words and Music by
DENNIS LAMBERT and BRIAN POTTER

Fmaj7
Em7
Dm7
ask for things, no dia - mond rings.
real good friends, right to the end.
So to - geth - er, like a hand in glove, like pag - es in a let - ter.
I'm a lone - ly man when she's gone.
F/G
Ain't no wom-an like the one I love.
She can build me
(Instrumental)
D.S. 1st Chorus
Cmaj7
A7
2nd ending;
Repeat 2nd Chorus and Fade

ALL DAY AND ALL OF THE NIGHT

Words and Music by
RAY DAVIES

Bright Rock
Strum Pattern: No. 1
Capo: Up One Fret (Actual Key: A♭)
Intro

APACHE

By JERRY LORDAN

ALL THROUGH THE NIGHT

Words and Music by
JULES SHEAR

Am7
G
To Coda
1, 2
Em
Bm
3
Em
D.S. al Coda
-ing all through– the night. Un- til ___ it ends, there is ___ no end. ___
There is ___ no end.
CODA
Em
Bm
G
Em
C
Am7
D7
Repeat with vocal ad lib. and Fade
there is ___ no end. ___

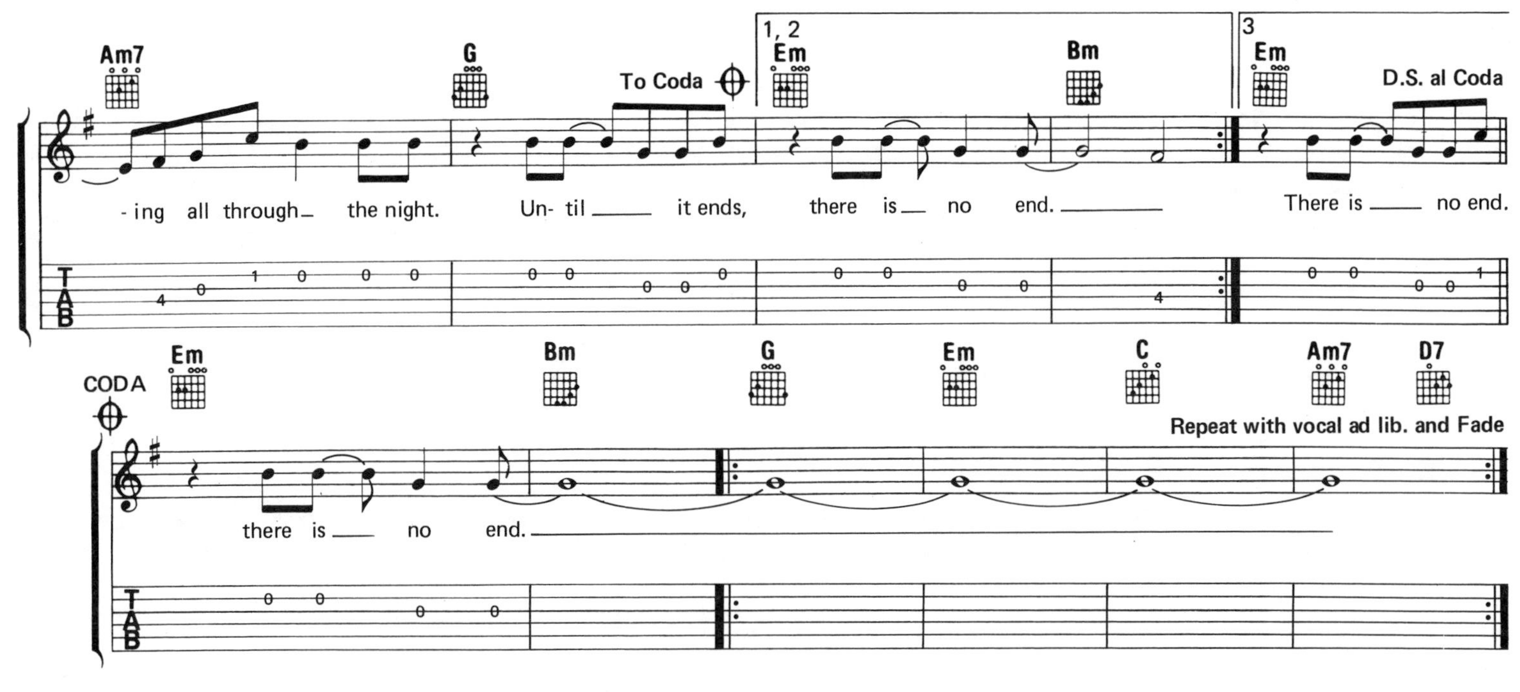

ALL I NEED IS A MIRACLE

Words and Music by
MICHAEL RUTHERFORD and CHRISTOPHER NEIL

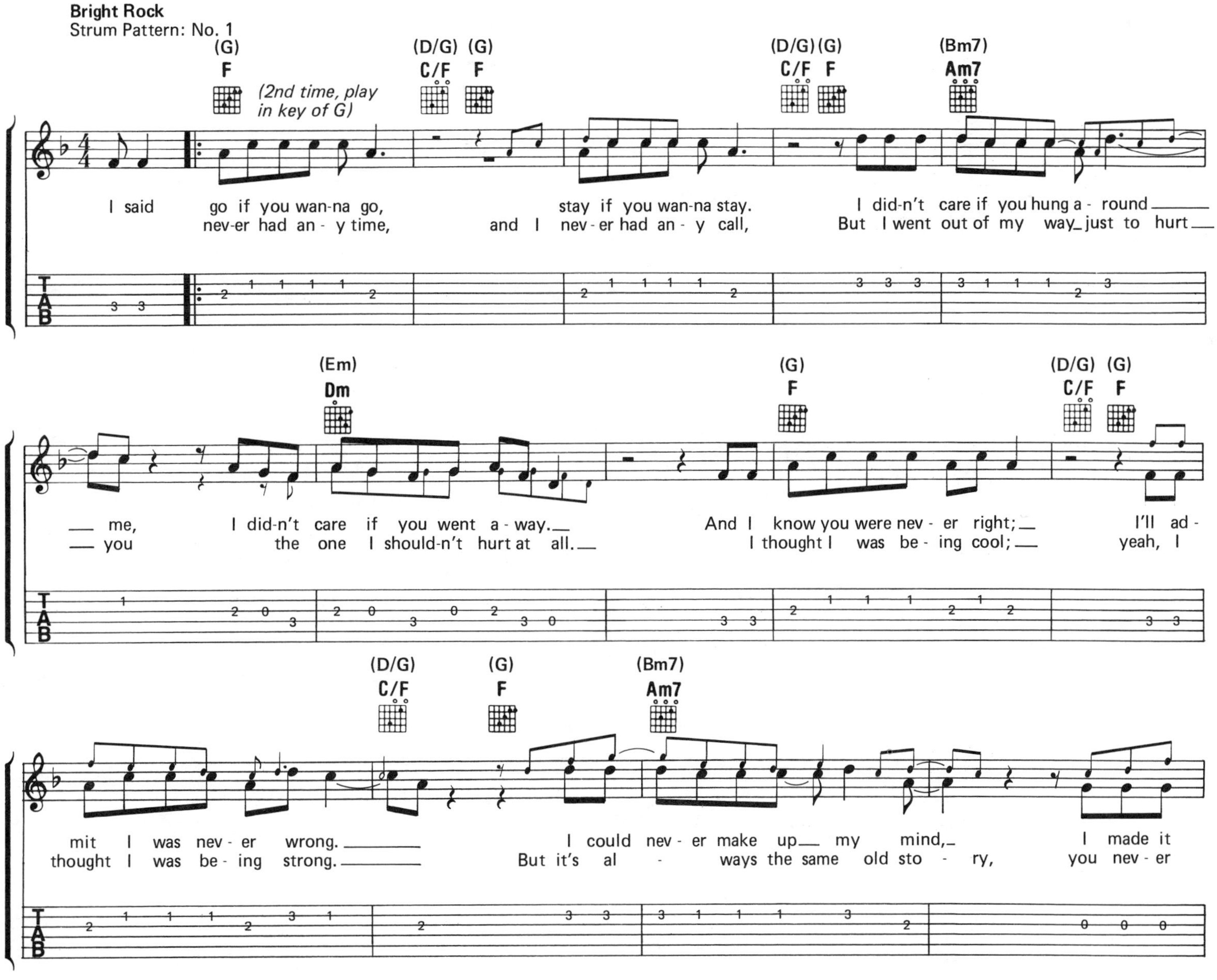

Bright Rock
Strum Pattern: No. 1
(G) F
(2nd time, play in key of G)
(D/G) C/F (G) F
(D/G) C/F (G) F
(Bm7) Am7
I said go if you wan-na go, stay if you wan-na stay. I did-n't care if you hung a - round ___
never had an - y time, and I nev-er had an - y call, But I went out of my way_ just to hurt ___
(Em) Dm
(G) F
(D/G) C/F (G) F
___ me, I did-n't care if you went a - way. ___ And I know you were nev - er right; ___ I'll ad -
___ you the one I should-n't hurt at all. ___ I thought I was be - ing cool; ___ yeah, I
(D/G) C/F
(G) F
(Bm7) Am7
mit I was nev - er wrong. ___ I could nev - er make up ___ my mind, ___ I made it
thought I was be - ing strong. ___ But it's al - ways the same old sto - ry, you nev - er

(Em) Dm
(C) Bb
(G/D) F/C
(C/E) Bb/D
up as I went a - long. And though I treat-ed you like a child, I'm gon-na miss you for the rest of my life.
know what you've got till it's gone. If I(2,3) ev-er catch up with you I'm gon-na love you for the rest of your life.
CHORUS
(G) F
(D/E) C/D
(D) C
(2nd time, key of D)
(G/B) F/A
(D/A) C/G
All I need is a mir - a-cle. All I need is you.
(G) F
(D) C
(G/B) F/A
(D/A) C/G
(G) F
To Coda
All I need is a mir - a-cle. All I need is you
(D) C
(G/B) F/A
(D/A) C/G
(G) F
1 C/D
modulate to key of G
2 D/E
modulate to key of A
All I need is a mir - a-cle, All I need is you. I
(Instrumental)
A
E/A
A
E/A
A
C#m7
F#m7
D.S. al Coda (Key of G)
And if I
CODA
D
G/B
D/A
G
Repeat and Fade
All I need is a mir - a-cle. All I need is you.

AT THE HOP

Words and Music by ARTHUR SINGER, JOHN MEDORA and DAVID WHITE

BACK IN THE U.S.A.

Words & Music by
CHUCK BERRY

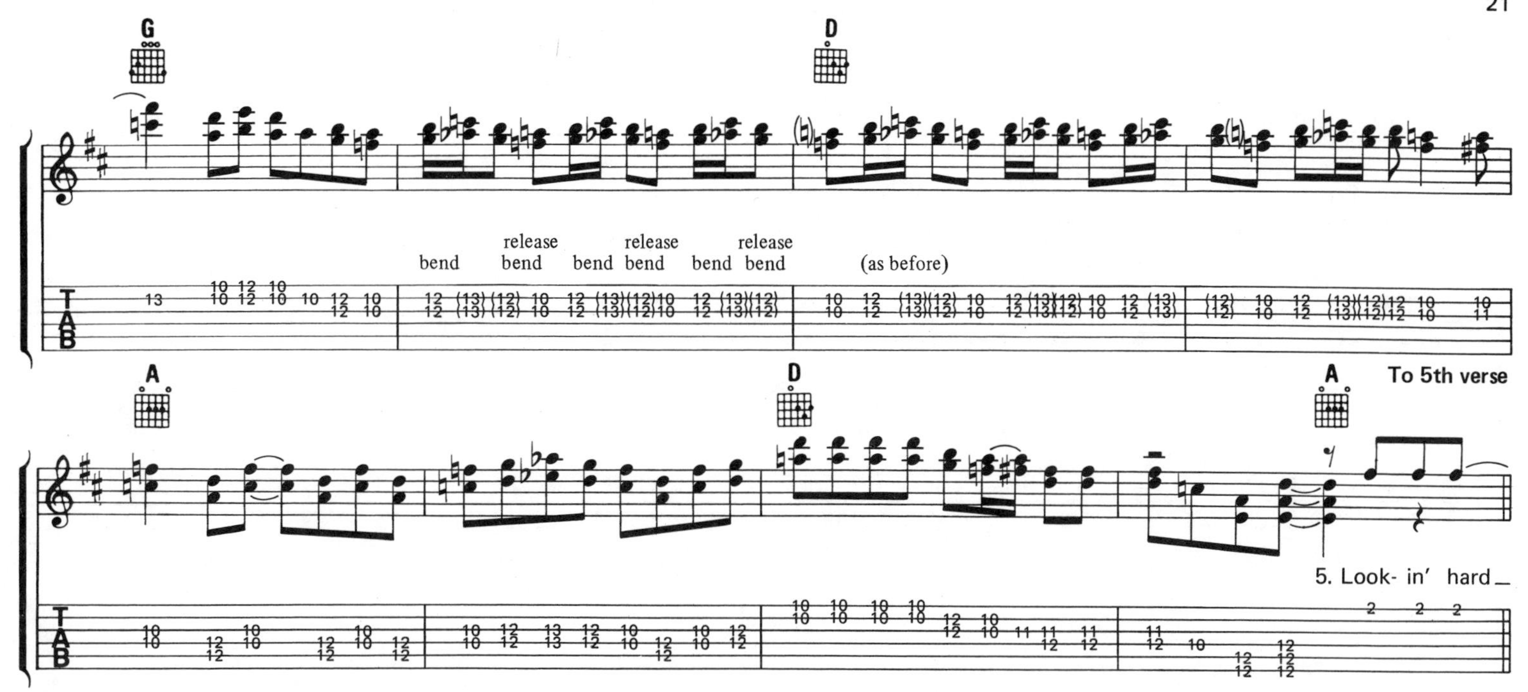

3. Did I miss the skyscrapers, did I miss the long freeway?
From the coast of California to the shores of the Delaware Bay.
You can bet your life I did, 'til I got back to the U.S.A.

4. *(Guitar solo)*

5. Lookin' hard for a drive-in, searchin' for a corner café,
where hamburgers sizzle on an open grill, night and day,
yeah, and a juke box jumpin' with records like in the U.S.A.

6. Well I'm so glad I'm livin' in the U.S.A.
Yes, I'm so glad I'm livin' in the U.S.A.
Anything you want, they got it right here in the U.S.A.

7. I'm so glad I'm livin' in the U.S.A.
Yes, I'm so glad I'm livin' in the U.S.A. (Fade)

BAND ON THE RUN

Words and Music by McCARTNEY

Em G C Em C Am
(Guitar)
There's a
C Fmaj7 C Fmaj7 C Fmaj7 C Fmaj7
D.S. al Coda
band on the run,
band on the run.
Well the
CODA
Fmaj7 Cmaj7 Fmaj7
coun-ty judge who held a grudge will search for-ev-er-more for the
C Fmaj7 C Fmaj7 C Fmaj7 C Fmaj7 Em G C
band on the run, the band on the run.
(Guitar)

BANG A GONG (GET IT ON)

Words and Music by
MARC BOLAN

Moderate Rock
Strum Pattern: No. 1

E A E A E

1. Well, you're dir - ty and clad in black, don't look back and I love you. You're dir - ty and sweet, oh yeah.
2.,3. *(see additional lyrics)*

A E

Well, you're slim and you're weak, you've got the teeth of a hy - dra up - on you. You're

A E G6 A E

dir - ty sweet and you're my girl.

CHORUS

Repeat, ad lib. for Fade

Get it on, bang a gong. Get it on. Get it on,

G6 A E

bang a gong. Get it on.

1, 2

3, 4

2. Well, you're built
3. Well, you're wind-

2. Well, you're built like a car;
You've got a hub cap diamond star halo.
You're built like a car, oh yeah.
Well, you're an untamed youth,
That's the truth, with your cloak full of eagles.
You're dirty sweet and you're my girl. *(Chorus)*

3. Well, you're windy and wild,
You've got the blues in your shoes and your stockings.
You're windy and wild, oh yeah.
Well, you're built like a car;
You've got a hub cap diamond star halo.
You're dirty sweet and you're my girl. *(Chorus)*

4. Well, you're dirty and sweet,
Clad in black, don't look back and I love you.
You're dirty and sweet, oh yeah.
Well, you dance when you walk.
So let's dance, take a chance, understand me.
You're dirty sweet and you're my girl. *(Chorus Fade)*

BECK'S BOLERO

C
B♭
D
C
D
C
E
D.C. al Coda
CODA
G
A
G
A
G
A
Play 7 times
(ad lib. Guitar solo)
THE BITCH IS BACK
Copyright © 1974 by Big Pig Music Ltd.
All Rights for the United States administered by Intersong–USA, Inc.
Words and Music by
ELTON JOHN and BERNIE TAUPIN
Moderate Rock
Strum Pattern: No. 1
Capo: Up One Fret (Actual Key: A♭)
Intro
G
1,2,3
Gsus
4
Gsus
(Guitar)
I was
I
G
D
G
just - i - fied when I was five, rais - in' Caine; I spit in your eye.
Eat meat on a Fri - day if that's all right. I e - ven like steak on a Sat-ur-day night. I can
en - ter - tain by pick - in' brains. Sell my soul by drop - pin' names. I
F
C
G
Times are chang - in', now the poor get fat, but the fe - ver's gon - na catch you when the bitch gets back. Uh huh!
bitch the best at your so - cial do's, I get high in the eve - nin' sniff - in' pots of glue. Ooh ooh!
don't like those! My God, what's that? Oh, it's full of nas - ty hab - its when the bitch gets back. Ooh - uh - huh!

1
Gsus G Gsus G Gsus G Gsus G Gsus G Gsus G
(Guitar)
2,3
Gsus G Gsus G D
(Guitar)
I'm a bitch, I'm a bitch, oh the
Em C D
bitch is back; stone cold so - ber, as a mat - ter of fact. I can bitch, I can bitch 'cause I'm
F D
D.C. al Coda
bet - ter than you. It's the way that I move; it's the things that I do, ohh.
CODA
G Gsus
(Guitar)
G7 F C G7 F C
Repeat and Fade
Bitch! Bitch! The bitch is back!

BLACKBIRD

Words and Music by
JOHN LENNON and PAUL McCARTNEY

Bright And Bouncy Shuffle
Strum Pattern: No. 10

Intro

G Am G/B G G Am G/B G

(Instrumental)

1.,3. Black-bird sing-ing in the dead of night.
2. Black-bird sing-ing in the dead of night.

C A7 D7 B7 Em Cm D A7 Cm G A7 To Coda

Take these bro-ken wings and learn to fly.
Take these sunk-en eyes and learn to see.
All your life, you were on-ly wait-ing for this

1. D7 G C G/B A D7 G

mo-ment to a-rise.

(Instrumental)

2. D7 G

mo-ment to be free.

F C/E Dm C B♭ C F C/E Dm C B♭ A7 D7

Black-bird, fly. Black-bird, fly, in-to the light of a dark black night.

G Am G/B G

night.

(Instrumental)

1. C A7 D7 B7 Em Cm

D A7 C Cm G/B A7 D7sus G
2
ritard.
a tempo
G Am G/B C G/B A7 D7sus
D.S. al Coda
CODA
D7 G C G/B A7 D7 G C G/B A7 D7 G
ritard.
mo-ment to a-rise. You were on-ly wait-ing for this mo-ment to a-rise.__ You were on-ly wait-ing for this mo-ment to a-rise.__
BLUE JEAN
©1984 Jones Music
Words and Music by
DAVID BOWIE
Medium Fast Rock
Strum Pattern: No. 1
C G D
Blue Jean, I just met a girl named Blue__ Jean. Blue Jean, she's got a
One day I'm gon-na write a po-em in a let-ter. One day I'm
G
cam-ou-flaged face and no mon-ey. Re-mem-ber, they al-ways let you down when you need 'em, Oh,
gon-na get that fac-ul-ty to-geth-er. Re-mem-ber, like ev-'ry-bod-y has to wait in line.__ Oh,
D C
Blue Jean, is heav-en an-y sweet-er than Blue Jean? She got a po-lice bike,
Blue Jean, look out world,_uh, you know, I've got mine. She got Lat-in roots

D
C
G
A
F♯m
she got turned up nose.
she got ev - 'ry - thing.
Some-times I feel like (oh,
the whole hu - man race,)
jazz - in' for Blue Jean. (oh,
and when my Blue Jean's
blue,)
Blue Jean can send me, (oh,
some-bod - y send me,)
To Coda
1
2
some - bod - y send me. (oh
some - bod - y send me.)
G11
Gmaj9
D.S. al Coda
(Guitar)
Some-times I feel like
CODA
Some-bod - y, some-bod - y, (oh,
some - bod - y send me,)
E(no3rd)
some-bod - y send me. (Oh
some - bod-y send me.) (Instrumental)

BLUE SUEDE SHOES

Words and Music by
CARL LEE PERKINS

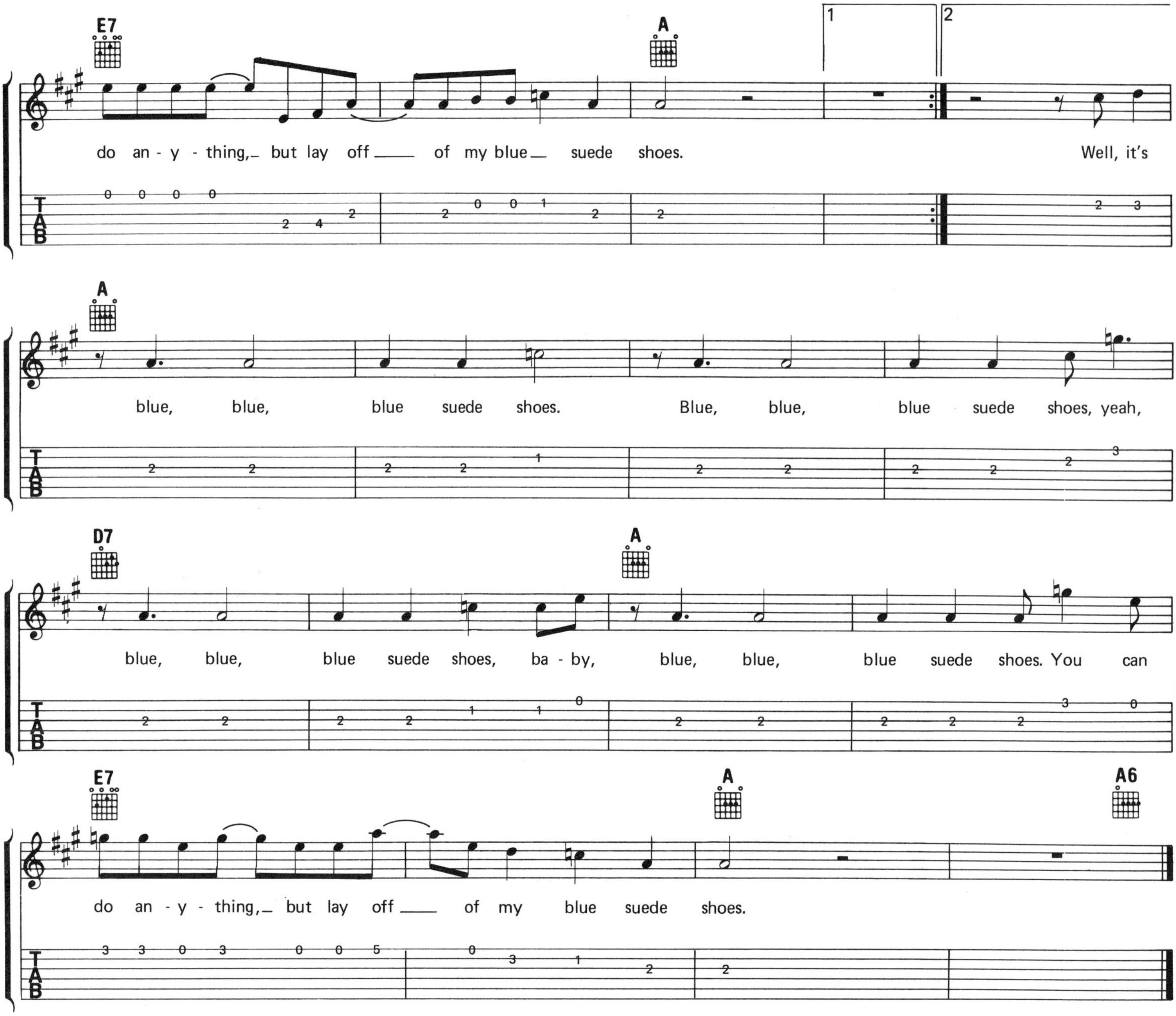

E7
A
1
2
do an - y - thing, but lay off of my blue suede shoes.
Well, it's
A
blue, blue, blue suede shoes. Blue, blue, blue suede shoes, yeah,
D7
A
blue, blue, blue suede shoes, ba - by, blue, blue, blue suede shoes. You can
E7
A
A6
do an - y - thing, but lay off of my blue suede shoes.

BO DIDDLEY

Words & Music by
ELLAS McDANIEL

Bo Diddley Beat
Strum Pattern: No. 12
Play 4 times

G
G
(Ad lib. rhythm guitar)
1. Bo Did - dley - 'll buy his ba - by a dia - mond ring.
2. Bo Did - dley caught a nan - ny goat,
3.,4. (see additional lyrics)

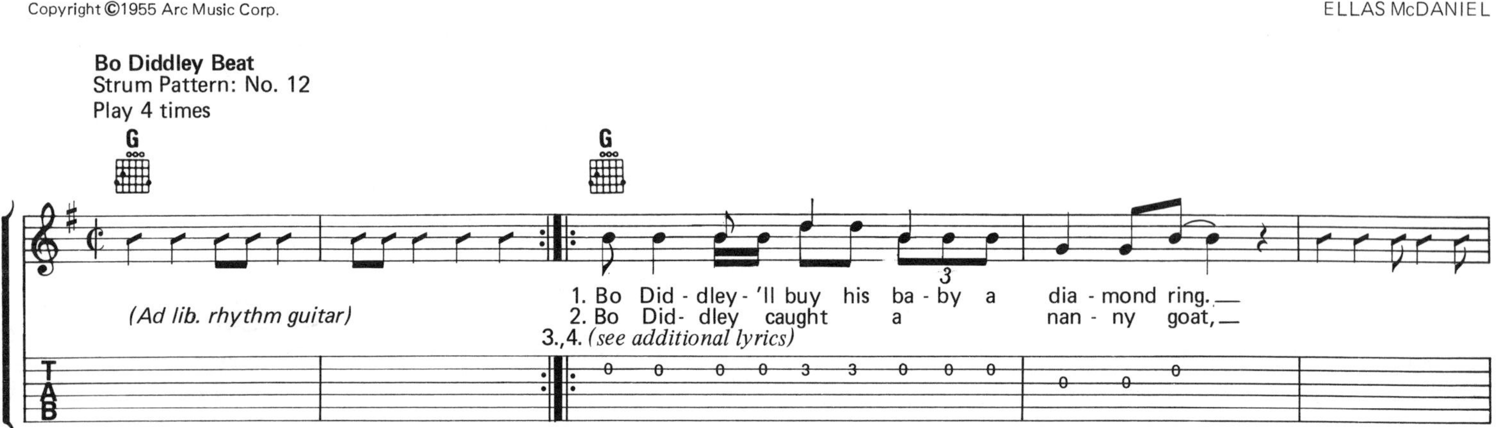

3. Mojo come to my house, a black cat bone.
Take my baby away from home.
Mother asked Mojo, where's he been?
"Up your house and gone again."

4. Bo Diddley, Bo Diddley, have you heard?
My pretty baby said she was a bird.

BODHISATTVA

Words and Music by
WALTER BECKER and DONALD FAGEN

G
Ebmaj7
A7+5
Dm7
F6
Ebmaj7
F6
G
1
Repeat w/ad lib. guitar
2
D.S. al Coda
(with repeats)
Bo - dhi -
CODA
Repeat and Fade
satt - va? Bo - dhi -

BORN TO BE WILD

Words and Music by
MARS BONFIRE

CAN'T BUY ME LOVE

Words and Music by
JOHN LENNON and PAUL McCARTNEY

F7
C7
I'll be sat - is fied.
Tell me that you want the kind of things that mon - ey just can't buy.
G7
F7
Tacet
F7
To Coda
C7
I don't care too much for mon - ey, mon - ey can't buy me love.
(Guitar solo)
C7
release bend
release bend
F7
C7
G7
F7
C7
D.S. al Coda
release bend
Buy me love
CODA
C7
Em
Am
Em
Can't buy me love, oh. Love, oh.
Am
Dm7
G7
C7
Can't buy me love, oh, oh.

CARELESS WHISPER

Words and Music by
GEORGE MICHAEL and ANDREW RIDGELEY

Dm
Gm7
Am7
B♭maj7
To Coda
should have known bet-ter than to cheat a friend,_ and waste a chance that I've_ been giv - en, so I'm nev-er gon-na dance a-gain_ the
1
Am7
Dm
Gm7
Am7
B♭maj7
Am7
way I dance_with you._
2
Am7
D.C. al Coda
(no repeat)
way I dance_with you, oh._
CODA
Am7
Dm
Repeat Intro and Fade
way I dance_with you._

CELEBRATE

Words and Music by
ALAN GORDON and GARRY BONNER

CHANTILLY LACE

Words and Music by
J. P. RICHARDSON

Bright Boogie Woogie
Strum Pattern: No. 8
Capo: Up One Fret (Actual Key: G♭)

Spoken verses (same changes as Chorus):

1. *Hello baby, yeah, this is the Big Bopper speakin'.*
   Ha, ha, ha, ha, ha, ha, oh you sweet thing.
   Do I what? Will I what? Oh, baby, you know what I like. (CHORUS)

2. *Uh, what's that, baby? But...but...but...oh, honey,*
   But...oh, baby, you know what I like. (CHORUS)

3. *What's that honey? Pick you up at eight? And don't be late?*
   But, baby, I ain't got no money, honey.
   Ha, ha, ha, ha, ha, oh all right, honey, you know what I like. (CHORUS)

CHILDREN OF THE GRAVE

Words and Music by FRANK IOMMI, WILLIAM WARD, JOHN OSBOURNE and TERENCE BUTLER

E(no3rd)
D.S. al Coda
(no repeats, lyric 2)
love comes flow - ing through.
CODA I
will they dis - ap - pear?
Em
G(no3rd)
C(no3rd)
D(no3rd)
N.C.
Em
G(no3rd)
Em
B(no3rd)
B♭(no3rd)
B(no3rd)
C♯(no3rd)
D(no3rd)
Em
G(no3rd)
Em
D(no3rd)
C♯(no3rd)
D(no3rd)
E
C(no3rd)
B(no3rd)
E
D.S. al Coda
(no repeats, lyric 3)
C(no3rd)
B(no3rd)
CODA II
chil - dren of the grave.
Em
G(no3rd)
C(no3rd)

D(no3rd)
E(no3rd)
G(no3rd)
(Guitar solo)
bend
release bend
C(no3rd)
8va
loco
Em
N.C.
Play 3 times

COOL JERK

Words and Music by
DONALD STORBALL

Bright Rock
Strum Pattern: No. 6
Capo: Up One Fret (Actual Key: E♭)

Intro

D Am7 A7 (Play 4 times) D Am7 A7 D

Cool Jerk We know a cat who can real - ly do the Cool Jerk

1 Am7 A7 | 2 A7 G7 Dm7 G Dm7

Well, this cat they're talk - ing a - bout I won - der who could it be.

G D

'Cause I know that I'm the heav - i - est cat, the heav - i - est cat you ev - er did see.

F♯m Bm F♯m Bm

When you see me walk - ing down the street none of the fel - lows want to speak,
When you see me walk - ing down the street they think twice and then they speak,

G A7 Tacet

On their fac - es they wear a sil - ly smirk, 'cause they know I'm the king of the Cool Jerk.
On their fac - es they don't wear that smirk, 'cause they know I'm the king of the Cool Jerk.

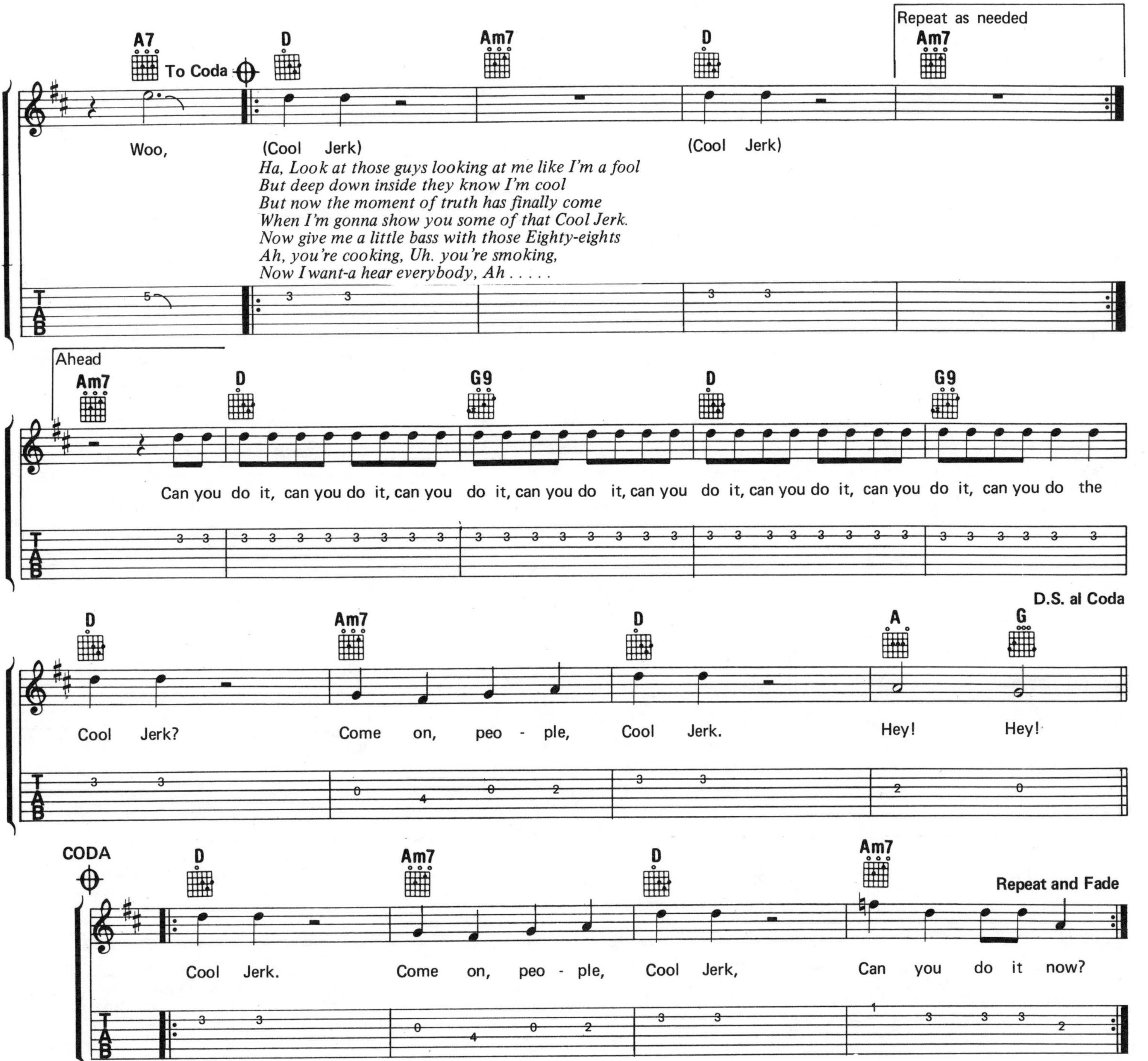
Repeat as needed
A7
To Coda
D
Am7
D
Am7
Woo,
(Cool Jerk)
(Cool Jerk)
Ha, Look at those guys looking at me like I'm a fool
But deep down inside they know I'm cool
But now the moment of truth has finally come
When I'm gonna show you some of that Cool Jerk.
Now give me a little bass with those Eighty-eights
Ah, you're cooking, Uh. you're smoking,
Now I want-a hear everybody, Ah . . . . .
Ahead
Am7
D
G9
D
G9
Can you do it, can you do it, can you do it, can you do it, can you do it, can you do it, can you do it, can you do the
D.S. al Coda
D
Am7
D
A
G
Cool Jerk?
Come on, peo - ple,
Cool Jerk.
Hey!
Hey!
CODA
D
Am7
D
Am7
Repeat and Fade
Cool Jerk.
Come on, peo - ple,
Cool Jerk,
Can you do it now?

CROCODILE ROCK

Words and Music by
ELTON JOHN and BERNIE TAUPIN

Fast Rock
Strum Pattern: No. 1

G Em C D7

(First time, just rhythm)

G Bm

1.,3. I re - mem - ber when rock was young, me and Su - sie had so much fun,
2. But the years went by and rock just died. Su - sie went and left me

C D

holding hands and skim-min' stones. Had an old gold Chev - y and a
for some for - eign guy. Long nights cry - in' by the rec-ord ma-chine, dream - in' of my Chev-y and my

G Bm

place of my own. But the big - gest kick I ev - er got was do - in' a thing called the Croc-o - dile
old blue jeans. But they'll nev - er kill the thrills we got burn - in' up to the Croc-o - dile

C D

Rock. While the oth - er kids were rock - in' 'round the clock, we were hop - pin' and bop - pin' to the
Rock. Learn - ing fast as the weeks went past, we real - ly thought the Croc - o - dile

Em A7

Croc - o - dile Rock. / Rock would last. } Well, Croc - o - dile Rock-in' is some - thin' shock - in' when your feet just can't keep

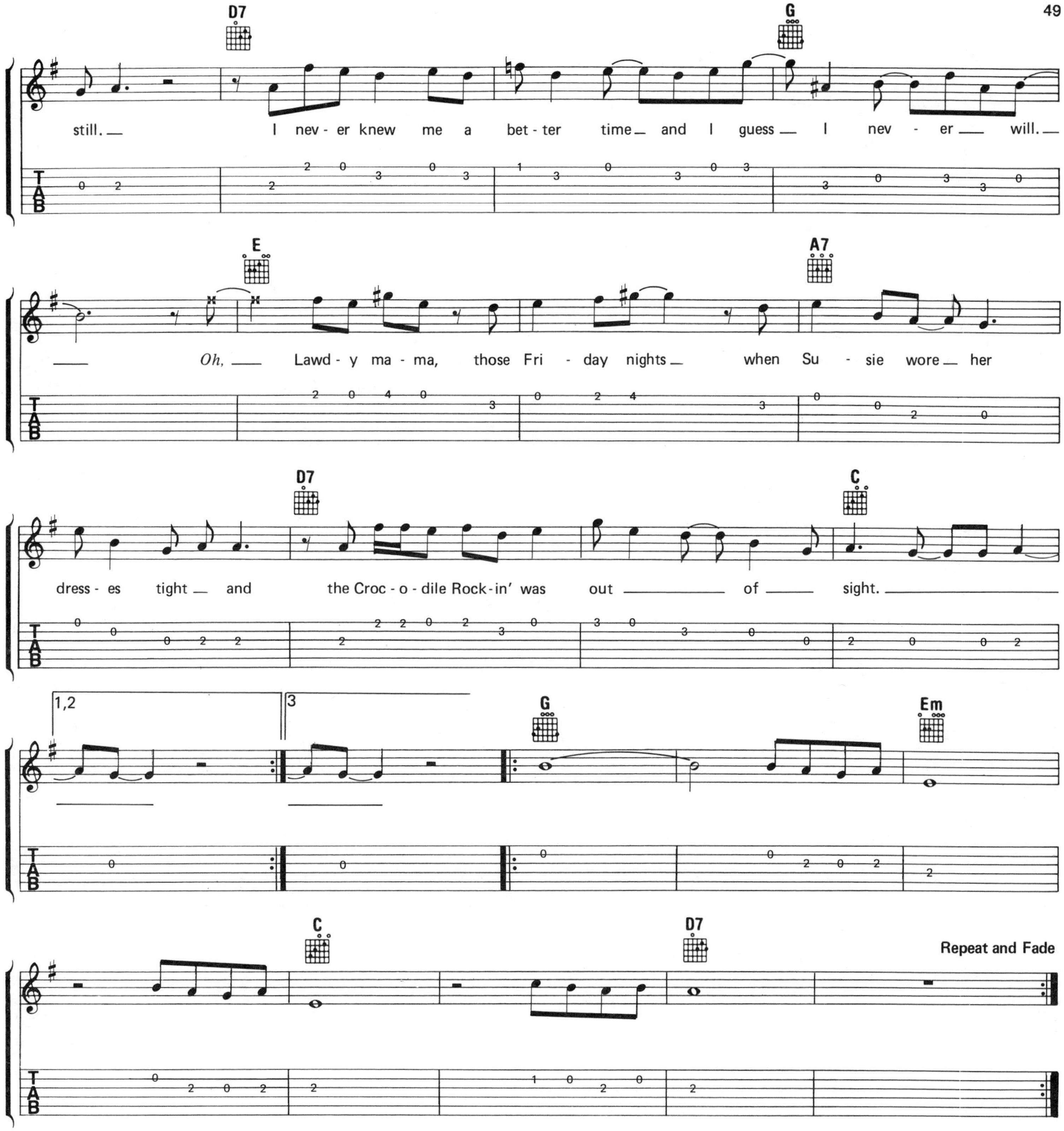

D7
G
still. I nev-er knew me a bet-ter time and I guess I nev-er will.
E
A7
Oh, Lawd-y ma-ma, those Fri-day nights when Su-sie wore her
D7
C
dress-es tight and the Croc-o-dile Rock-in' was out of sight.
1,2
3
G
Em
C
D7
Repeat and Fade

DAY TRIPPER

Words and Music by
JOHN LENNON and PAUL McCARTNEY

Moderate Rock
Strum Pattern: No. 1

Tacet

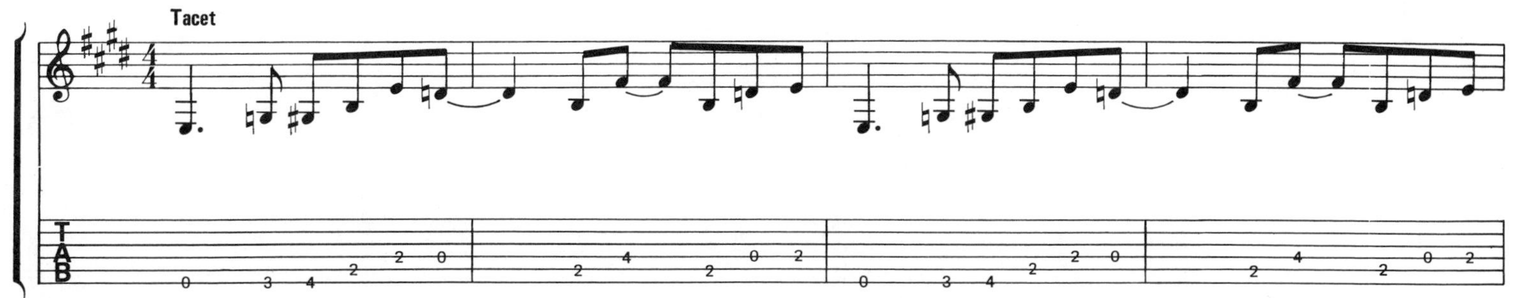

E7
Got a good rea - son for tak - ing the eas - y way out.
She's a big teas - er. She took me half the way there.
Tried to please her. She on - ly played one night stands.
A7
E7
Got a good rea - son for tak - ing the eas - y way out, now.
She's a big teas - er. She took me half the way there, now.
Tried to please her. She on - ly played one night stands, now.
She was a
F#
day trip - per, one way tick - et, yeah.
(3rd verse:) Sun-day driv - er,
It took me
A7
G#7
C#7
B7
(3rd time)
To Coda
so long to find out, and I found out.
(2nd time to Instrumental)
B
Play 3 times
D.C. al Coda (3rd verse)
(Instrumental)
Ah
CODA
Play 4 times
E7
Repeat and Fade
Day trip - per, day trip - per, yeah.

DEE

By RANDY RHOADS

Moderate Waltz
Strum Pattern: No. 18

DOCTOR! DOCTOR!

Ab Fm7 Bb Gm Ab Fm7
Doc - tor, Doc - tor, can't you see I'm burn - ing, burn - ing; oh Doc - tor, Doc - tor, is this love I'm
Bb Gsus G Ab Bb
To Coda
feel - ing? Fev - er breathe your love on me, take a - way my name.
Ab Bb G C Eb Bb/D
D.S. al Coda (2nd ending)
Fev - er lay your hands on me, nev - er be the same. Oh
CODA
C Eb Bb/D C
Come with me and make be - lieve we can tra - vel to
Eb Bb/D C Eb Bb/D
Repeat and Fade
e - ter - ni - ty,
(Instrumental)

DOCTOR, MY EYES

Words and Music by
JACKSON BROWNE

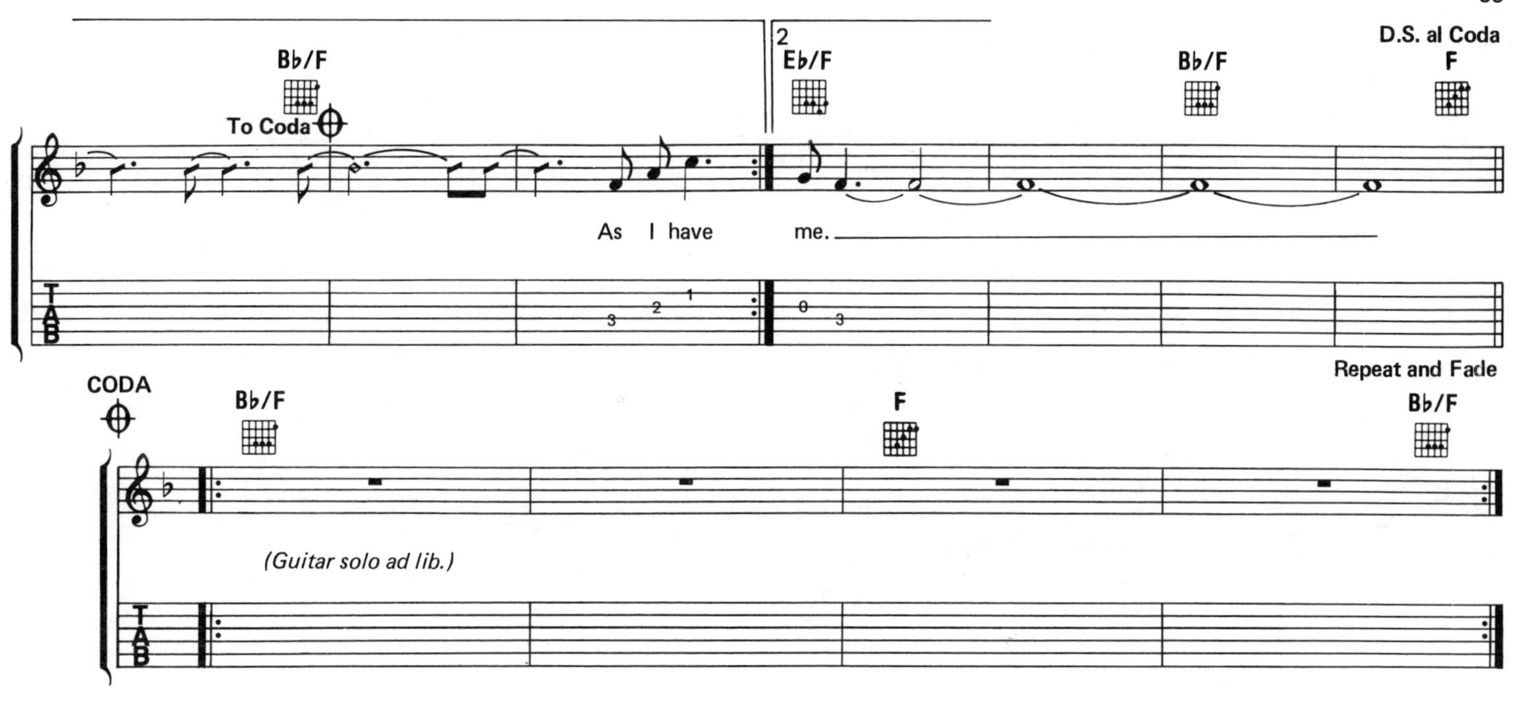

DIZZY MISS LIZZIE

Words and Music by
LARRY WILLIAMS

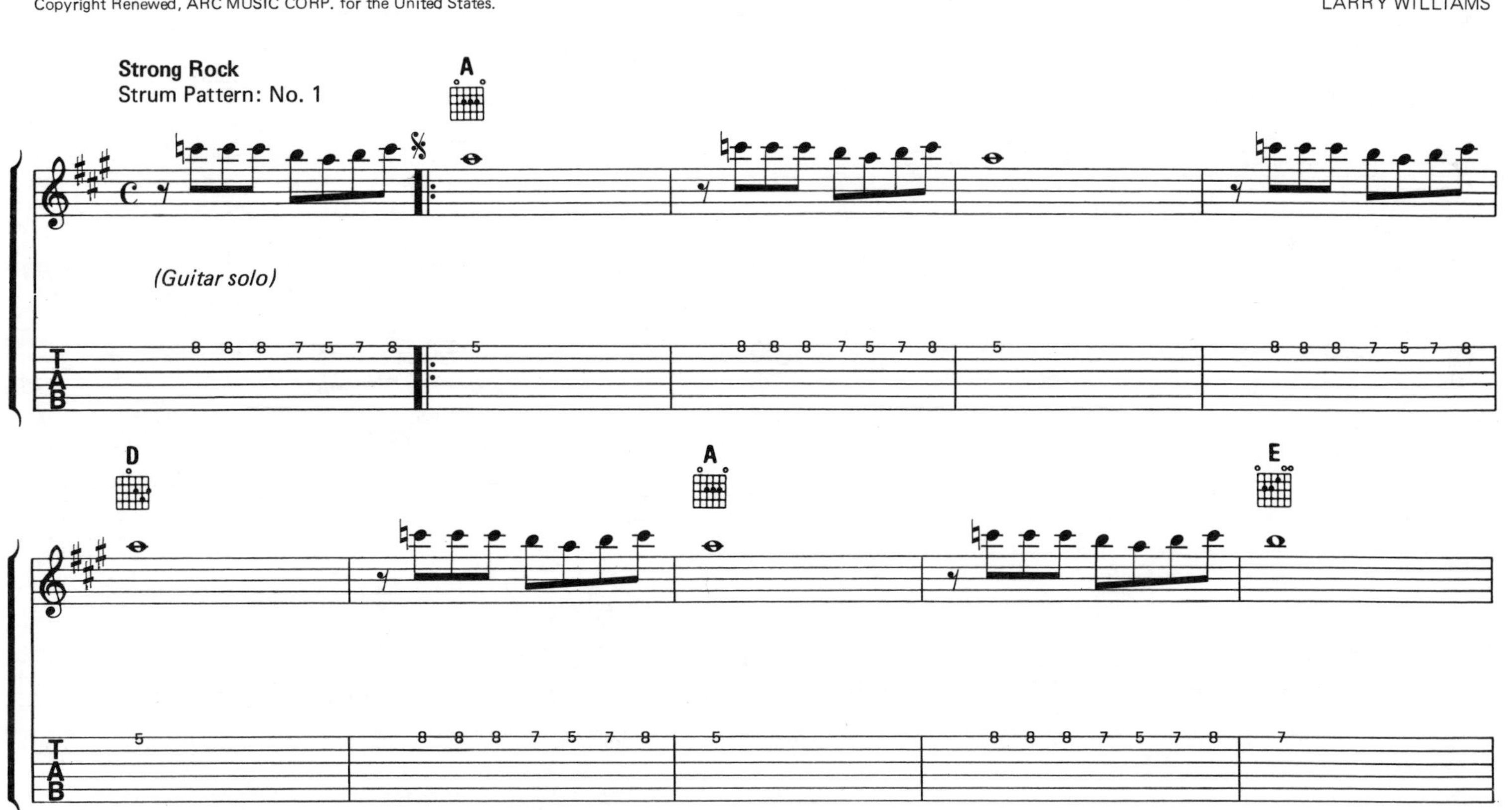

D A E7 A
You make me diz-zy, Miss Liz - zie, the way you rock and roll.
You make me diz-zy, Miss Liz - zie, when you call my name.
Run and tell your ma - ma, I want you to be my bride.
D A
You make me diz-zy, Miss Liz - zie, when you do the stroll.
Woo, ba - by, say, you're driv-in' me in - sane.
Run and tell your broth-er, ba - by don't run and hide.
E D 1,3 A E7
Come on, Miss Liz - zie, love me 'fore I grow too old.
Come on, come on, come on ba-by, I wan-na be your lov - in'
You make me diz-zy Miss Liz-zie, girl I wan-na mar - ry you.
Come on, give me
A D
fe - ver. Put your lit - tle hand in mine. You make me diz-zy Miss Liz - zie.
(3rd:) diz - zy
A E D
Oh, girl, you look so fine. Just a-rock-in' and a - roll - in', girl I said I wish you were mine.
A
Last time To Coda
(Guitar solo)
2 A E
D.S. al Coda
(3rd verse)
man.
(Guitar solo)
CODA A6
T
A
B

DOIN' IT (ALL FOR MY BABY)

Words and Music by
MIKE DUKE and PHIL CODY

Slow Rock Shuffle
Strum Pattern: No. 7

C G/B Am7 C/G F C/E
Ear - ly in the morn - in'___ I'm still in bed.___ She comes to me
La - ter in the eve - nin'___ it's been a bus - y day. She lays her head___ up -

Dm7 F/G C G/B Am7 C/G
with sweet af - fec - tion.___ Wakes___ me with kiss - es,___ "Hel - lo, sleep - y___ head,"___
on my wear - y shoul - der. Lis - ten to her laugh-ing,___ snug - gle up___ and say,___

F C/E Dm7 C/E F F/G Em7 Am7 Dm7 F/G
and gets me mov - in' in the right di - rec - tion.
"Now I'm with you ba - by your lone - li - ness is o - ver."
I do my best to give her love that lasts for - ev - er.___

Em7 Am7 Dm7 F/G C Am7 Fmaj7 Em7 Dm7 F/G
It seems like ev - 'ry - thing I do I'm___ do - in' bet - ter.___ Do - ing it all for my ba - by

C Am7 Dm7 F C/G C Am7 Bb F
'cause she's as fine___ as she can be.___ I'm do - ing it all for my ba - by,___ for

Dm7 C/E F F/G C To Coda 1 F/G 2 F G D.S. al Coda
ev - 'ry - thing she does for me.___ ___

CODA

C Am7 F Em Dm7 F/G

Do - in' it, (do - in' it) do - in' it, (do - in' it) do - in' it, do - in' it, do - in' it, yeah

C Am7 F Em Dm7 F/G C Am7

Do - in' it, (do - in' it) do - in' it, (do - in' it) ooh, ooh, ooh. Do - in' it all for my

Fmaj7 Em7 Dm7 F/G C Am7 Fmaj7 Em7 Dm7 F/G Repeat ad lib. and Fade

ba - by. Do - in' it all for my ba - by. Do - in' it all for my ba - by. She's as fine as she can be.

DON'T BE CRUEL

Words and Music by
OTIS BLACKWELL and ELVIS PRESLEY

Medium Bright Shuffle
Strum Pattern: No. 9
Intro Play 3 times

(Played an octave lower on a 6-string bass)

D

You know I can be found sit - ting home all a - lone
Baby, if I made you mad for some-thing I might have said

G D Em7

if you can't come a - round, at least, please tel - e - phone. Don't be cruel
please let's forget the past, the fu-ture looks bright a - head. Don't be cruel

A7 1 D 2 D G

to a heart that's true.
to a heart that's true. I don't want no oth - er love,

A7 G A7 D
ba - by, it's just you I'm think-ing of.
G
Don't stop think - ing of me, don't make me feel this way, come on o-ver here and love me, you
walk up to the preach-er, and let us say, "I do." Then you'll know you have me, and I'll
D Em7 A7 D
know what I want you to say. Don't be cruel to a heart that's true. Why
know that I'll have you. Don't be cruel to a heart that's true. I don't
G A7 G A7 1 D
should we be a - part? I real - ly love you, ba - by, cross my heart. Let's
want no oth - er love. Ba - by, it's just you I'm think - ing
2 D Em7 A7 D
of. Don't be cruel to a heart that's true.
Em7 A7 D D7
Don't be cruel to a heart that's true. I don't
G A7 G A7 D D6/9
want no oth - er love, ba - by, it's just you I'm think-ing of.

DON'T YOU (FORGET ABOUT ME)

Words and Music by
KEITH FORSEY and STEVE SCHIFF

CODA
D E D A D E
But you walk on by,___ will you call my name?___ When you walk a-way,___
As you walk on by,___ will you call my name?___ or will you walk a-way?___
D A D E D A
Will you walk on by? Come on and call my name.___
D E D A D
Will you call my name? I say ooh-
E D A D
Repeat and Fade
la, la, la, la,___ la, la, la, la,___ la, la, la, la, la, la, la, la, la.

DO YOU WANT TO DANCE?

Words and Music by
ROBERT FREEMAN

2
C
D.S. al Coda
Well, do you
CODA
F/G
C
F
C
Well, do you, do you, do you, do you wan - na dance? Do you, do you, do you, do you
F
C
F
C6
F/G
wan - na dance? Do you, do you, do you, do you want to dance?
G7
C

ELECTRIC AVENUE

Words and Music by
EDDY GRANT

Medium Rock
Strum Pattern: No. 2
Capo: Up One Fret (Actual Key: B♭)

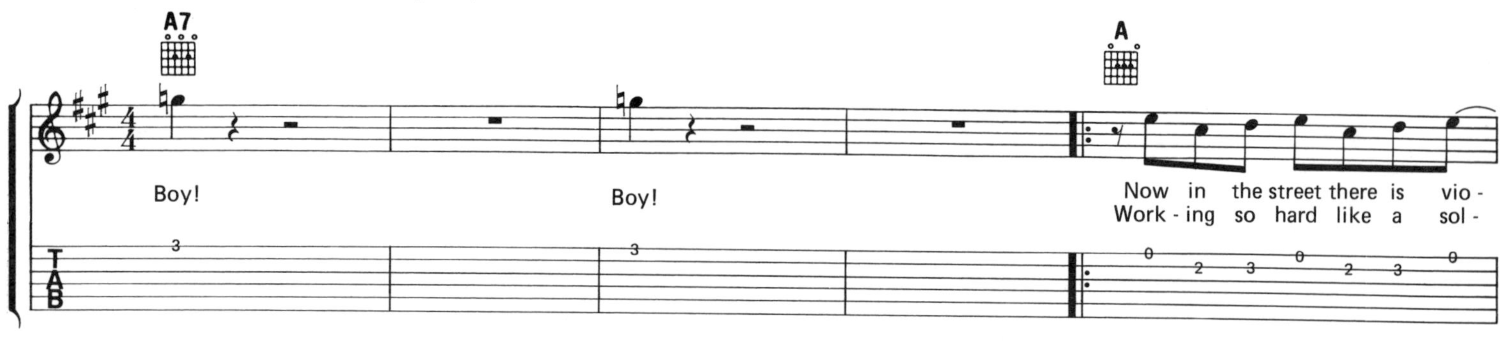

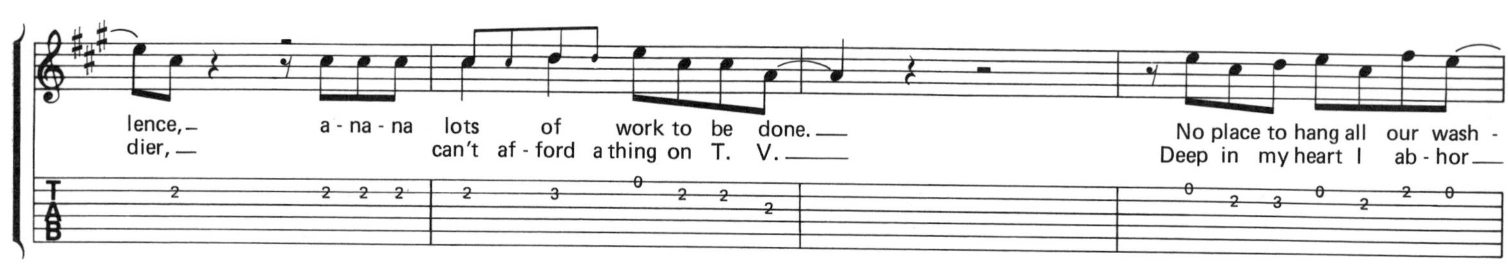

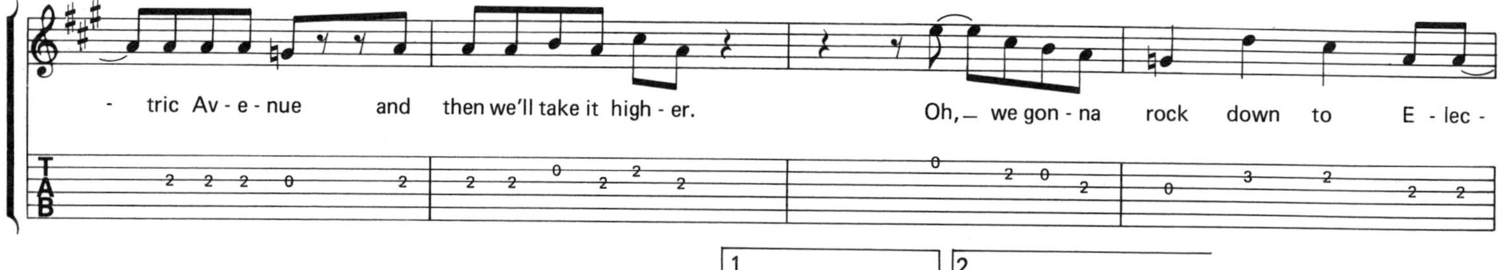

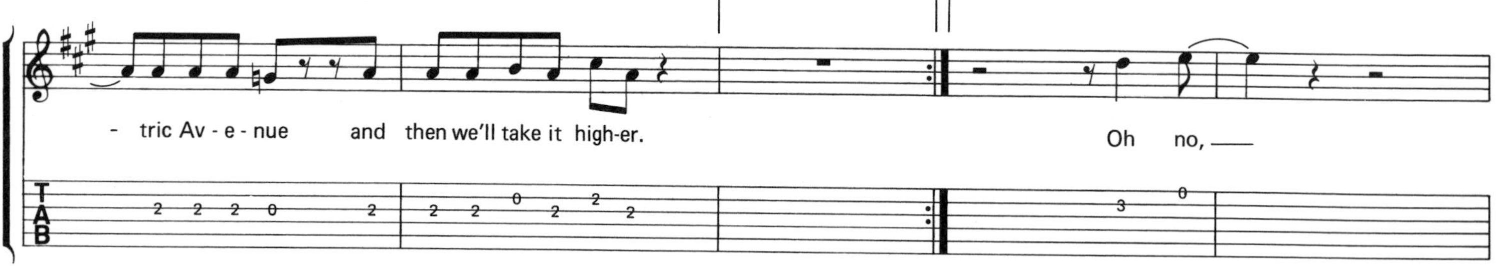

1
2
rock down to E - lec - tric Av - e - nue and then we'll take it high-er. Oh, — we gon-na
Who is to blame in what coun - try? Nev - er can get to the one. — Deal-ing in mul - ti-pli - ca -
- tion and they still can't feed ev-'ry - one. — Oh, no, — we're gon-na rock down to E - lec - tric Av - e - nue and
then we'll take it high - er. Oh, — we gon-na rock down to E - lec - tric Av - e - nue and
then we'll take it high-er. Ho! Out in the streets, Out in the streets,
Out in the day-time,
Out in the play-ground,
D.S. and Fade
out in the night, Oh — we gon - na in the dark side of town. Oh, — we gon-na

EVERY BREATH YOU TAKE

Words and Music by
STING

Moderately
Strum Pattern: No. 1
Capo: Up One Fret (Actual Key: A♭)

Eb
F
-ly see your face. I look a-round but it's you I can't re-place. I feel so cold and I long for your em-brace.
Eb
G
Em
I keep cry-ing ba-by, ba-by please.
C
Dsus
1 Em
2 G
D.S. al Coda
CODA
Em
C
Dsus
Em
Ev-'ry move you make, ev-'ry step you take, I'll be watch-ing you.
Em
C
Dsus
G
Repeat and Fade
I'll be watch-ing you.

EVERYTHING SHE WANTS

Words and Music by
GEORGE MICHAEL

Medium Rock
Strum Pattern: No. 1
Capo: Up Two Frets (Actual Key: G♭)

Intro

E7sus E7 Am7 D9 E7sus E

Ah ah ah. Oh yeah.

Am7 D9 E7sus E Am

Some - bod - y told me, boy, ev - 'ry-thing she wants is
Some peo - ple work for a liv - ing. Some peo-ple work for fun; girl,

D9 E7sus E Am

ev - 'ry-thing she sees. I guess I must have loved you, be - cause I said you were the per - fect girl
I just work for you. They told me mar-riage was a give and take. Well, you've shown me you can take, you've got some

D9 E7sus E Am D9

for me, ba-by. And now we're six months old - er, and ev-'ry-thing you want and ev-'ry-thing you see
giv-ing to do. And now you tell me that you're hav-ing my ba - by. I'll tell you that I'm hap-py if you want me to. But

E7sus E Am D9

is out of reach, not good e - nough. I don't know what the hell you want from me. Oh uh uh huh,
one step fur-ther and my back will break. If my best is - n't good e-nough, then how can it be good e - nough for

E7sus E Am D9 E7sus E

uh uh huh oh oh oh oh oh oh, uh huh uh huh, doo doo doo la la la la la. Oh oh oh
two? I can't work an-y hard-er than I do.

Am D9 Am B7+5 B7
oh oh oh, uh huh, uh huh, doo doo doo la la la la la.
Some-bod-y
(Instrumental)
Em Am B7+5 B7 Em
tell me, oh, why I work so hard for you.
To Coda
E7sus
Am7
Tacet
Oh! Oh! Why do I do the things I do?
Tacet
I'd tell you if I
Em Am D9 Am7
Tacet
D.S. al Coda
knew. My God, I don't e-ven think that I love you.
CODA
B7+5 B7 Em Am
Some-bod-y tell me, oh, why I work
B7 Em Am
Repeat and Fade
so hard for you. Oh, to give you mon-ey.

EVERYTIME YOU GO AWAY

Words and Music by
DARYL HALL

F Dm Gm C 1 F
Ev'-ry-time you go a-way, you take a piece of me with you. (Guitar)
Bb(add9) Csus C 2 F Bbmaj7
(Instrumental) (Guitar) (Instrumental)
Csus C Dm A7
I can't go on singing the same theme,
Bb Bdim F
'cause baby, can't you see we got ev'-ry-thing go-ing on and on and on. Ev'-ry-time you
Dm Gm C F
Repeat and Fade
go a-way, you take a piece of me with you. Ev'-ry-time you

EIGHT DAYS A WEEK

Words and Music by
JOHN LENNON and PAUL McCARTNEY

FOXY LADY

Words and Music by
JIMI HENDRIX

FAMILY MAN

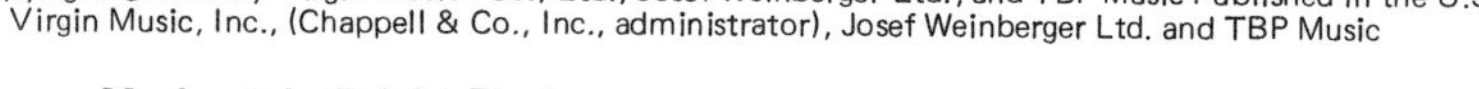

Words and Music by TIM CROSS, RICK FENN, MIKE FRYE, MIKE OLDFIELD, MORRIS PERT, and MAGGIE REILLY

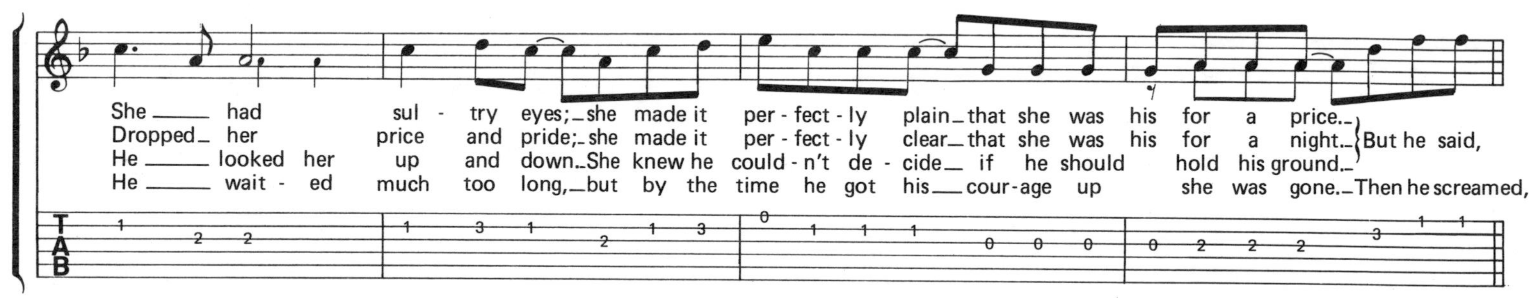

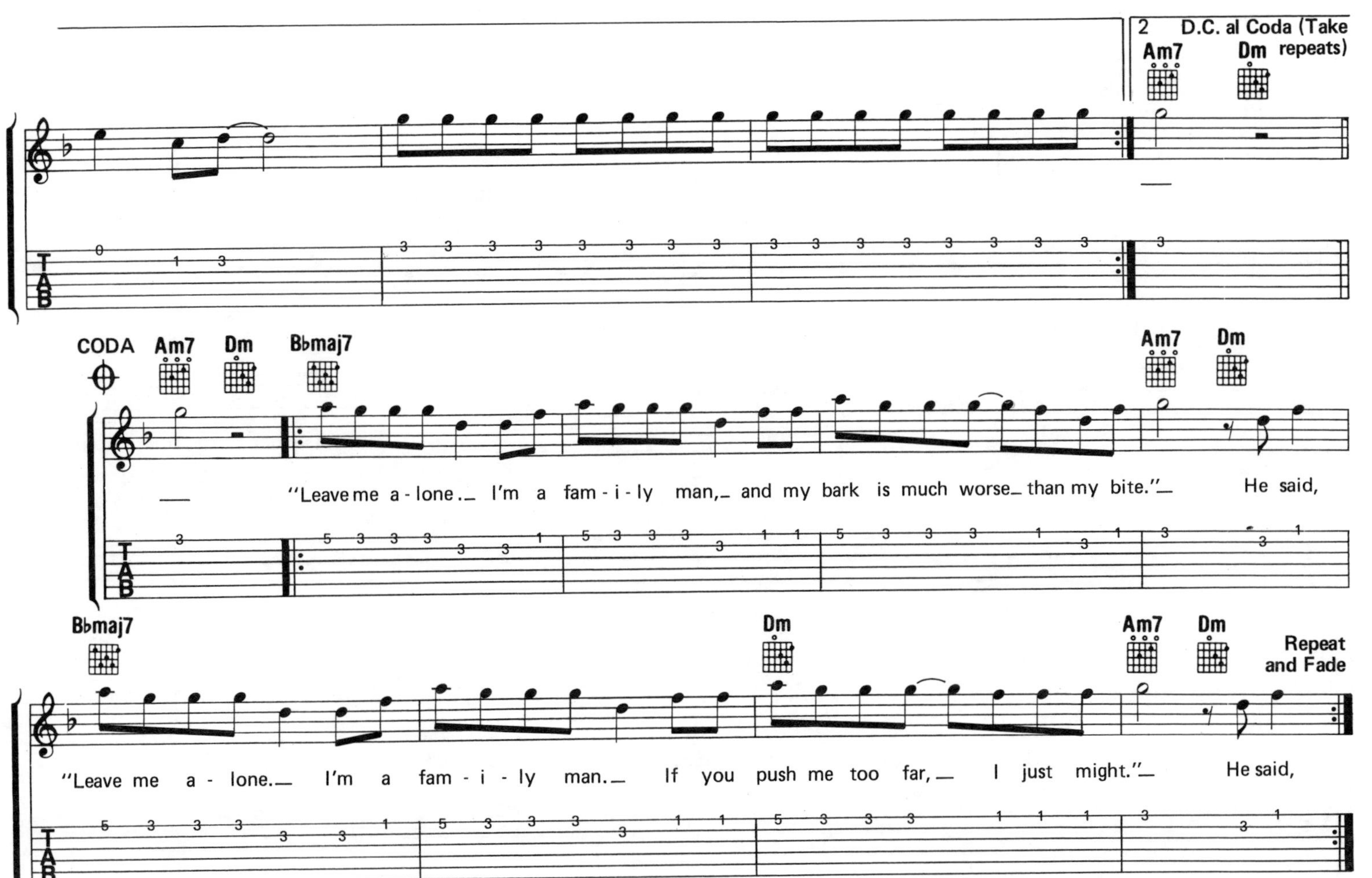
2 D.C. al Coda (Take repeats)
Am7
Dm
CODA
Bbmaj7
"Leave me a-lone._ I'm a fam-i-ly man,_ and my bark is much worse_ than my bite."_ He said,
"Leave me a-lone._ I'm a fam-i-ly man._ If you push me too far,_ I just might."_ He said,
Repeat and Fade

FLASHDANCE . . . WHAT A FEELING

Lyrics by KEITH FORSEY and IRENE CARA
Music by GIORGIO MORODER

Moderate Rock Ballad
Strum Pattern: No. 5
Capo: Up Three Frets (Actual Key: B♭)

G D Am Em C
First, when there's noth - ing but a slow glow - in' dream, that your fear seems to
lone I have cried si - lent tears full of pride in a world made of

G F C D
hide deep in - side your mind. All a -
steel, made of

Faster Moderate Rock Strum Pattern: No. 1

F C F
stone.

C/D D C D G D Am Em
Well, I hear the mu - sic, close my eyes, feel the rhy - thm. Wrap a -
I hear the mu - sic, close my eyes, I am rhy - thm. In a

C G F C/D D Em D
round, take a hold of my heart.
flash it takes hold of my heart.
What a feel - ing.

C D Em D C D G Am7 G/B C
Be - in's be - liev - in' I can have it all now I'm danc - ing for my life.

C/D D7 Em D C D Gm D
Take your pas - sion and make it hap - pen

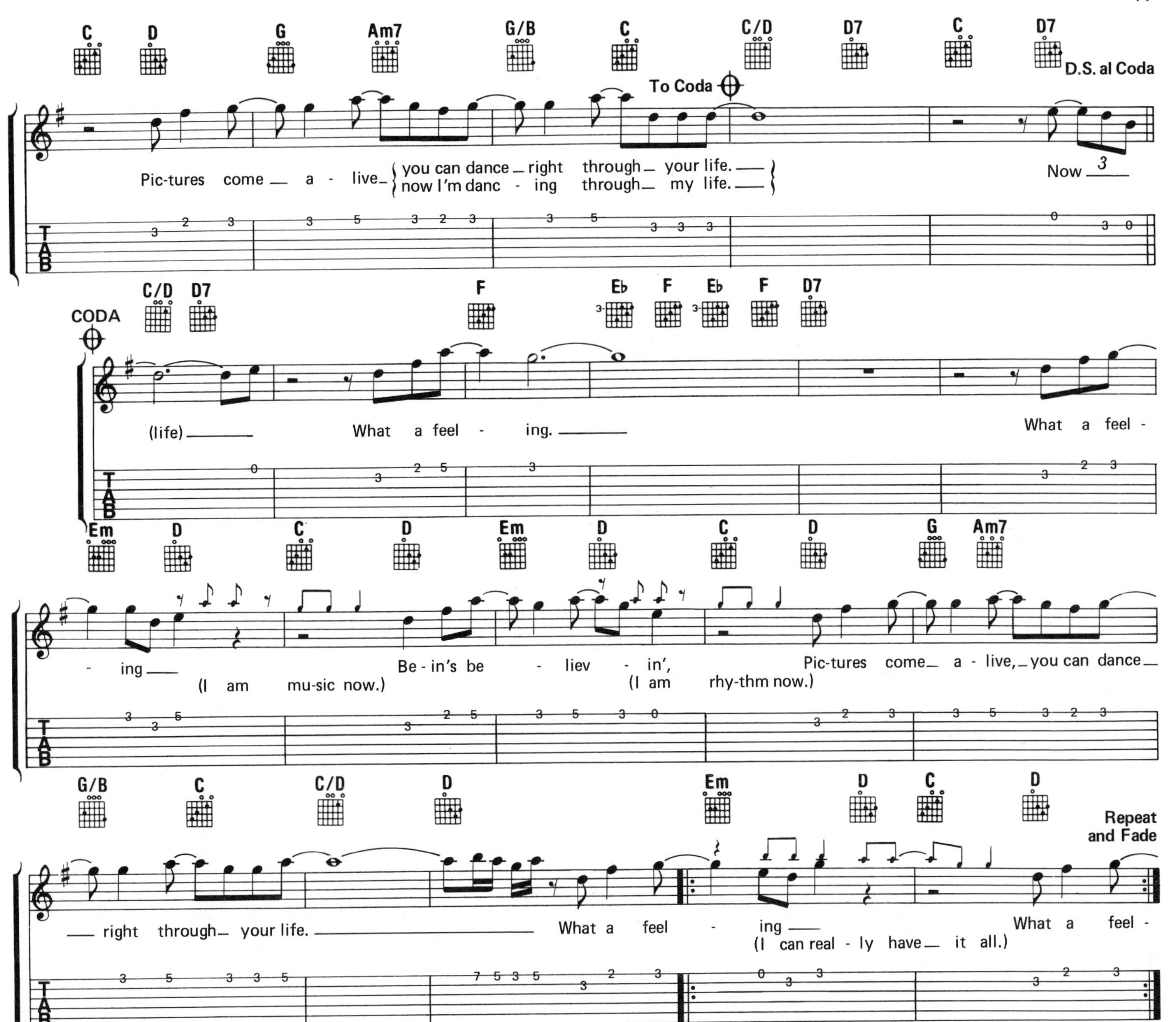
C D G Am7 G/B C C/D D7 C D7
To Coda
D.S. al Coda
Pic-tures come — a - live — { you can dance — right through — your life. — / now I'm danc - ing through — my life. — }
Now 3
CODA
C/D D7 F Eb F Eb F D7
(life) — What a feel - ing. — What a feel -
Em D C D Em D C D G Am7
- ing — Be - in's be - liev - in', Pic-tures come — a - live, — you can dance —
(I am mu-sic now.) (I am rhy-thm now.)
G/B C C/D D Em D C D
Repeat and Fade
— right through — your life. — What a feel - ing — What a feel -
(I can real - ly have — it all.)

FIRE

By JIMMY HENDRIX

D
C
A
Oh,_ move o-ver, Rov-er, and let Jim - i take o - ver. Yeah, you know what I'm
talk - in' 'bout. Yeah!_ Get on with it, ba - by!
(Guitar solo)
E
B(no3rd)
D.S. al Coda
CODA
(Guitar solo)
A(no3rd)
Repeat with ad lib. guitar and Fade

FUNKYTOWN

Words and Music by
STEVEN GREENBURG

E
Got-ta move on.
(Guitar)
(Tremolo bar)
Em7
Won't you take me to
(uh) funk-y town.
Won't you take me to
(uh) funk - y town.
Won't you take me to
(uh) funk - y town.
Won't you take me to
1
E
(uh) funk - y town.
2
A
G
A
1,2,3
4
E
D.S. al Coda
Got -
funk - y town.
Well, I
CODA
E
Repeat and Fade
C♯(no3rd) D(no3rd)
Got-ta move on.
(Instrumental)
Got - ta move on.
(Instrumental)

FREE BIRD

Words and Music by
ALLEN COLLINS and RONNIE VAN ZANT

Moderately/Slow Rock Ballad
Strum Pattern: No. 5

If I leave__ here to - mor - row, would you still re - mem - ber me?
Bye, bye ba - by it's been a sweet love, though this feel - ing I can't change.

For I must be__ trav - 'ling on now 'cause there's too man - y plac - es I've got to see.__
But please don't take__ it so bad - ly, 'cause the Lord knows I'm to blame.__

But if I stayed__ here with you, girl, things just could - 'nt be the same.

'Cause I'm as free__ as a bird now, and this bird you can - not change.

And this bird you can - not change.____ And this bird you can - not change.____

1. Lord knows I can't change.__

2. Lord knows I can't change.__ Lord help me, I can't change.

FOREVER MAN

Words and Music by
JERRY LYNN WILLIAMS

CODA
C Dm Bb C Dm Bb C
man. Try to be_ your for - ev - er man_ 'rev - er man,_ 'rev - er man,_ 'rev - er man._
For - ev - er man._
Repeat with vocal ad lib. and Fade
Dm Bb C Dm Gm Bb C Dm
'rev - er man,_ 'rev - er man,_ 'rev - er___ man. Try to be_ your for - ev - er man._
For - ev - er man._

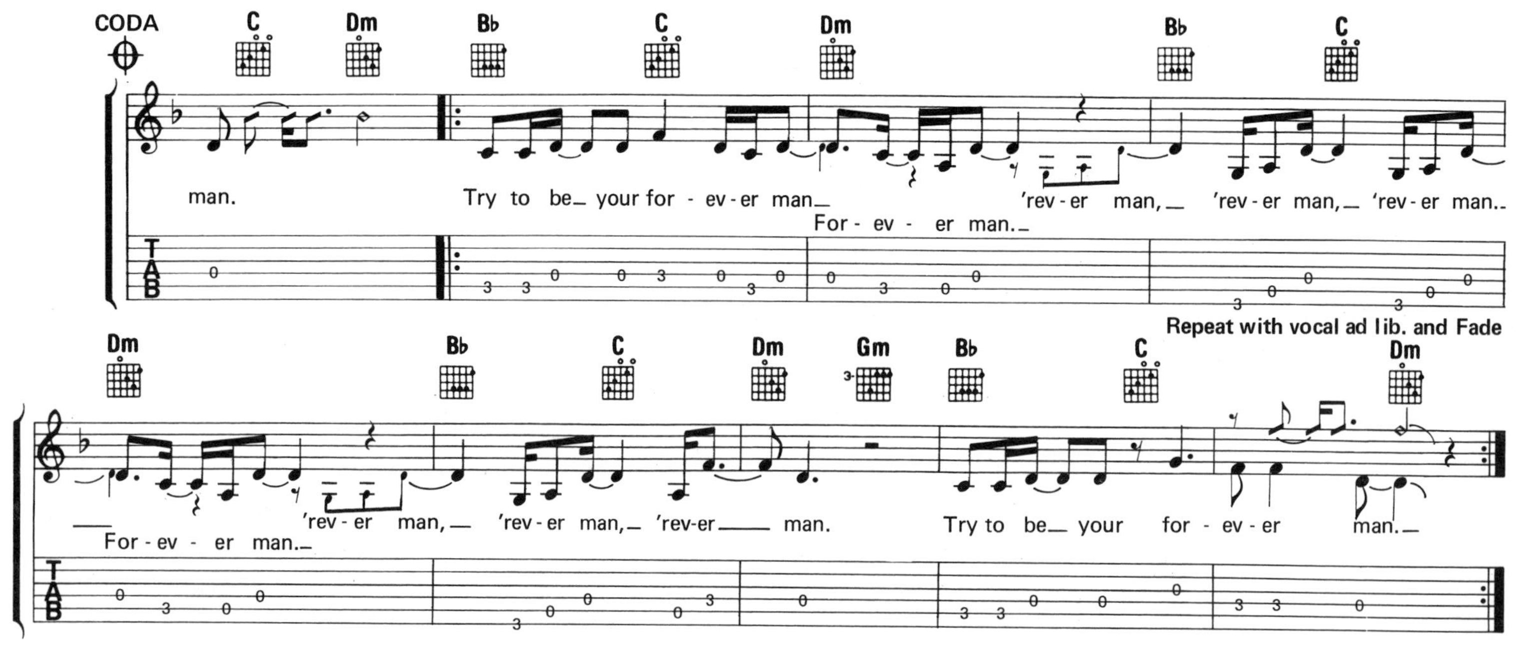

GET BACK

Words and Music by
JOHN LENNON and PAUL McCARTNEY

Moderate Rock
Strum Pattern: No. 1

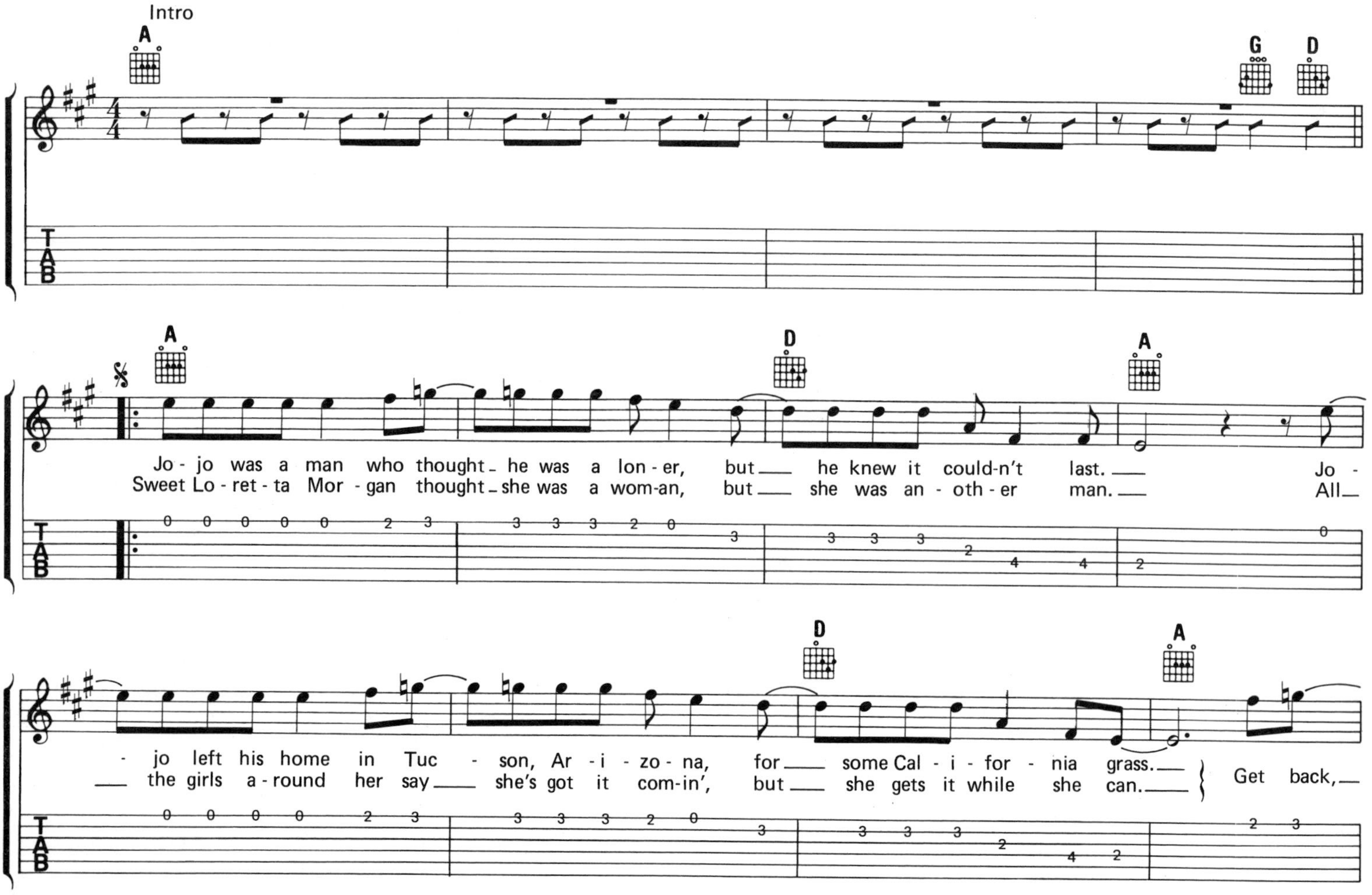

Intro
A G D
A D A
Jo - jo was a man who thought_ he was a lon - er, but___ he knew it could-n't last.___ Jo -
Sweet Lo - ret - ta Mor - gan thought_ she was a wom-an, but___ she was an - oth - er man.___ All_
D A
- jo left his home in Tuc - son, Ar - i - zo - na, for___ some Cal - i - for - nia grass.___
___ the girls a - round her say___ she's got it com-in', but___ she gets it while she can.___
Get back,_

D A G D
get back, get back, get back to where you once be - longed. Get back,
A D A
get back, get back, get back to where you once be - longed.
(Get back, Jo - jo.)
(Get back, Lo - ret - ta.)
A D A G D
(Guitar solo)
(bend)
A D A G D A
Get back, get back,
D A G D A
get back to where you once be - longed. Get back, get back, get back
1 D 2 D
to where you once be - longed.
to where you once be - longed.
D.S., ad lib. vocals and Fade

GLORIA

Words and Music by
VAN MORRISON

Steady, Moderate Rock
Strum Pattern: No. 2
Intro

E G6 D G6 A G6 E D A E D A E D A

(Continuous guitar backup throughout song.)

Like to tell you 'bout my ba - by. Y'know she comes a - round.
She comes a-round here, just a - bout mid - night.

She 'bout five feet four, a-from her head to the ground.
She make me feel so good, Lord, I wan-na say she make me feel al - right.

Y' know she comes a-round here, a - just - a - bout mid - night.
She comes walk - in' down my street; a - well, she comes to my house.

She make me feel so good, Lord. She make me feel all right. And her name is G
She knock up - on my door. And then she comes to my room. Then she make me feel

all right. L O R I - I - I - I,

2nd time to next strain

G - L - O - R - I - A. (Glo - ri - a.) G - L - O - R - I - A. (Glo - ri - a.)

E D A E D A E D A E D A

To Coda

I'm gon - na shout it all night. (Glo - ri - a.) I'm gon - na shout it ev - 'ry day. (Glo - ri - a.) yeh, yeh,

Play 6 times Play 4 times

E D A E D A D E D A E

D.S. al Coda (2nd verse)

yeh, yeh, yeh, yeh. *(Guitar solo)*

CODA

E D A E D A E D A E D A

(Double-time Drum Beat)

yeh, yeh, yeh, so good, all right, feels so good, all right,

Play 4 times

E D A E D A E D A E D A D E

yeah. *(Guitar rhythm figure)* *(Guitar solo)*

GLORIA

Original Words and Music by GIANCARLO BIGAZZI and UMBERTO TOZZI
English Lyrics by TREVOR VEITCH

G
D
E7
A
D/E
E7
leave them hang-ing on the line
call-ing Glo-ri - a,
Glo-ri- a,
I think they've got your
num-ber,
I think they've got the
a - li - as
that you've been liv-ing un-der.
But you real - ly don't re -
F#m
B7
mem-ber,
was it some-thing that they
said,
or the voic-es in your
head
call-ing Glo-ri - a.
1
2
A/E
D/A
Glo-ri - a,
Glo-ri - a.
Repeat and Fade

GOOD LOVIN'

Words and Music by
RUDY CLARK and ART RESNICK

E A7 D G A
need, all I, I real - ly need: Now gim - me that
(Good lov - in'.)
G D G A G D G A G D
2nd time, D.S. al Coda
good, good lov - in'. All I need is love. Good lov - in', ba - by.
(Good lov - in'.) (Good lov - in'.) (Good
CODA
D E A Tacet D G A G D
Play 8 times
(Instrumental)
Good love. Good
D G A G A D D G A G A D
love.
GOT TO GET YOU INTO MY LIFE
Copyright ©1966 NORTHERN SONGS LIMITED
All Rights Controlled and Administered by BLACKWOOD MUSIC INC. under license from ATV MUSIC (MACLEN)
Words and Music by
JOHN LENNON and PAUL McCARTNEY
Moderate Rock Shuffle
Strum Pattern: No. 7
Intro
G F/G C G
(Instrumental)
G F/G
I was a - lone, I took a ride, I did - n't know what I would find there.
You did - n't run, you did - n't hide, you knew I want - ed just to hold you.
What can I do, what can I be, when I'm with you I want to stay there.

G
F/G
An - oth - er road where may - be I could see an - oth - er kind of mind there.
And had you gone, you knew in time we'd meet a - gain for I had told you.
If I am true, I'll nev - er leave, and if I do I know the way there.
Bm Bm(maj7) Bm7 Bm6 Bm Bm(maj7) Bm7 Bm6
Ooh, then I sud - den - ly see you. Ooh, did I tell you I need you?
Ooh, you were meant to be near me. Ooh, and I want you to hear me.
Ooh, then I sud - den - ly see you. Ooh, did I tell you I need you?
C C/B Am7 D7 G
1
2,3
Ev - 'ry sin - gle day of my life.
Say we'll be to - gether ev - 'ry day.
Ev - 'ry sin - gle day of my life.
G C D
Got to get you in - to my life.
(Instrumental)
G
To Coda
D.S. al Coda
(Guitar solo)
CODA
G
G F/G C G
Repeat and Fade
I was a - lone I took a ride, I did - n't know what I would find there.
(Horn, ad lib. vocal)

GREAT BALLS OF FIRE

Words and Music by
OTIS BLACKWELL and JACK HAMMER

Bright Rock
Strum Pattern: No. 1

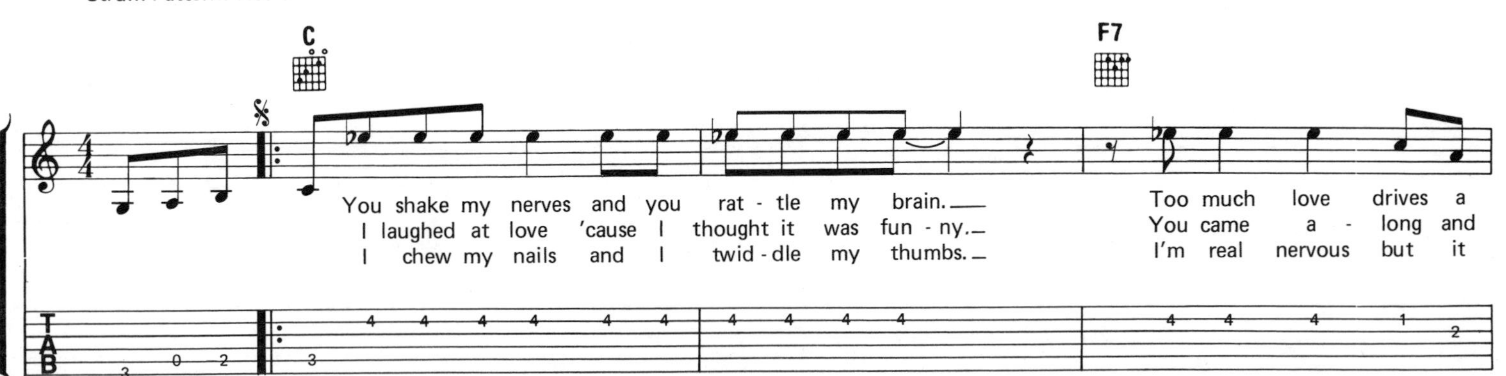

GUITAR BOOGIE SHUFFLE

By ARTHUR SMITH

A HARD DAY'S NIGHT

Words and Music by
JOHN LENNON and PAUL McCARTNEY

HEARTBREAKER

Words and Music by
CLIFF WADE and GEOFF GILL

Fast Hard Rock
Strum Pattern: No. 1
Capo: Up One Fret (Actual Key: Fm)

Em D C Am Bm D
Your love is like a tidal wave spinnin' over my head,
Your love has set my soul on fire, burnin' out of control.

Em D C Am Bm D
drownin' me in your promises that are left unsaid.
You taught me the ways of desire. Now it's taken its toll.

Tacet* Tacet Tacet
Em D C Am Bm
You're the right kind of sinner to release my inner fantasy,

Tacet Tacet Tacet
Em D C Am Bm
the invincible winner, and you know that you were born to be.

Tacet
Em F♯m G Am Bm C Bm
You're a heartbreaker, dream maker, love taker. Don't you mess around with me. You're a

Em Tacet F♯m G Tacet Am Tacet Bm To Coda C Bm Em
heartbreaker, dream maker, love taker. Don't you mess around, no, no, no.

*All Tacets last time only.

G
1
Em
2
Em
G
D
Em
Bm
Am
1
G
F♯m
Em
D
C
2
N.C. (Tacet 3)
(Guitar)
B(no3rd)
D.S. al Coda
CODA
C
Bm
Em
G
1 Am
C
Bm
mess a-round with me. You're a heart-break-er, dream mak-er, love tak-er. Don't you mess a-round with me. You're a
2 Am
C
Bm
Em
G
Am
love tak-er, heart-break-er.
(Guitar)
Repeat with ad lib. guitar
C
a.h.
Bm
Em
G
a.h.
Am
C
Bm
Em
(sounds)

HEARTBREAK HOTEL

By MAE BOREN AXTON,
TOMMY DURDEN and ELVIS PRESLEY

3. Now, the bellhop's tears keep flowing, the desk clerk's dressed in black.
They've been so long on Lonely Street they'll never, never look back,
and they're so, and they're so lonely, oh they're so lonely,
they're so lonely, they could die.

4. Well now, if your baby leaves you and you've got a tale to tell.
Well, just take a walk down Lonely Street to Heartbreak Hotel, where you will be
you'll be so lonely, baby, well you'll be lonely,
you'll be so lonely, you could die.

HELLO, MARY LOU

Words and Music by
GENE PITNEY and C. MANGIARACINA

HERE COMES THE SUN

D
G
E7
D
Here comes the sun, doo 'n' doo doo, here comes the sun, and I say, it's all right. (Guitar)
G
D
G
D
A
To Coda
D
1
A7
2
A7
F
(Guitar solo)
C
G
D
A7
F
C
Sun, sun,
G
D
Play 5 times
A7
D.S. al Coda
sun, here it comes.
(Instrumental)
CODA
D
G
E7
Here comes the sun, doo 'n' doo doo, here comes the sun.
D
G
D
G
D
A
Dm7
C
G
D
It's all right. (Guitar)
(Guitar)

HEY JUDE

Words and Music by
JOHN LENNON and PAUL McCARTNEY

HARD HABIT TO BREAK

Words and Music by
JOHN LEWIS PARKER and STEVE KIPNER

Moderately Slow Rock Ballad
Strum Pattern: No. 5

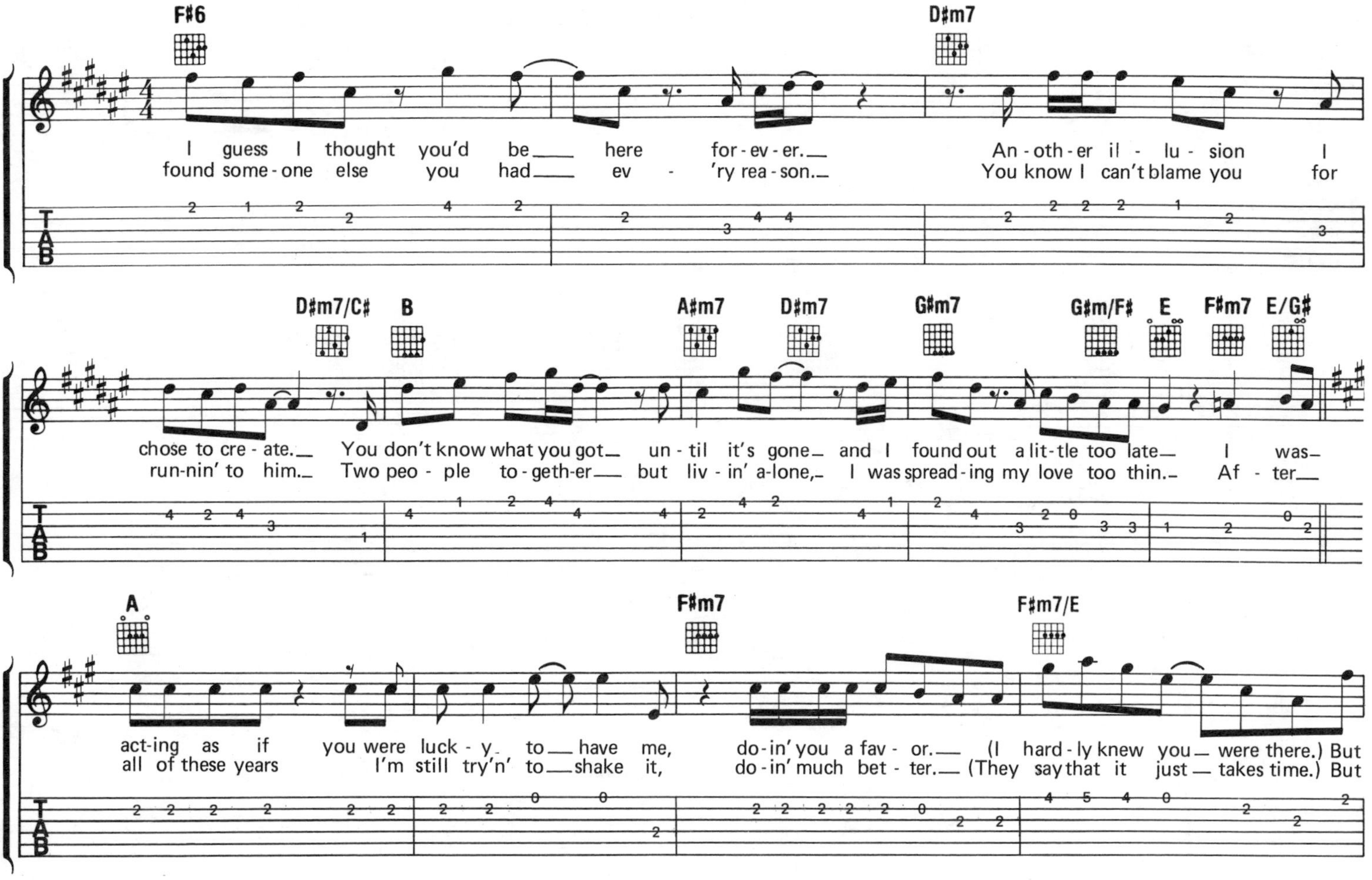

F♯6 D♯m7

I guess I thought you'd be here for - ev - er. An - oth - er il - lu - sion I
found some - one else you had ev - 'ry rea - son. You know I can't blame you for

D♯m7/C♯ B A♯m7 D♯m7 G♯m7 G♯m/F♯ E F♯m7 E/G♯

chose to cre - ate. You don't know what you got un - til it's gone and I found out a lit - tle too late. I was
run-nin' to him. Two peo - ple to - geth - er but liv - in' a - lone, I was spread - ing my love too thin. Af - ter

A F♯m7 F♯m7/E

act - ing as if you were luck - y to have me, do - in' you a fav - or. (I hard - ly knew you were there.) But
all of these years I'm still try'n' to shake it, do - in' much bet - ter. (They say that it just takes time.) But

D C#m7 F#m7 Bm7 Bm7/A G Am7 G/B C
then you were gone, and it all was wrong, had no i-dea how much I cared.
deep in the night, it's an end-less fight, I can't get you out of my mind.
Now, be-ing with-out you takes a
Em7/B F/A Fm6/Ab C Em7
lot of get-ting used to; Should learn to live with it, but I don't want to. Be-ing with-out you is all a big mis-take; in-
F/A Fm6/Ab F/G G Ab Bb/D
To Coda
stead of get-ting eas-i-er, it's the hard-est thing to take. I'm ad-dict-ed to you babe, you're a hard ha-bit to break.
C Abmaj7 Gm7 Cm7 Fm7 G7sus G7 Eb/Ab Bb/Ab Eb/Ab Ab G7sus G7
You
Can't go on. Just can't go on, on,
D.S. al Coda
Modulate up ½ step to Db
Eb/Ab Bb/Ab Eb/Ab Ab G7sus G7 Am7 Fm/Ab Eb/G Ebm/Gb F/Bb Ebm/Gb F7sus C/E B/D#
can't go on. Just can't go on, on.
CODA
A B/A A B/A E/A B/A A B/A F#/G# Ab
Repeat and Fade
hard ha-bit to break. Such a hard ha-bit to break, I'm ad-dict-ed to you. You're a

HI-HEEL SNEAKERS

Words and Music by
ROBERT HIGGENBOTHAM

HIT ME WITH YOUR BEST SHOT

Words and Music by
EDDIE SCHWARTZ

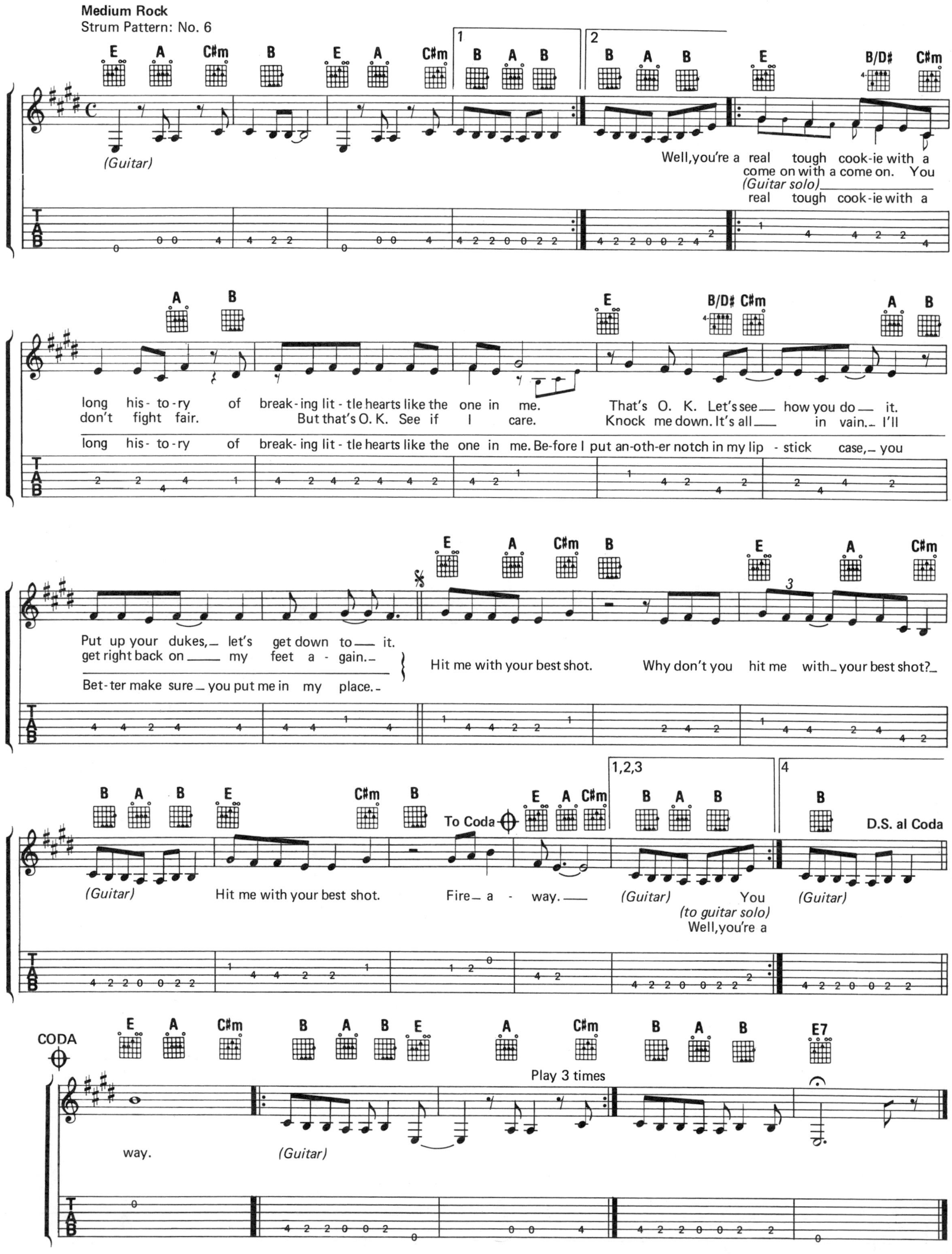

Medium Rock
Strum Pattern: No. 6

E A C#m B E A C#m | 1. B A B | 2. B A B | E B/D# C#m

(Guitar)

Well, you're a real tough cook-ie with a
come on with a come on. You
(Guitar solo)
real tough cook-ie with a

A B E B/D# C#m A B

long his-to-ry of break-ing lit-tle hearts like the one in me. That's O. K. Let's see how you do it.
don't fight fair. But that's O. K. See if I care. Knock me down. It's all in vain. I'll

long his-to-ry of break-ing lit-tle hearts like the one in me. Be-fore I put an-oth-er notch in my lip-stick case, you

E A C#m B E A C#m

Put up your dukes, let's get down to it.
get right back on my feet a-gain.
Bet-ter make sure you put me in my place.
Hit me with your best shot. Why don't you hit me with your best shot?

B A B E C#m B To Coda E A C#m | 1,2,3 B A B | 4 B D.S. al Coda

(Guitar) Hit me with your best shot. Fire a-way. (Guitar) You (Guitar)
(to guitar solo)
Well, you're a

CODA

E A C#m B A B E A C#m B A B E7

Play 3 times

way. (Guitar)

HOLDING BACK THE YEARS

Words by MICK HUCKNELL
Music by MICK HUCKNELL and NEIL MOSS

2. Holding back the years,
Chance for me escape from all I've known.
Holding back the tears,
'Cause nothing here has grown.
I've wasted all my tears,
Wasted all those years.
Nothing had the chance to be good,
Nothing ever could.

3. *(First 9 bars instrumental solo)*
Well I've wasted all my tears,
Wasted all of those years.
And nothing had a chance to be good,
'Cause nothing ever could.

HONKY CAT

Words and Music by
ELTON JOHN and BERNIE TAUPIN

G
hmm, hmm, oh, the change is gon-na do me good.
1,3
B7
You bet-ter get back, hon-ky cat, liv-in' in the cit-y ain't where its at; it's like
E7
D7
try'n' to find gold in a sil-ver mine; it's like try'n' to drink
G
whis-key, oh, from a bot-tle of wine.
To Coda
Well, I
2
G
D.C. al Coda
They said,
CODA
D7
G
Repeat and Fade
Get back, hon-ky cat, get back, hon-ky cat, get back. Ooh.

HOUND DOG

Words and Music by
JERRY LEIBER and MIKE STOLLER

HURT SO BAD

Words and Music by TEDDY RANDAZZO,
BOBBY HART, and BOBBY WILDING

I CAN SEE FOR MILES

Words and Music by
PETER TOWNSHEND

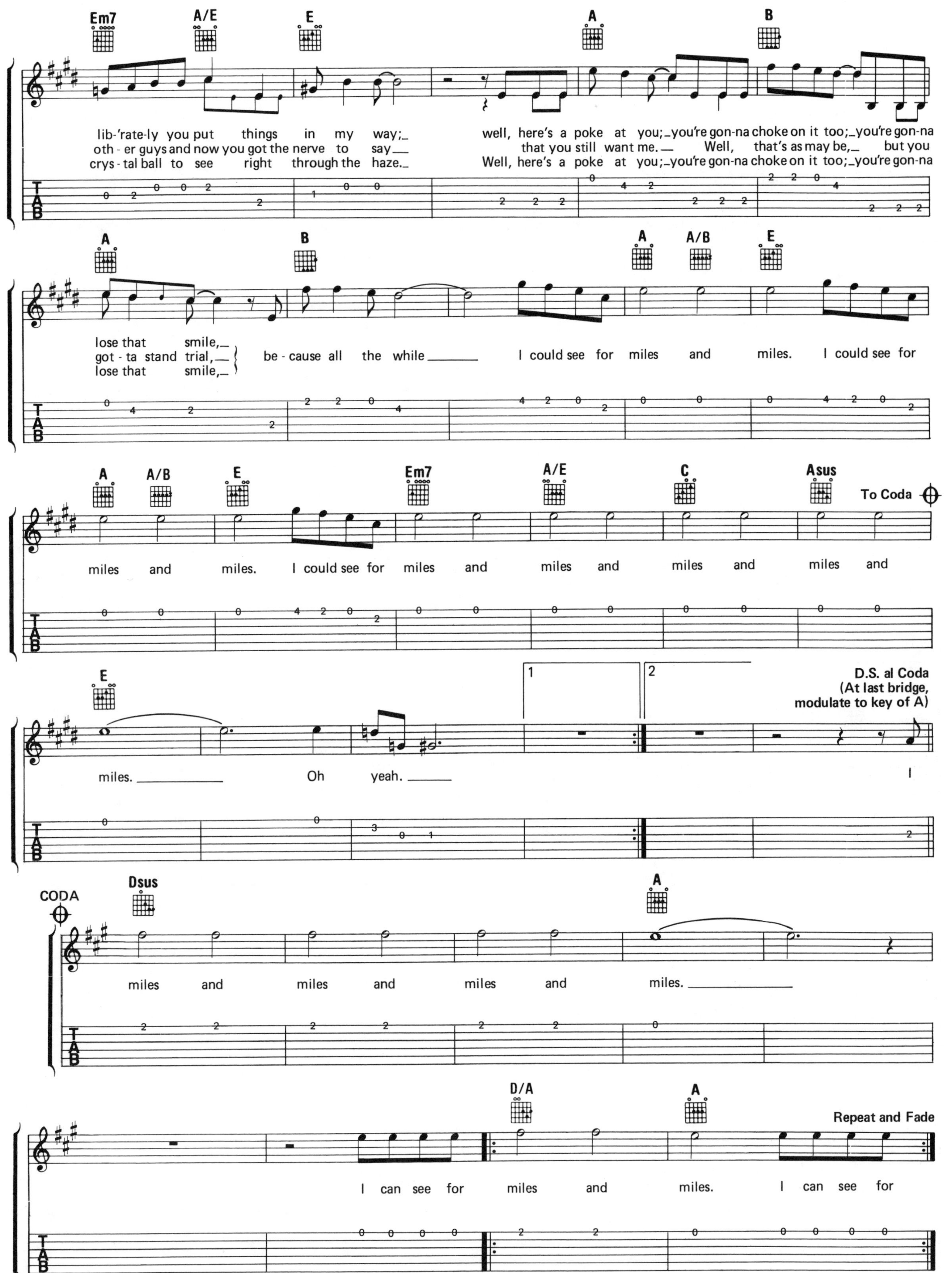
Em7 A/E E A B
lib-'rate-ly you put things in my way;_ well, here's a poke at you;_you're gon-na choke on it too;_you're gon-na
oth - er guys and now you got the nerve to say_ that you still want me._ Well, that's as may be,_ but you
crys - tal ball to see right through the haze._ Well, here's a poke at you;_you're gon-na choke on it too;_you're gon-na
A B A A/B E
lose that smile,_
got - ta stand trial,_
lose that smile,_
be - cause all the while I could see for miles and miles. I could see for
A A/B E Em7 A/E C Asus
To Coda
miles and miles. I could see for miles and miles and miles and miles and
E
1
2
D.S. al Coda
(At last bridge,
modulate to key of A)
miles._ Oh yeah._ I
CODA
Dsus A
miles and miles and miles and miles._
D/A A
Repeat and Fade
I can see for miles and miles. I can see for

I CAN'T GO FOR THAT (NO CAN DO)

Words and Music by DARYL HALL, JOHN OATES and SARA ALLEN

CODA
can't go for that, can't go for that.
(Instrumental)
Repeat and Fade
No, I can't go for that,
No, I can't
I FEEL FINE
Copyright ©1964 NORTHERN SONGS LIMITED
All Rights Controlled and Administered by BLACKWOOD MUSIC INC. under license from ATV MUSIC (MACLEN)
Words and Music by
JOHN LENNON and PAUL McCARTNEY
Bright Rock
Strum Pattern: No. 6
(Guitar solo)
G7
Ba - by's good to me, you know, she's hap - py as can be,
Ba - by says she's mine, you know, she tells me all the time.
D
you know, she said so.
I'm in love with her
C7
G
and I feel fine.
1
2
G
Bm
I'm so glad that

C
D
G
Bm
C
D
she's my lit- tle girl.
She's so glad, she's tell - ing all the world that her
G7
D
ba - by buys her things, you know, he buys her dia - mond rings, you know, she said so.
C
G
To Coda
G7
She's in love with me and I feel fine.
(Guitar solo)
D7
D.S. al Coda
CODA
D
C
G7
Repeat and Fade
She's in love with me and I feel fine.
(Guitar)

IF SHE KNEW WHAT SHE WANTS

Words and Music by
JULES SHEAR

Steady Rock
Strum Pattern: No. 1
Capo: Up Two Frets (Actual Key: B)

E B D A

(Guitar)

(Ooh_______________)

D E A D E A D E

If she knew_ what she wants
(He'd be giv-ing it to her)
If she knew_

A D E A D E

_____ what she needs
(He could give her that too)
If he knew_ what she wants
(But he can't see through her)
If she knew_

F#m F#m/E B7/D# D E/G# A

_____ what she wants he'd be giv-ing it to_ her, giv-ing it to her. But she wants_ ev-'ry-thing
(He can pre-

D E A D E A

Or there's noth-ing she wants
tend to give her ev-'ry-thing)
(She don't want to sort it out)
He's cra-zy for this girl
(But she

D E F#m F#m/E B7/D# D E

If she knew_ what she wants he'd be giv-ing it to_ her, giv-ing it_ to_ her._
don't know what she's look-ing for)

D
F#m
E/G#
A
I'd say her val-ues are cor-rupt-ed, but she's o - pen to change. Then one day
No sense think-ing I could re-ha-bil-i-tate her when she's fine, fine, fine. She's got so man-
E
she's sat-is-fied and the next I'll find her cry-ing, and it's noth-ing she can ex-plain.
y i-deas trav-'ling a-round in her head, she does-n't need noth-ing from mine.
(Guitar)
B/D#
If she knew what she wants
(He'd be
giv-ing it to her)
If she knew what she needs
(He could give her that too)
(But he
can't see through her)
F#m/E
B7/D#
To Coda
he'd be giv-ing it to her, giv-ing it to her.
E/D
A/C#
(giv-ing it to her)
Some have a style that they
un-der-stand why

D
A/C#
F#m
1 E
work hard to re-fine, so they walk a crook-ed line. But she won't
an-y-one would have to try to walk a line when they could fly.
2 E
B/D#
D
A
D.S. al Coda
(Guitar)
CODA
D
E
A
giv-ing it to her. But she wants ev-'ry-thing Or there's noth-ing she wants
(He can pre-tend to give her ev-'ry-thing) (She don't
F#m
F#m/E
B7/D#
He's cra-zy for this girl If she knew what she wants he'd be giv-ing it to her,
want to sort it out) (But she don't know what she's look-in' for)
giv-ing it to her. He'd be giv-ing it to her He could give her that too
A(add9)
But he can't see through her. Ooh Giv-ing it to her, giv-ing it to her now.

IF YOU LOVE SOMEBODY SET THEM FREE

Words and Music by
STING

G
Am7
Dm9
if you love some - one set them free.
Set them free.
(Free, free, set them free)
Set them free.
Set them free.
To Coda
If it's a mir-ror you want,
Dm7
Fsus
F
C/E
C
Gm7
You can't con - trol an in - de - pen - dent heart,
(Can't love what you can't keep)
them free)
y' can't tear the one you love a - part.
(can't love what you can't keep)
For - ev- er con-di-tioned to be -
lieve that we can't live, we can't live here and be hap-py with less.
With so man- y rich-es, so man - y souls, with
D.S. al Coda
Repeat and Fade with vocal ad lib.
CODA
ev-'ry-thing we see that we want to pos - sess. If you need some-bod-y,
free.
Set them
(Free, free, set them free)

I'M A MAN

Words and Music by
ELLAS McDANIEL

G C G C G C G C G C
To 2nd verse, Fade
I'm a man, spelled M. A. N. Man.

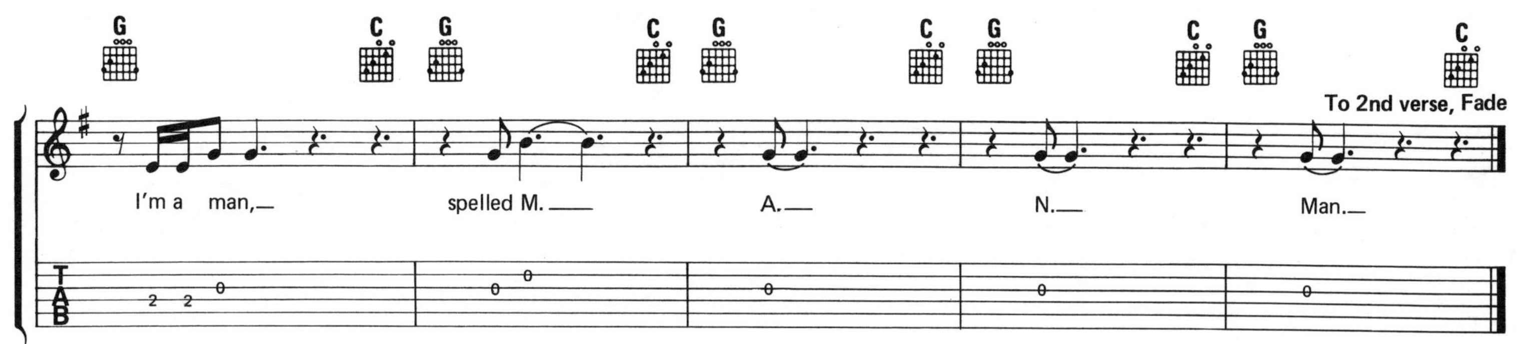

2. I'm goin' down to Kansas soon
Bring back the second cousin, Little John the Conqueroo,
I'm a man, spelled M. A. N. Man.
Ohh, Ohh, aah, aah.
The line I shoot will never miss.
The way I make love to 'em, they can't resist.
I'm a man. I spell M. A. N. Man. *(fade)*

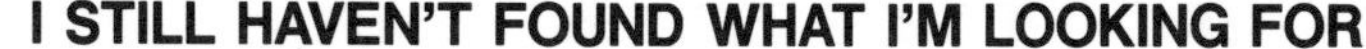

I STILL HAVEN'T FOUND WHAT I'M LOOKING FOR

Words by BONO
Music by U2

Moderately Disco/Funk
Strum Pattern: No.s13
Capo: Up One Fret (Actual Key: D♭)

Intro

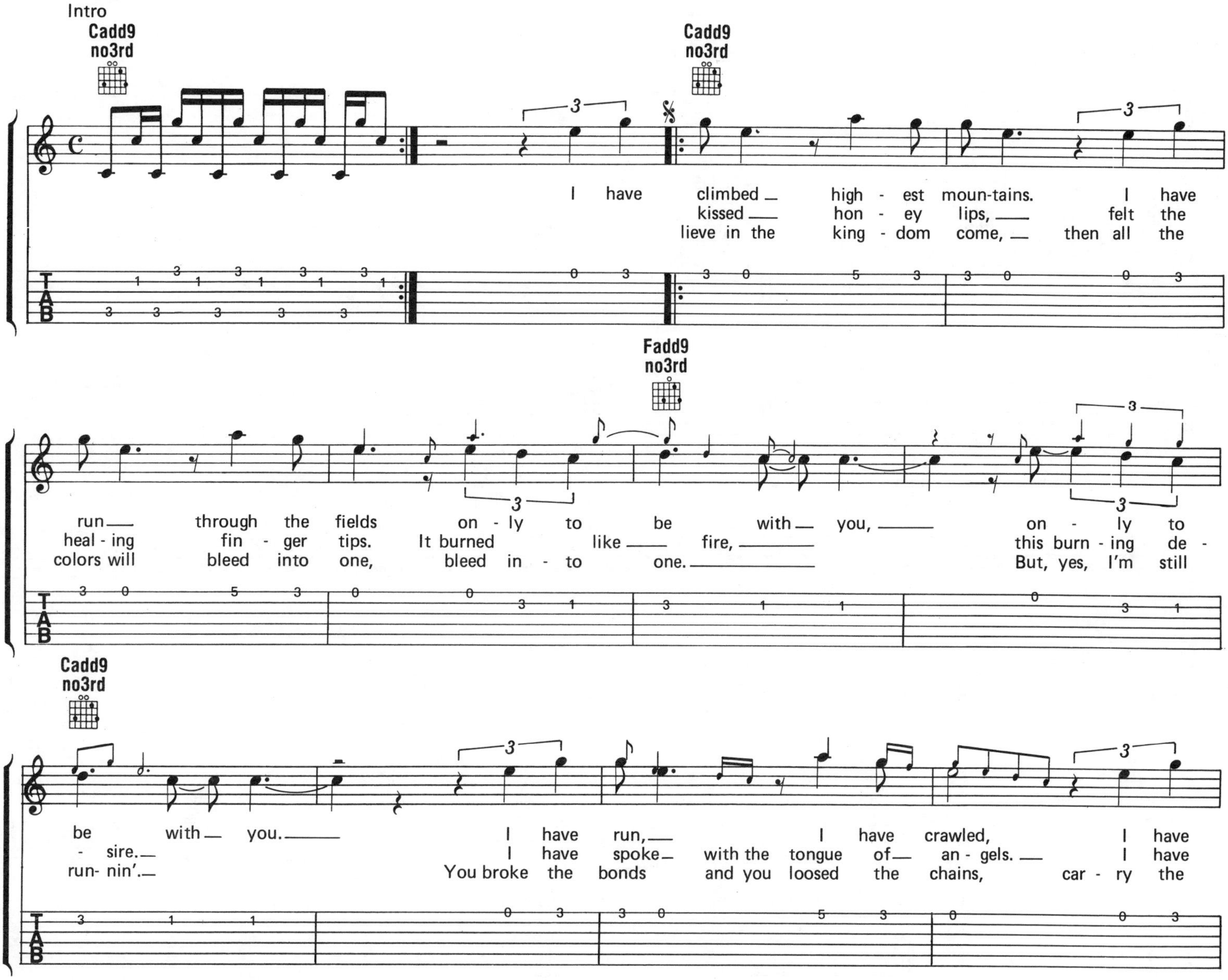

Cadd9 no3rd
Cadd9 no3rd
Fadd9 no3rd
Cadd9 no3rd
I have climbed high - est moun-tains. I have run through the fields on - ly to be with you, on - ly to be with you.
kissed hon - ey lips, felt the heal - ing fin - ger tips. It burned like fire, this burn - ing de - sire.
lieve in the king - dom come, then all the colors will bleed into one, bleed in - to one. But, yes, I'm still run-nin'.
I have run, I have crawled, I have
I have spoke with the tongue of an - gels. I have
You broke the bonds and you loosed the chains, car - ry the

Fadd9 no3rd
sealed these cit-y walls, these cit-y walls, on-ly to
held the hand of the dev-il. It was warm in the night. I was cold as
cross of my shame, of my shame. You know I be-
Cadd9 no3rd
Gsus
Fadd9 no3rd
be with you.
a stone.
lieve it.
But I still have-n't found what I'm look-
C
Csus
C
Gsus
C/F
C
ing for. But I still have-n't found what I'm look-
C
Csus
To Coda
1 C
2 Cadd9 no3rd
C
Csus
C
Csus
C
ing for. I have
(Guitar)
F
C
D.S. al Coda
I be-
CODA
C
Gsus
Fadd9 no3rd
C
Csus
1 C
2 C
Csus
Repeat and Fade
But I still have-n't found what I'm look-ing for. But I still

IT'S SO EASY

Words and Music by
BUDDY HOLLY and NORMAN PETTY

I'M YOUR MAN

Words and Music by
GEORGE MICHAEL

If you're gonna do it – you know what I say?
If you're gonna do it don't throw it away
Don't throw it baby
Because
I'll be your boy, I'll be your man,
I'll be the one who understands,
I'll be your first, I'll be your last,
I'll be the only one you ask,
I'll be your friend, I'll be your toy,
I'll be the one who brings you joy,
I'll be your hope, I'll be your pearl
I'll take you half way round the world!
I'll make you rich – I'll make you poor
Just don't use the door

Do it with me . . . .

Additional lyric on final chorus – (To Fade.)

IT'S NOT OVER ('TIL IT'S OVER)

Words and Music by ROBBIE NEVIL, JOHN VAN TONGEREN and PHIL GLADSTON

A
A/E
D
A
8va
(Instrumental)
It's not o - ver 'til it's o - ver.
A/E
Bm
E
A
A/E
It's not o - ver 'til we get it right.
(Instrumental)
D
E
A
A/E
Bm
E
It's not o - ver 'til it's o - ver.
It's not o - ver 'til we get it
D
A
E
D
E
right.
The odds are a - gainst us,
but y'-know, we still stand a chance.
A
E
Bm
CHORUS
There's no giv - ing up, no giv - ing in.
It's not o - ver.
(Instrumental)
Repeat Chorus with vocal ad lib. and Fade
A/E
D
D/E
E
Bm
E
It's not o - ver 'til it's o - ver.
It's not o - ver, 'til we get it right.

IT'S STILL ROCK AND ROLL TO ME

Words and Music by
BILLY JOEL

Moderately Fast Rock/Shuffle
Strum Pattern: No. 7

C Em B♭ F

What's the mat - ter with the clothes I'm wear - ing? "Can't you tell that your tie's too wide?"
What's the mat - ter with the car I'm driv - ing? "Can't you tell that it's out of style?"
How a - bout a pair of pink side - wind - ers and a bright o - range pair of pants?
What's the mat - ter with the crowd I'm see - ing? "Don't you know that they're out of touch?"

C Em B♭ F

May - be I should buy some old tab col - lars? "Wel - come back to the age of jive.
Should I get a set of white wall tires? "Are you gon - na cruise the mir - a - cle mile?
Well you could real - ly be a Beau Brum - mel, ba - by, if you just give it half a chance.
Should I try to be a straight 'A' stu - dent? "If you are, then you think too much."

Em Am Em D G

Where have you been hid - in' out late - ly, hon - ey? You can't dress trash - y till you spend a - lot of mon - ey."
Now - a - days you can't be too sent - i - men - tal. Your best bet's a true ba - by blue Con - ti - nen - tal."
Don't waste your mon - ey on a new set of speak - ers. You get more mile - age from a cheap pair of sneak - ers."
"Don't you know a - bout the new fash - ion, hon - ey? All you need are looks and a whole lot of mon - ey." It's the

C Em B♭ F Am G To Coda C

Ev - 'ry - bod - y's talk - in' 'bout the new sound. Fun - ny, but
Hot funk, cool punk, e - ven if it's old junk,
Next phase, new wave dance craze, an - y - ways,
next phase, new wave dance craze, an - y - ways,
it's still rock and roll to me.

1 | 2,3

G F

Oh, it does - n't mat - ter what they say in the pa - pers, 'cause it's
(Instrumental solo)

E7
Am
G
F
al - ways been the same old scene.
There's a new band in town but you can't get the sound from a
E7
Ab
Eb
F
G
D.S. al Coda
sto - ry in a mag - a - zine,
aimed at your av - er-age teen.
Oooh!
(2nd time only)
CODA
C
Em
Bb
F
G
C9
Tacet
Tacet
Tacet
Tacet
Tacet
Ev - 'ry -bod - y's talk - in' 'bout a new sound. Fun - ny, but it's still rock and roll to me.

I WANNA ROCK

Words and Music by
D. SNIDER

Fast Rock
Strum Pattern: No. 1

A G D E G A G D E C

I wan-na rock, (rock!) I wan-na rock, (rock!) I want to

A G D E G A G D E C A A7

To Coda

rock, (rock!) I wan-na rock, (rock!) Turn it down-you say, well
There's a feel - in' that I

D/A G/A A G D A

all I got to say to you is time and time a - gain I say no, (no) no, no, no, no, no.
get from noth-in' else, and there ain't noth-in' in the world that makes me go, (go) go, go, go, go, go.

A7 D G A G D

Tell me not to play. Well, all I got-ta say to when you tell me not to say, I say no, (no) no, no, no, no,
Turn the pow - er up, I've wait-ed for so long so I could hear my fav - 'rite song, so let's go, (go) go, go, go, go,

A G D G D

no. So if you ask me why I like the way I play it,
go. When it's like this I feel the mu - sic shoot - in' through me,

G 1 C G A Tacet 2 C G A D.S. al Coda

there's on - ly one thing I can say to you. I wan-na rock
there's noth-in' else that I would rath - er do. I wan-na rock

CODA
D
E
C
A
E
G
A
I wan-na rock,— (rock,) rock, (rock,) rock, (rock!) I wan-na rock,— (rock,) rock, (rock,)
E
C
A
E
G
A
rock, (rock!) I want to rock, (rock,) rock, (rock,) rock, (rock!) I wan-na rock,— (rock,) rock, (rock,)
E
C
A
G
D
E
G
A
G
rock, (rock!) I wan-na rock! I wan-na rock,— (rock!)
D
E
C
A
G
D
E
G
A
G
D
E
C
Repeat and Fade
I wan-na rock,— (rock!) I want to rock, (rock!) I wan-na rock—

I WANT TO HOLD YOUR HAND

Words and Music by
JOHN LENNON and PAUL McCARTNEY

C D C D
I can't hide, I can't hide. Yeah,
G D E(no3rd) B(no3rd)
you got that some - thing, I think you'll un - der - stand. When
G D E(no3rd) B(no3rd)
I say feel that some - thing, I want to hold your hand.
C D G Em
I want to hold your hand,
1 C D G
I want to hold your hand.
2 C D B7 C D C G
I want to hold your hand, I want to hold your hand.
T
A
B

I WON'T STAND IN YOUR WAY

Words and Music by
BRIAN SETZER

Fm6
C
G
C
just a lit-tle boy who's ea - si-ly led a - stray.
D7
Dm
Well, aren't you that sa - ame lit-tle girl who al - ways gets her
1 G
2 Ab7
G7
Tacet
D.S. al Coda
way? I, I got a wa - a - a - ay? I - I - I - I I got a
CODA
Fmaj7
Fm6
Bb9
won't stand in your way I won't stand in your way I
Dm7
G7
C
Fm
C
B6/9
C6/9
won't stand in your way an - y more.

JIVE TALKIN'

Words and Music by
BARRY GIBB, ROBIN GIBB and MAURICE GIBB

CODA
C
F
C
Love talk - in' is all ver - y fine — yeah. Jive talk - in' just is - n't a crime, — and if there's
Bb
C
some - bod - y you'll love 'til you die — then all that jive talk - in' just gets in your eye. —
1,2,3
4
Repeat and Fade
Do be lu bu loop do be lu bu loop do do — do — do doot doot do doot do. Jive talk - in'.

JUMP (FOR MY LOVE)

Words and Music by
MARTI SHARRON, G. SKARDINA and S. MITCHELL

A D/A E/A A D/A E/A
my touch. Jump, if you wan-na taste my kiss-es in the night, then jump for
A D/A E/A A D/A E/A
my love. Jump! I know my heart can make you hap-py. Jump in. You know these arms can
A D/A E/A A D/A E/A
fill you up. Jump! If you wan-na taste my kiss-es in the night, then jump for
A To Coda G
my love.
D.C. al Coda
(to 3rd verse)
CODA
A E/A A E/A C G/C C G/C G/F C/F G/F C/F
When you are next to me, Oh, I come a-live.
Oh, it feels so right.
E7sus A E/A A E/A A D/A E/A
Your love burns in-side.
Come to me if you want me to-night.
Jump!
TAB

A D/A E/A A D/A E/B A
Jump in if you wan - na taste my kiss- es in the night, then jump, jump, jump. Oooh yeah.
F Bb/F C/F F Bb/F F
You know my heart can make you hap-py. Jump! You know these arms can fill you up. Jump in.
Bb/F C/F F Bb/F C/F F
You wan - na taste my kiss - es in the night, then jump, jump, for my love. Jump!
Repeat with vocal ad lib. and Fade

JUST A GIGOLO

Original German Text by JULIUS BRAMMER
English Words by IRVING CAESAR
Music by LEONELLO CASUCCI

Moderate Rock/Shuffle
Strum Pattern: No. 7
Capo: Up One Fret (Actual Key: A♭)

KID CHARLEMAGNE

Words and Music by
WALTER BECKER and DONALD FAGEN

3. Now the patrons have all left you in the red.
Your low-rent friends are dead; life can be very strange.
All those Day-Glow freaks who used to paint the face;
They've joined the human race. Some things will never change.

Son, you were mistaken, you are obsolete;
Look at all the white men on the street.

4. Clean this mess up or else we'll all end up in jail.
Those test tubes and the scale, just get them all out of here.
Is there gas in the car? Yes, there's gas in the car.
I think the people down the hall know who you are.

Careful what you carry 'cause the man is wise;
You are still an outlaw in their eyes,

KING OF PAIN

Words and Music by
STING

A Gmaj7 1,2,3 A Gmaj7 4 A Gmaj7 Bm A Bm A
There's a king on a throne with his eyes torn out.
There's a blind man look- ing for a sha-dow of doubt.
There's a rich man sleep - ing on a gold- en bed.
There's a skel - e - ton chok - ing on a crust of bread.
C
(Instrumental)
Bm A Bm A Bm A Bm A
There's a red fox torn by a hunts - men's pack. (That's my soul up there.) There's a
Gmaj7 A Gmaj7 A F#m Gmaj7 F#m7
Tacet
black-winged gull with a bro - ken back. (That's my soul up there.) There's a lit - tle black spot on the sun
F#m
D.S. al Coda
to - day. It's the same old thing as yes - ter - day. I have
CODA
Dmaj7 Gmaj7 D E7sus Dmaj7 Gmaj7 Dmaj7 E7sus
Repeat and Fade
king of pain. king of pain.

LADY MADONNA

Words and Music by
JOHN LENNON and PAUL McCARTNEY

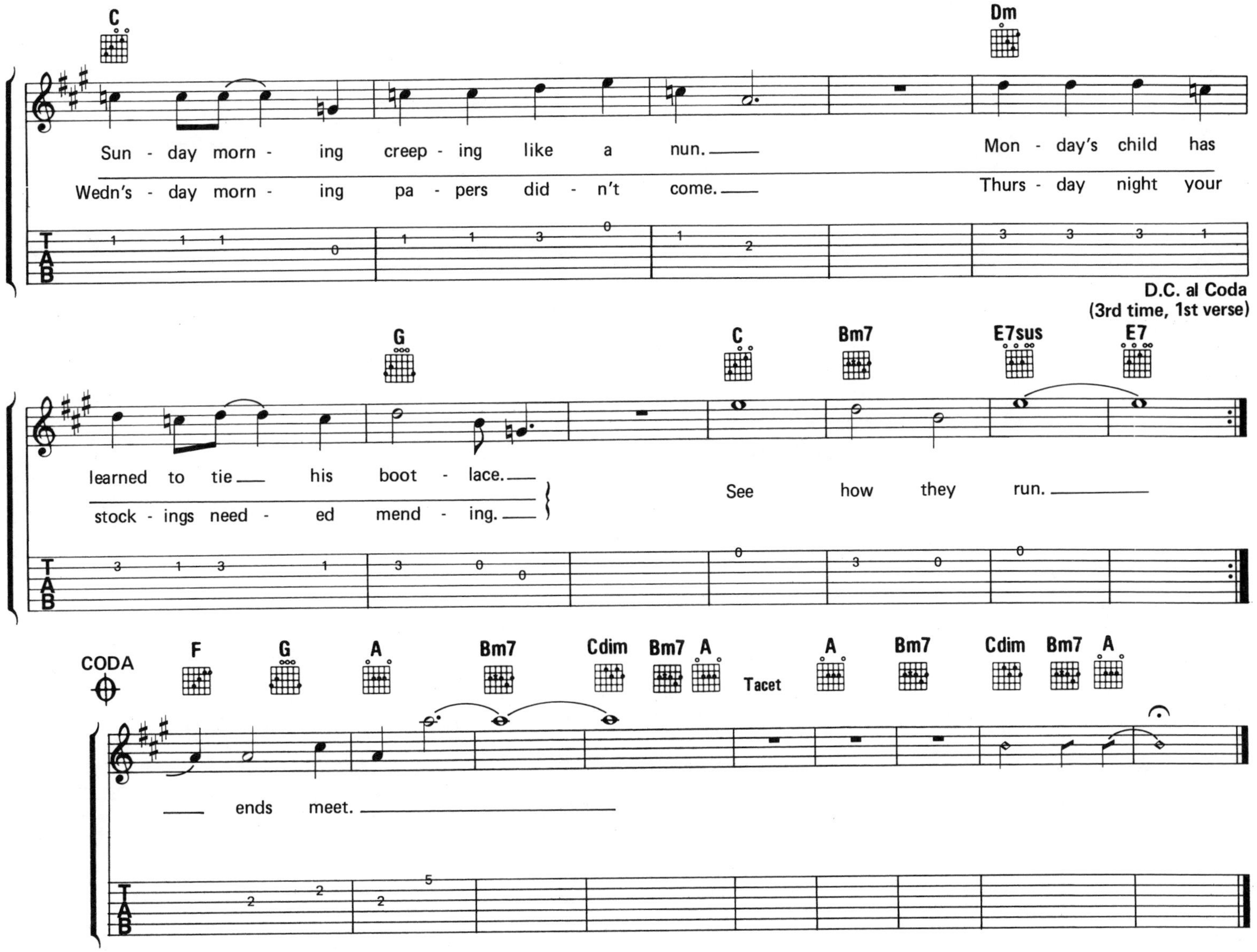

C
Dm
Sun - day morn - ing creep - ing like a nun.
Mon - day's child has
Wedn's - day morn - ing pa - pers did - n't come.
Thurs - day night your
D.C. al Coda
(3rd time, 1st verse)
G
C
Bm7
E7sus
E7
learned to tie his boot - lace.
stock - ings need - ed mend - ing.
See how they run.
CODA
F
G
A
Bm7
Cdim
Bm7
A
Tacet
A
Bm7
Cdim
Bm7
A
ends meet.

LAND OF A THOUSAND DANCES

Words and Music by
CHRIS KENNER and ANTOINE DOMINO

Fast Rock
Strum Pattern: No. 1

D
VERSE
(Guitar riff throughout verse)
You got to know how to po - ny,
like Bo - ny Ma - ro - nie.
Do the mashed po - ta - ter,
do the al - li - ga - tor.
Put your

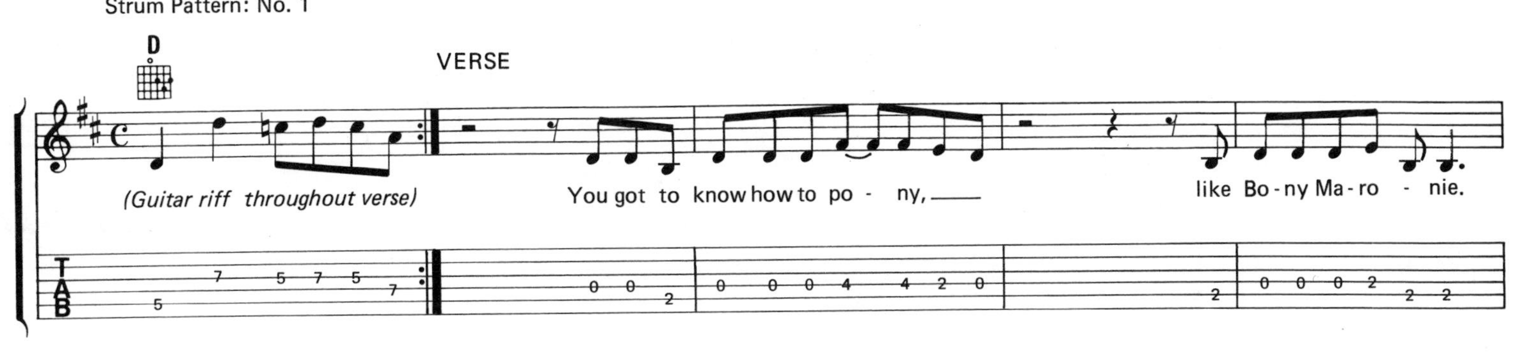

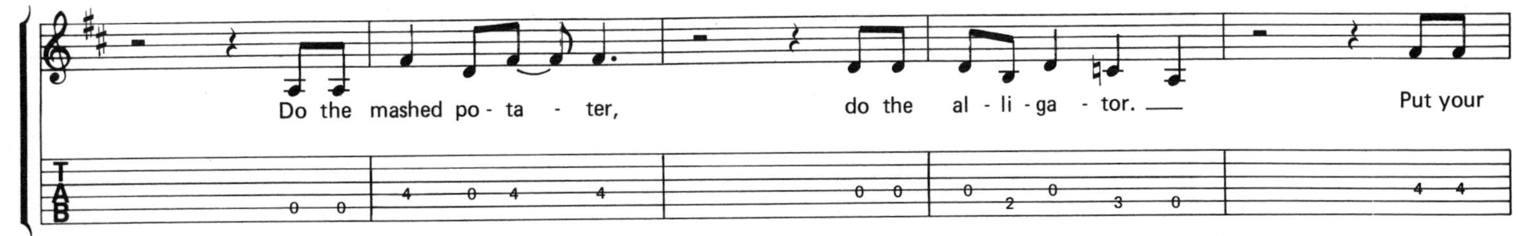

hands on your hips, yeah. Let your back-bone slip. Do the wa-tu-si,
Tacet
like my lit-tle Lu-cy. Ow! Ugh!
CHORUS
D
Na na na na na na na na na na na na na na na na na na na.
Spoken: I need somebody to help me say it one time. C'mon y'all, let's say it one more time.
Na na na na na na na na na na na na na na na na na na na Ow!
1
Ugh! D'you know I feel all right, huh! Feel pret-ty good y'all huh ha!
2
Ow!
Spoken ad lib.:
Baby have a party twisting with Lucy. Roll over on your back, do that jerk.
With long tall Sally doing the watusi. I like it like that watch me work, y'all.
Repeat and Fade

LAYLA

Words and Music by
ERIC CLAPTON and JIM GORDON

LESSONS IN LOVE

Words and Music by MARK KING, ROLAND GOULD and WALLY BADAROU

Am7
B7♯5(♯9)
1
E
D
2,3
Em
bet - ter for
lose it,
les - sons in love.
If we
Cmaj7
Am7
B7
Em
lose the time be - fore us,
the fu - ture will ig - nore us.
We should
Fade
Cmaj7
Am7
B7♯5(♯9)
E
D
C
use it; we could lose it, yeah.
Les - sons in love.
Lost with - out
E
D
A7
C
G
F
love.
Les - sons in
love. When will you ev - er
love, when there's no - where left to
love; don't let your spir - it
love; I'll wait 'til you re -
1,2,3
4
D.S. and Fade
C
D
D
Em
Am
Bm
learn? Les - sons in
turn. Les - sons in
burn. Les - sons in
turn.
All the

LET'S DANCE

Lyric and Music by BOWIE

Moderate Disco/Funk
Strum Pattern: No. 4
Capo: Up One Fret (Actual Key: B♭m)

Am Em7 Am Am11

Let's dance. Let's dance. Put on your red shoes

Am6 F6 Am

and dance the blues. Let's dance to the song they're play - ing — on the ra - di - o —

Am11 Am6 F6

Let's sway while col-or lights up your face. Let's sway,

Am G C D

sway thru' the crowd to an emp-ty space. — If you say run, I'll run with you.

C D G C/D D C/D D G

If you say hide, we'll hide, be-cause my love for you —

Em7 C D

— would break my heart — in two — If you should fall — in-to my arms and trem - ble like a

Am
Am11
Am6
To Coda
flow - er. Let's dance, for fear your grace should fall. Let's
F6
Am
Am11
dance, for fear to - night is all. Let's sway, you could look in - to my eyes.
Am6
F6
Am
D.S. al Coda
Let's sway un - der the moon - light, the ser - i - ous moon - light.
CODA
Am11
Am6
dance. Put on your red shoes and dance the blues. Let's
F6
Am
Repeat and Fade
dance.

LET THE GOOD TIMES ROLL

Words and Music by
LEONARD LEE

Moderate Shuffle
Strum Pattern: No. 7
Capo up one fret (Actual key: D♭)

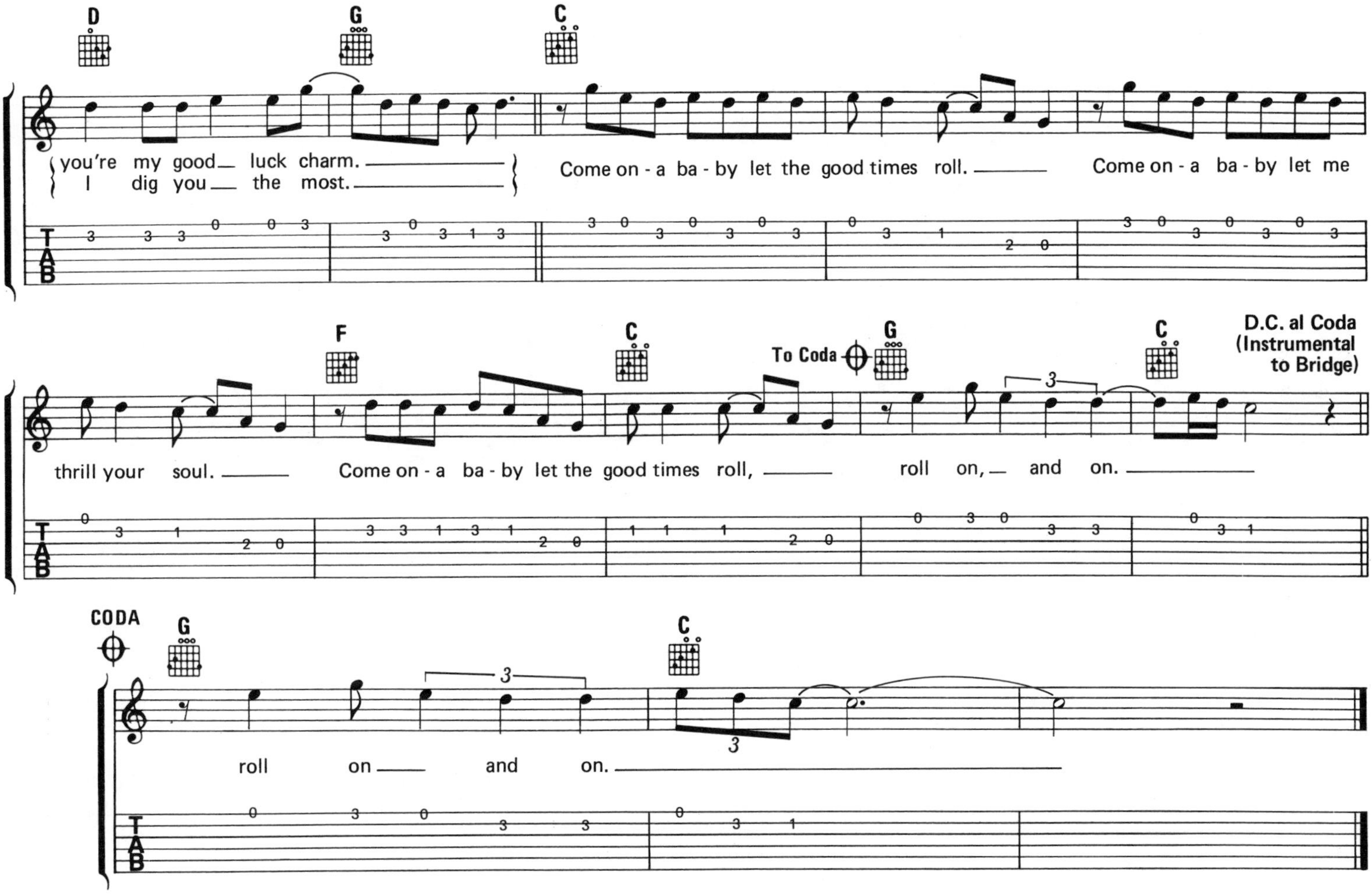

D G C

you're my good luck charm.
I dig you the most.

Come on-a ba-by let the good times roll. Come on-a ba-by let me

F C To Coda G C D.C. al Coda (Instrumental to Bridge)

thrill your soul. Come on-a ba-by let the good times roll, roll on, and on.

CODA G C

roll on and on.

LET THE GOOD TIMES ROLL

Words and Music by
SAM THEARD and FLEECIE MOORE

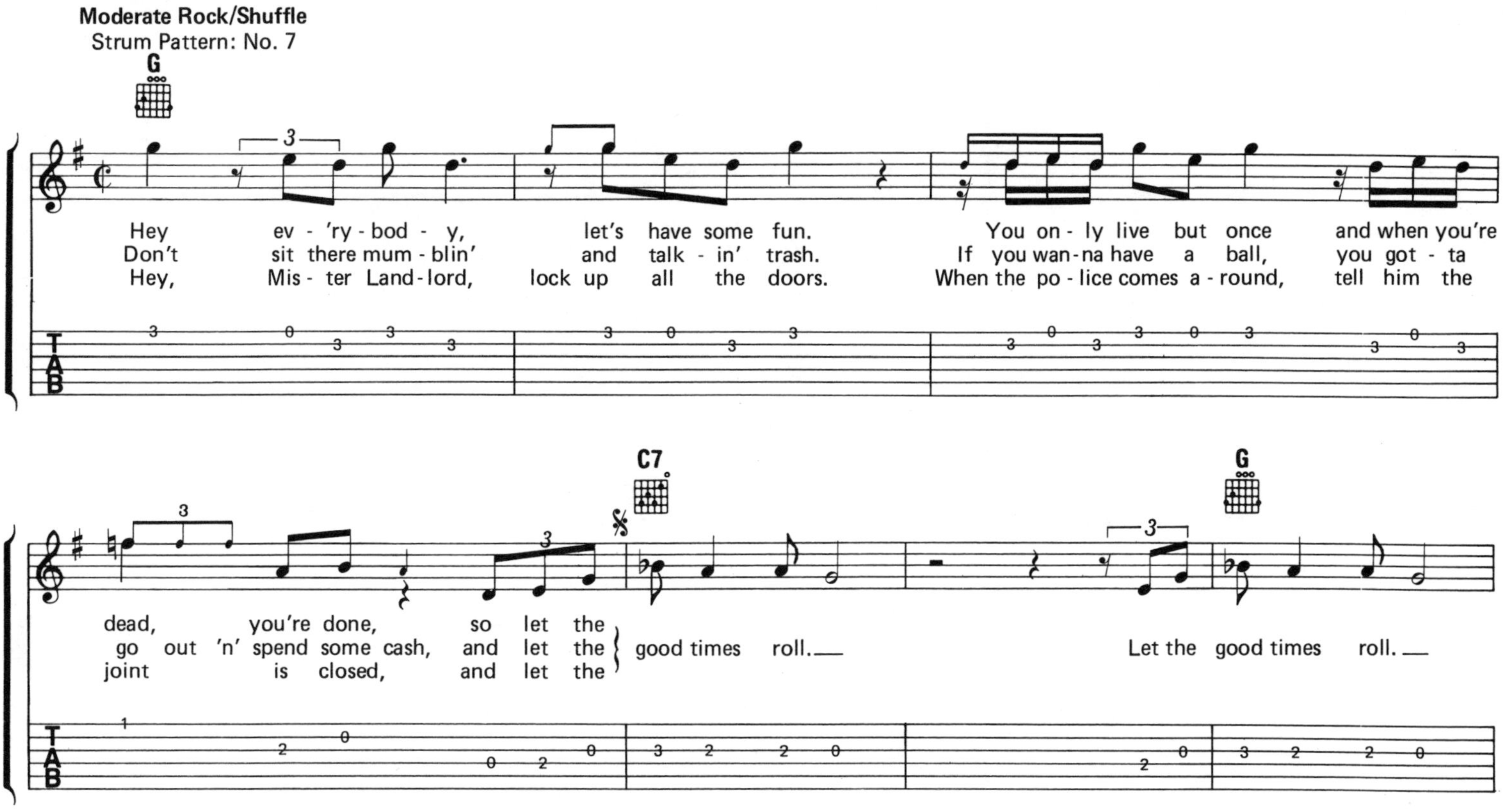

Moderate Rock/Shuffle
Strum Pattern: No. 7

G

Hey ev-'ry-bod-y, let's have some fun. You on-ly live but once and when you're
Don't sit there mum-blin' and talk-in' trash. If you wan-na have a ball, you got-ta
Hey, Mis-ter Land-lord, lock up all the doors. When the po-lice comes a-round, tell him the

C7 G

dead, you're done, so let the
go out 'n' spend some cash, and let the
joint is closed, and let the
good times roll. Let the good times roll.

Am7
D7
G
To Coda
Don't care if you're young or old, get to-geth'r and let the good times roll.
G
Tacet
Hey, y'all, tell ev-'ry-bod-y, Mis-ter Jor-dan's in town. I got a dol-lar 'n' a quar-ter 'n' I'm just rar-in' to clown. But
don't let no - bod-y play me cheap. I got fif-ty cents more that I'm gon-na keep. So let the
D.S. al Coda
CODA
G/B
C
C#dim
Hey, no mat-ter wheth-er it's rain-y weath-er,
G/D
Em7
G7
F7
E7
Bb7
birds of a feath-er got-ta stick to-geth-er; so get your-self un-der con-trol, go out
A7
D7b9
Ab7
G13
and get to-geth-er and let the good times roll.

LONG TALL SALLY

By ENOTRIS JOHNSON, RICHARD PENNIMAN and ROBERT BLACKWELL

Bright Boogie Shuffle
Strum Pattern: No. 8
Capo: Up One Fret (Actual Key: F)

LIVING IN AMERICA

Words and Music by
DAN HARTMAN and CHARLIE MIDNIGHT

Medium Funk
Strum Pattern: No. 4

D9 C6 D9 C6 After D.C.: no repeat

8va lower
(Bass riff for verse)

Verses 1 & 2:
D9 C6 D9 C6
Super highways coast to coast
trans-con-ti-nen-tal o-ver-load just

1,3,4
D9 C6 D9 C6
eas-y to get an-y where on the

2,5
D9 C6 D9 C6
slide be-hind the wheel. How does it feel when there's

(verse continues)
G7 A
no des-ti-na-tion that's too far. And some-where on the way you might find out who you are.

CHORUS
F G D9 C6 D9 C6 F
Liv-ing in A-mer-i-ca, eye-to-eye, station to sta-tion. Liv-ing in A-mer-i-ca,

G D9 C6
hand-to-hand a-

1,2 To next strain
D9 C6
cross the na-tion.

3,4 *etc.* Repeat ad lib. and Fade
D9 C6
cross the na-tion.

F C Bb7
Liv-ing in A-mer-i-ca, got to have a cel-e-bra-tion!

1
D(no3rd) C6
Rock my soul.

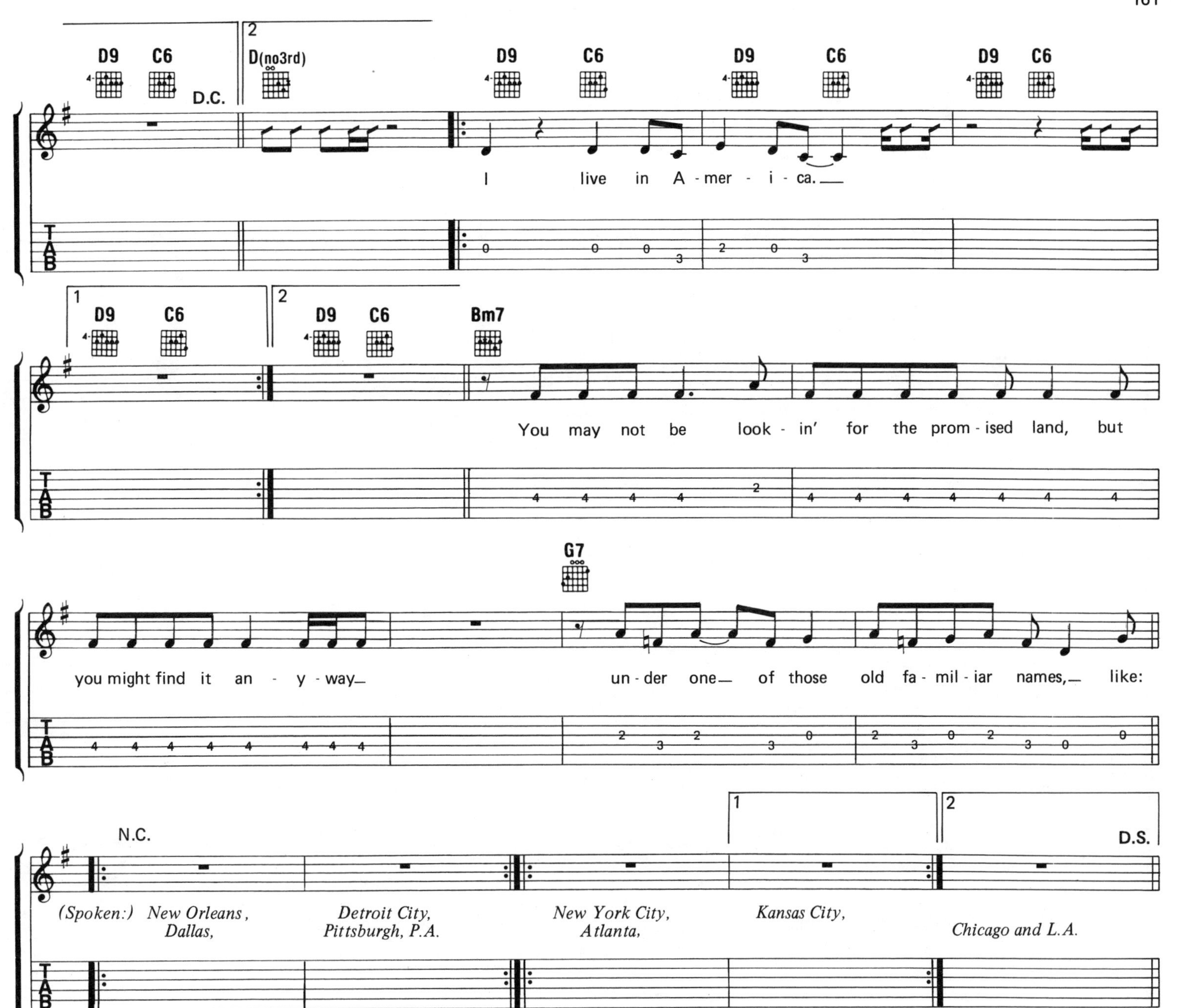

2. Smokestack, fatback,
Many miles of railroad track.
All-night radio,
Keep runnin' through your rock-and-roll soul.
All-night diners keep you awake
On black coffee and a hard roll.
You might have to walk a fine line;
You might take the hard line.
Everybody's workin' overtime. *(To Chorus)*

LOLA

Words and Music by
RAYMOND DOUGLAS DAVIS

E
said, "Dear boy, won't you come home with me?" Well, I'm not the world's most pas - sion - ate guy but when I
said, "Dear boy, I'm gon - na make you a man." Well, I'm not the world's most mas - cu - line man, but I
Repeat and Fade on D.S.
A D E A D C D
looked in her eyes, well, I al-most fell for my
know what I am, and I'm glad I'm a man and so is
Lo - la, la la la la Lo - la, la la la la Lo - la.
E A C#m B A C#m B A C#m B
I pushed her a-way, I walked to the door. I fell to the floor. I got
E G#7 C#m B E
down on my knees then I looked at her, and she at me. Well, that's the way that I want it to stay, and I
A D E A E
al-ways want it to be that way for my Lo - la, la la la la Lo - la. Girls will be boys, and boys will be girls, it's a
A D E A
D.S. and Fade
mixed up, mud-dled up, shook up world ex - cept for Lo - la, la la la la Lo - la. Well,

LAY DOWN SALLY

Words and Music by
ERIC CLAPTON, MARCY LEVY and GEORGE TERRY

D
E
Lay down, Sal - ly. No need to leave so soon. I've been try - ing all
A
A7
3rd time, D.S. to Chorus, Repeat Guitar riff and Fade
night long just to talk to you.
(Guitar)
The
I
LOUIE, LOUIE
Copyright ©1957 Limax Music, Inc.
Copyright Renewed, assigned to Limax Music, Inc. and American Berry Music
Words and Music by
RICHARD BERRY
Moderate Rock
Strum Pattern: No 1
Intro
CHORUS
A D Em D
(Rhythm Guitar riff - throughout tune)
Lou-ie, Lou-ie, oh no, say, we got-ta go.
Yeah yeah yeah yeah yeah, said a -Lou-ie, Lou-ie, oh, ba-by, well, we got-ta go.
To Coda
A
Three
Me
fine lit - tle girl, she waits for me. Me catch the ship a - cross the sea. Me
nights and days I sail the sea. I think of girl, oh, con - stant - ly. A -
see Ja - mai - ca, the moon a - bove. It won't be long, me see me love, to
sail that ship out all a - lone. Me nev - er know how I'll make it home.
on that ship, I dream she there. I smell the rose a - in her hair.
take her in my arms a - gain. I'll tell her I'll nev - er leave her here.
A -
Last Time, D.S. al Coda

THE MAGIC BUS

Words and Music by
PETER TOWNSHEND

Bo Diddley-type Beat
Strum Pattern: No. 12
Capo: Up One Fret (Actual Key: A♭)

Bb G F C G Bb F

(Rhythm guitar)

G Bb F G Bb G Bb G Bb G F C

G Bb F G Bb F C G

Ev - 'ry - day I get in the queue;
Thank you, driv-er, for get - tin' me here.
(Too much, the

F C G Bb G C G F C

mag - ic bus!) to get on the bus that takes me to you.
You'll be an in - spec - tor, have no fear.
(Too much, the mag-ic bus!)

Additional verses:

Three pence and six pence every day, (Too much, the magic bus!)
Just to drive to my baby. (Too much, the magic bus!)
Three pence and six pence each day; (Too much, the magic bus!)
Drive my baby every way. (Too much, the magic bus!)

Now I got my magic bus. (Too much, the magic bus!)
I said, "Now I got my magic bus." (Too much, the magic bus!)
I drive my baby every way. (Too much, the magic bus!)
Each time I go a different way. (Too much, the magic bus!)

Every day you'll see the dust,
I drive my baby in the magic bus.

(Repeat Chorus and Fade)

MAGGIE MAY

Words and Music by
ROD STEWART and MARTIN QUITTENTON

3. You lured me away from home,
'cause you didn't want to be alone.
You stole my heart; I couldn't leave you if I tried.

I suppose I could collect my books and go on back to school.
Or steal my daddy's cue and make a living out of playin' pool.
Or find myself a rock 'n' roll band that needs a helping hand.
Oh Maggie, I couldn't have tried any more.

4. You made a first-class fool out of me.
I'm blind as a fool can be.
You stole my heart, but I love you anyway.

MAGIC CARPET RIDE

Words and Music by
RUSHTON MOREVE and JOHN KAY

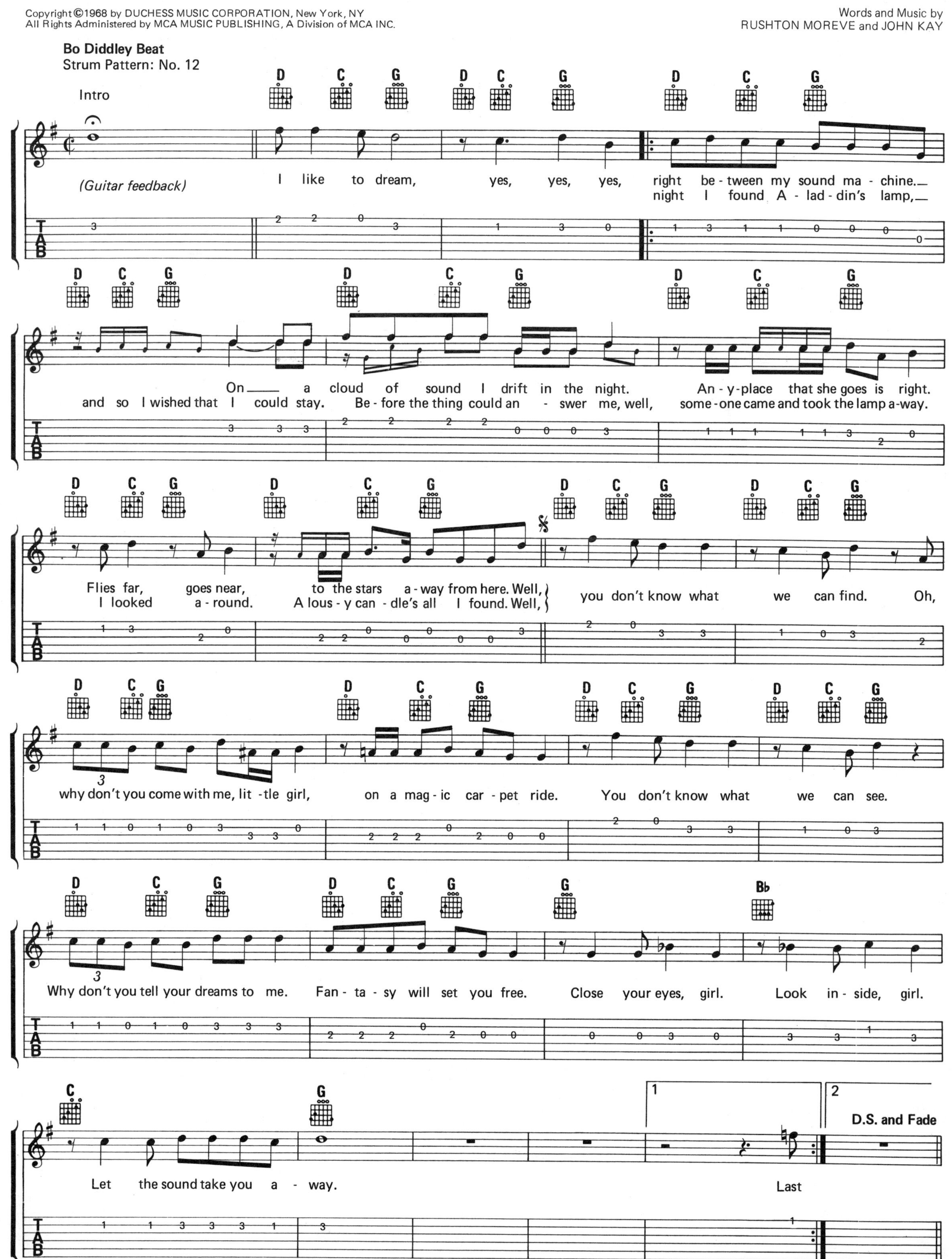

MAMA TOLD ME NOT TO COME

Words and Music by
RANDY NEWMAN

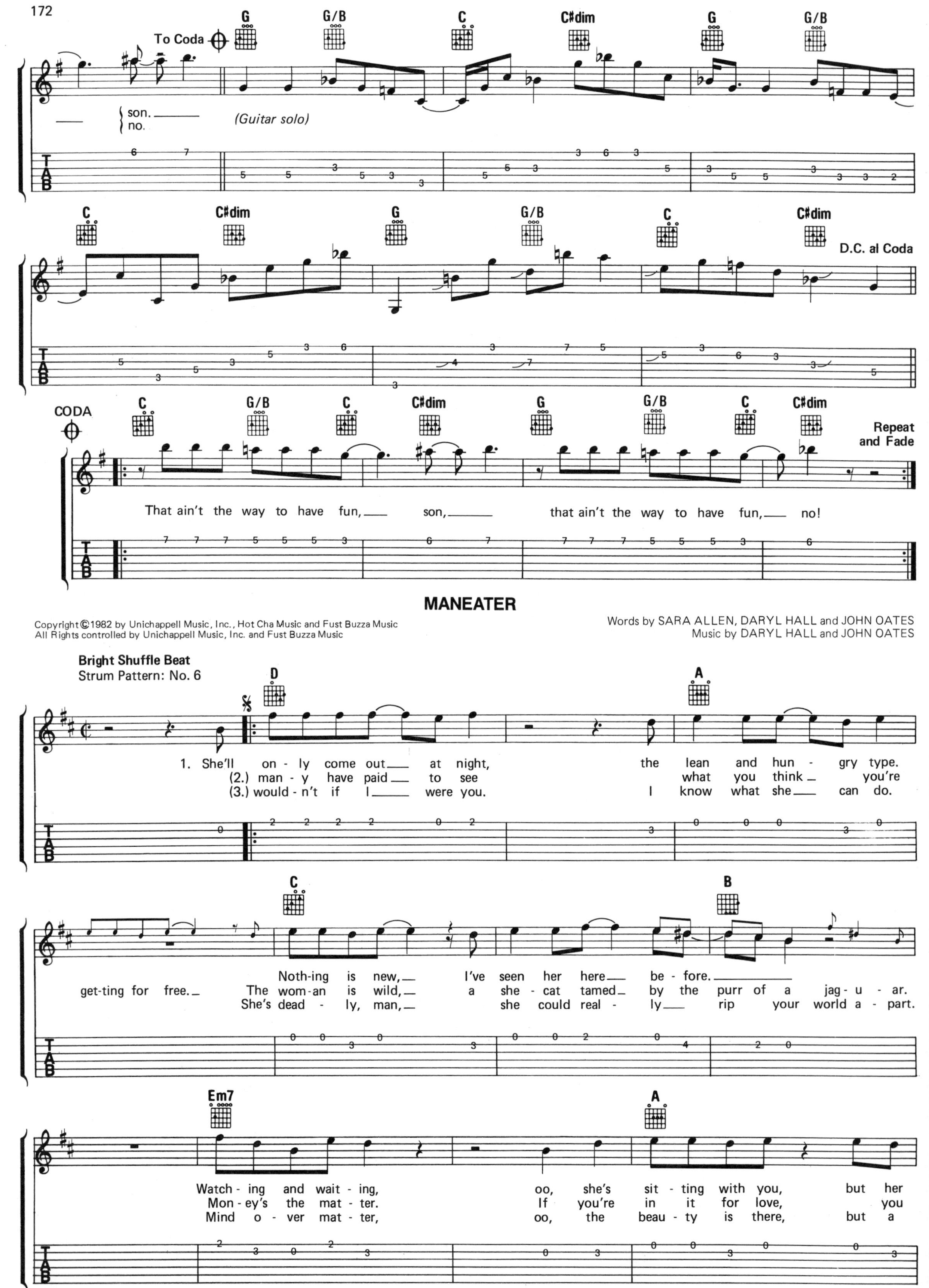
To Coda
G
G/B
C
C#dim
son.
no.
(Guitar solo)
D.C. al Coda
CODA
That ain't the way to have fun, son, that ain't the way to have fun, no!
Repeat and Fade
MANEATER
Copyright © 1982 by Unichappell Music, Inc., Hot Cha Music and Fust Buzza Music
All Rights controlled by Unichappell Music, Inc. and Fust Buzza Music
Words by SARA ALLEN, DARYL HALL and JOHN OATES
Music by DARYL HALL and JOHN OATES
Bright Shuffle Beat
Strum Pattern: No. 6
D
A
1. She'll on - ly come out at night, the lean and hun - gry type.
(2.) man - y have paid to see what you think you're
(3.) would - n't if I were you. I know what she can do.
C
B
Noth-ing is new, I've seen her here be - fore.
get-ting for free. The wom-an is wild, a she - cat tamed by the purr of a jag - u - ar.
She's dead - ly, man, she could real - ly rip your world a - part.
Em7
A
Watch - ing and wait - ing, oo, she's sit - ting with you, but her
Mon - ey's the mat - ter. If you're in it for love, you
Mind o - ver mat - ter, oo, the beau - ty is there, but a

B♭dim
Bm
F♯m7
1
Bm7
eyes are on the door.
ain't gon-na get too far.
beast is in the heart.
2. So
2,3
B
CHORUS
Bm
A
Oh, here she comes.
Watch out, boy, she'll
G
F♯
chew you up.
Oh, here she comes.
She's a man-eat-er.
Bm
A
Oh, here she comes.
Watch out boy, she'll
Em7
G
chew you up.
Oh, here she comes.
She's a man-eat-er.
A
Bm
D.S., Repeat Chorus and Fade
(Instrumental)
3. I

MANIAC

Music and Lyric by
MICHAEL SEMBELLO and DENNIS MATKOSKY

Moderately Fast
Strum Pattern: No. 1
Capo: Up One Fret (Actual Key: E♭m)

C
Dm7
Bbmaj7
C
- er danced_ be fore.
She's a ma - ni - ac, ma - ni - ac
on the
I sure
Dm7
C
Bbmaj7
C
Gm7
To Coda
floor,
know
and she's danc - ing like_ she's nev - er danced_ be - fore.
1
2
Dm9(#5)
Dm6/9
On the
(Guitar)
bend
release bend
Dm9
Dm9(#7)
Bbmaj7
C/Bb
Bbmaj9
(bend)
(release bend)
Dm
A
Dm9(#5)
Dm6/9
Dm9
○= Hammer on with right-hand finger
Dm9(#7)
Bbmaj7
C/Bb
Bbmaj9
Dm
D.S. al Coda (lyric 1)
(bend)
(bend)

CODA
Bbmaj7
C
Dm7
She's a ma - ni - ac, ma - ni - ac I sure know

C
Bbmaj7
C
Dm7
Repeat and Fade
and she's danc - ing like she's nev - er danced be - fore.
She's a ma-

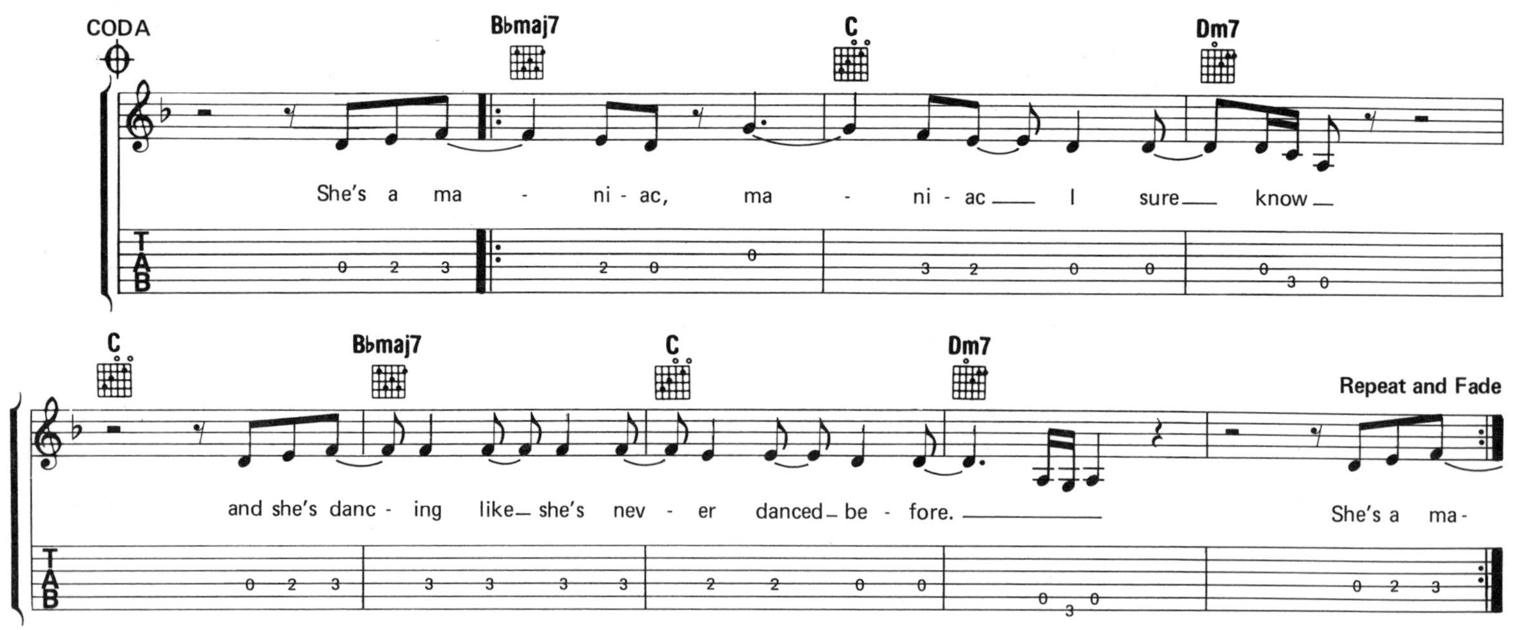

MISSING YOU

Words by JOHN WAITE
Music by JOHN WAITE, CHAS SANDFORD and MARK LEONARD

Medium Rock
Strum Pattern: No. 1

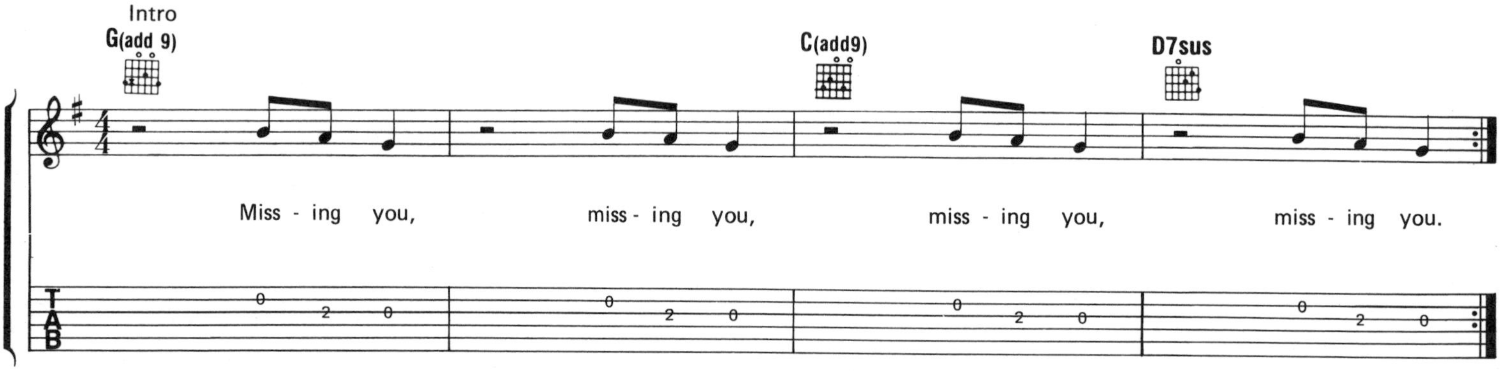

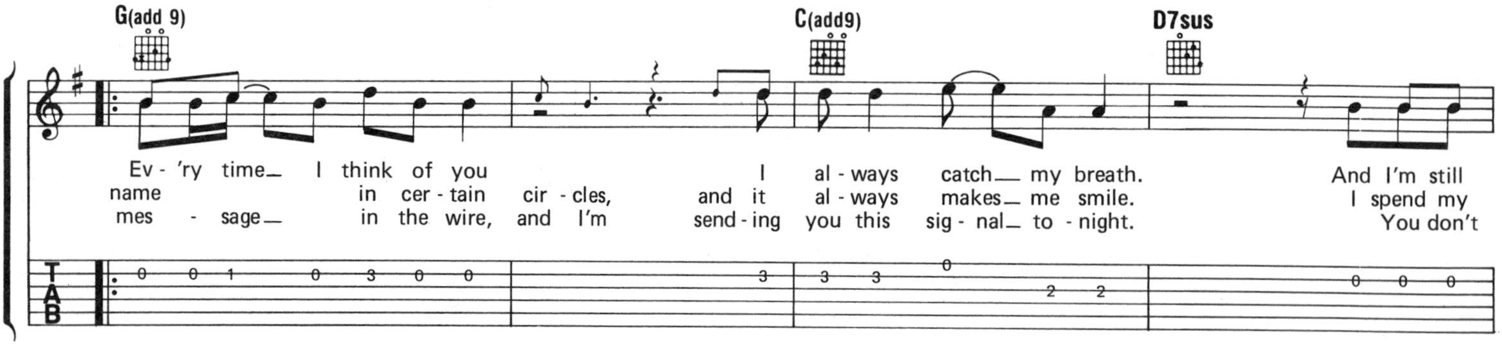

Intro
G(add 9)
C(add9)
D7sus
Miss - ing you, miss - ing you, miss - ing you, miss - ing you.

G(add 9)
C(add9)
D7sus
Ev - 'ry time I think of you I al - ways catch my breath. And I'm still
name in cer - tain cir - cles, and it al - ways makes me smile. I spend my
mes - sage in the wire, and I'm send - ing you this sig - nal to - night. You don't

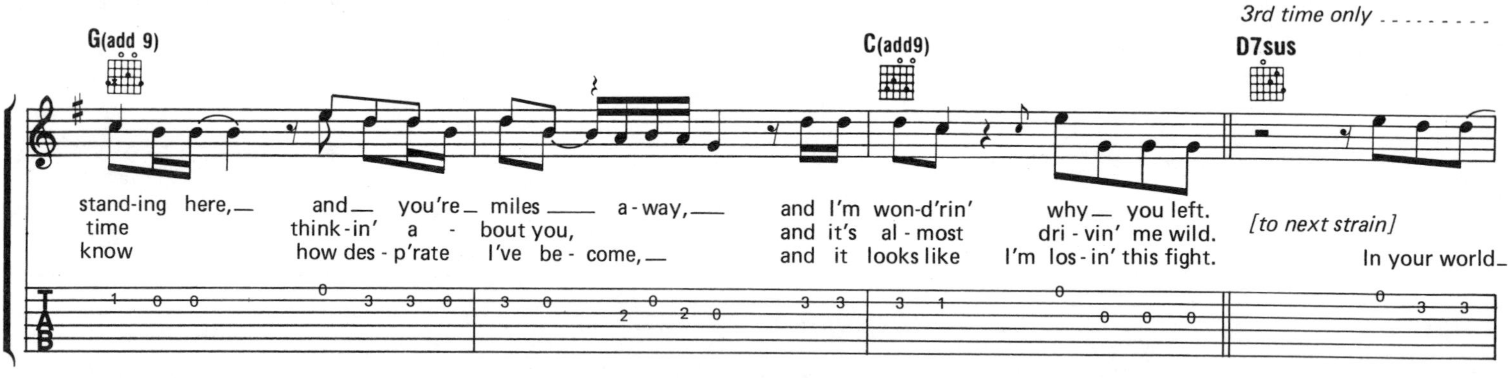

3rd time only
G(add 9)
C(add9)
D7sus
stand-ing here, and you're miles a - way, and I'm won-d'rin' why you left.
time think-in' a - bout you, and it's al - most dri - vin' me wild.
know how des - p'rate I've be - come, and it looks like I'm los - in' this fight.
[to next strain]
In your world

G(add 9)
C(add9)
D7sus
I have no mean - ing, though I'm try - in' hard to un - der - stand.
And there's a
And there's a
And it's my
Em
C
1
D
storm that's rag - in' through my fro - zen heart to - night.
heart that's break - in' down this long dis - tance line to - night.
heart that's break - in' down this long dis - tance line to - night.
I hear your
2,3
D
G(add 9)
C(add9)
I ain't miss - in' you at all, since you've been gone a - way.
D7sus
G(add 9)
C(add9)
I ain't miss - in' you, no mat - ter what I might say.
no mat - ter what my friends say.
D7sus
Em
C(add9)
3. There's a
(continue:)
And there's a mes - sage that I'm send - ing out like a tel - e - graph to your
D7sus
A
C6
soul. And if I can't bridge this dis - tance, stop this heart - break o - ver -
T
A
B

D7sus
G(add 9)
C(add9)
load. I ain't miss - in' you at all,
since you've been gone a - way,
I ain't miss - in' you,
no mat - ter what my friends
G
say. I ain't miss - in' you. I ain't miss - in' you. I can
Em11
C6
lie to my - self. And there's a storm that's rag - in' through my fro - zen heart to -
night. I ain't miss - in' you at all. (Ad lib.vocal)
Repeat and Fade

MONEY

Words and Music by
ROGER WATERS

MEMPHIS, TENNESSEE

Words and Music by
CHUCK BERRY

3. Help me, information, more than that I cannot add,
only that I miss her and all the fun we had.
But we were pulled apart because her mom did not agree,
and tore apart our happy home in Memphis, Tennessee.

4. Last time I saw Marie, she's waving me good-bye,
with hurry-home-drops on her cheek that trickled from her eye.
Marie is only six years old. Information, please,
try to put me through to her in Memphis, Tennessee.

"MIAMI VICE" THEME

By JAN HAMMER

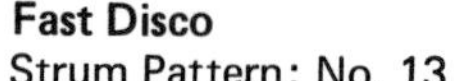

Tacet

f p f p

G C

mf mf

A(no3rd) F/A Dsus/A D/A Dsus/A D/A A

mp mf

F/A Dsus/A D/A Dsus/A D/A A G

C/G Csus/G C Csus/G C/G G C7

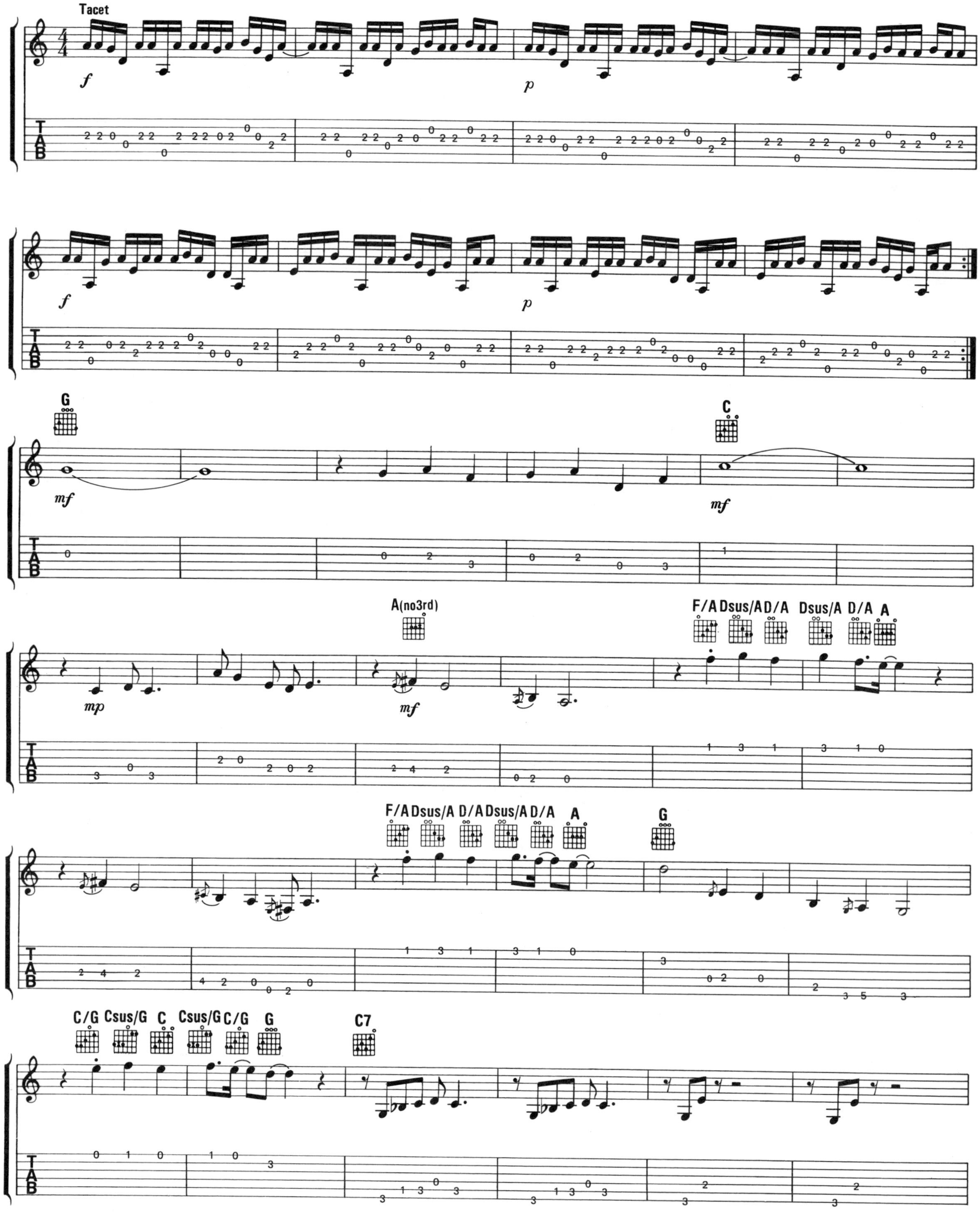

A(no3rd)
(Guitar)
(Guitar)
bend
release bend
G
C
bend
release bend
A(no3rd)
G(no3rd)
mp
f
C

MORNING TRAIN (NINE TO FIVE)

Words and Music by
FLORRIE PALMER

Dm7 G7 Dm7 G7 Dm G Dm G B♭ Am7
takes me to a mov - ie or to a res - tau-rant. Slow dan-cin'! An-y - thing I want. On - ly when he's with me,
Dsus D B♭maj7 Am7 Dsus D D7
D.S. al Coda
I catch a light. On - ly what he gives me, makes me feel all right.
CODA
F♯m7/B B7 Emaj7 F♯m B F♯m7/B
All day I think of him, dream-ing of him con - stant - ly. I'm cra - zy
B7 Emaj7 E6 E7 Amaj7
mad for him and he's cra-zy mad for me. When he steps off
Dmaj7 Gmaj7 Cmaj7 Gmaj7 Cmaj7 Em7
that train, a - maz - ing - ly full of fight. He works all day to
G C Em G C Em Dsus D7
D.S. and Fade
earns his pay so we can play all night.

MY LIFE

Words and Music by
BILLY JOEL

Bm
F#7
D7
I never said you had to of-fer me a sec-ond chance.
I nev-er said I was a vic-tim of cir - cum-stance.
E7
F#
G
D/F#
I still be-long;
don't get me wrong.
And you can speak your mind, but not on my time.
A7
To Coda
D.S. al Coda (with repeats)
CODA
D
my time.
I don't care what you say an-y-more; this is my life.
G
A
Go a-head with your own life; leave me a-lone.
D9
(Instrumental)
C9
F13
Bb
(Keep it to your-self, it's my life.)
life.)
Repeat and Fade

MY OLD SCHOOL

Words and Music by
WALTER BECKER and DONALD FAGEN

Moderate Rock
Strum Pattern: No. 1
Capo: Up One Fret (Actual Key: A♭)

G Em C

I re - mem - ber__ the thir - ty - five sweet good-byes__ when you put me on the
O - le - an - ders__ grow-ing out - side her door,__ soon they're gon-na
Cal - i - for - nia__ tum-bles in - to the sea,__ that - 'll be the

D G

Wol - ver - ine__ up to Ann - an-dale. It was still Sep - tem - ber__ when your
be in bloom__ up in Ann - an-dale. I can't stand__ her__
day I go__ back to Ann - an-dale. Tried to warn__ you__ a- bout

Em C D G

dad-dy was quite sur - prised__ to find you with the work - ing girls__ in the coun - ty jail.
do-ing what she did be - fore,__ liv-ing like a gyp - sy queen in a fair - y tale.
Chi-no and Dad - dy Gee,__ but I can't seem to get__ to you through the U.__ S. mail.

C D

I was smok-ing with the boys up - stairs__ when I heard a-bout the whole af - fair,__ I said,
Well, I hear the whis-tle but I can't go;__ I'm gon-na take her down to Mex - i - co.__ She said,
Well, I hear the whis-tle but I can't go;__ I'm gon-na take her down to Mex - i - co.__ She said,

G Em G Em C D Am7

"Oh, no,__ Wil-liam and Ma - y won't do."__
"Oh, no,__ Gua-da - la - ja - ra won't do."__
"Oh, no,__ Gua-da - la - ja - ra won't do."__

Well, I did not think the girl__

Bm7
Em
D
Am7
could be so cruel,
and I'm nev - er go - ing back
Bm7
1,2
G
Tacet
3
G
to my old school.
school.
D
Em7
Am7
Bm7
Em7
(Guitar)
D
Em7
Am7
Bm7
Em7
Repeat with guitar ad lib. and Fade

MY GENERATION

Words and Music by
PETER TOWNSHEND

* 4th verse, modulate one whole-step up to key of A.
** 5th verse repeats in key of B♭ (one half-step up from A).

NADINE

By CHUCK BERRY

2. I saw her from the corner when she turned and doubled back,
she started walkin' toward a coffee-colored Cadillac.
I's pushin' through the crowd, try'n' to get to where she's at,
and I was campaign shoutin' like a southern diplomat. (CHORUS)

3. Downtown, searchin' for her, lookin' all around,
saw her gettin' in a yellow cab headin' uptown.
I caught a loaded taxi, paid up everybody's tab,
flipped a twenty dollar bill and told him "Catch that yellow cab." (CHORUS)

4. She moves around like a wayward summer breeze.
Go, driver, go, go on 'n' catch her for me please.
Movin' through the traffic like a mounted cavalier,
leanin' out the taxi window, tryin' to make her hear. (CHORUS)

NEUTRON DANCE

Words and Music by
ALLEE WILLIS and DANNY SEMBELLO

E
Oh, I'm just burn - in', do - in' the Neu - tron Dance.
D.C. al Coda
To Coda
I'm just burn - in', do - in' the Neu - tron Dance.
CODA
Tacet
(Tacet)
Woo ooh. Woo I'm on fi -
D.S. al Coda
re, Yeah! Well, I'm on fi - re, yeah! And it's
CODA
I know there's a pot of gold for me. All I got to do
is just be - lieve. I'm so hap - py, do - in' the Neu - tron Dance.

1.
And I'm just burn - in', do - in' the Neu - tron Dance.
2.
Repeat and Fade
Whoo ooh. Whoo ooh.
I'm so hap - py,
I'm just burn - in'.

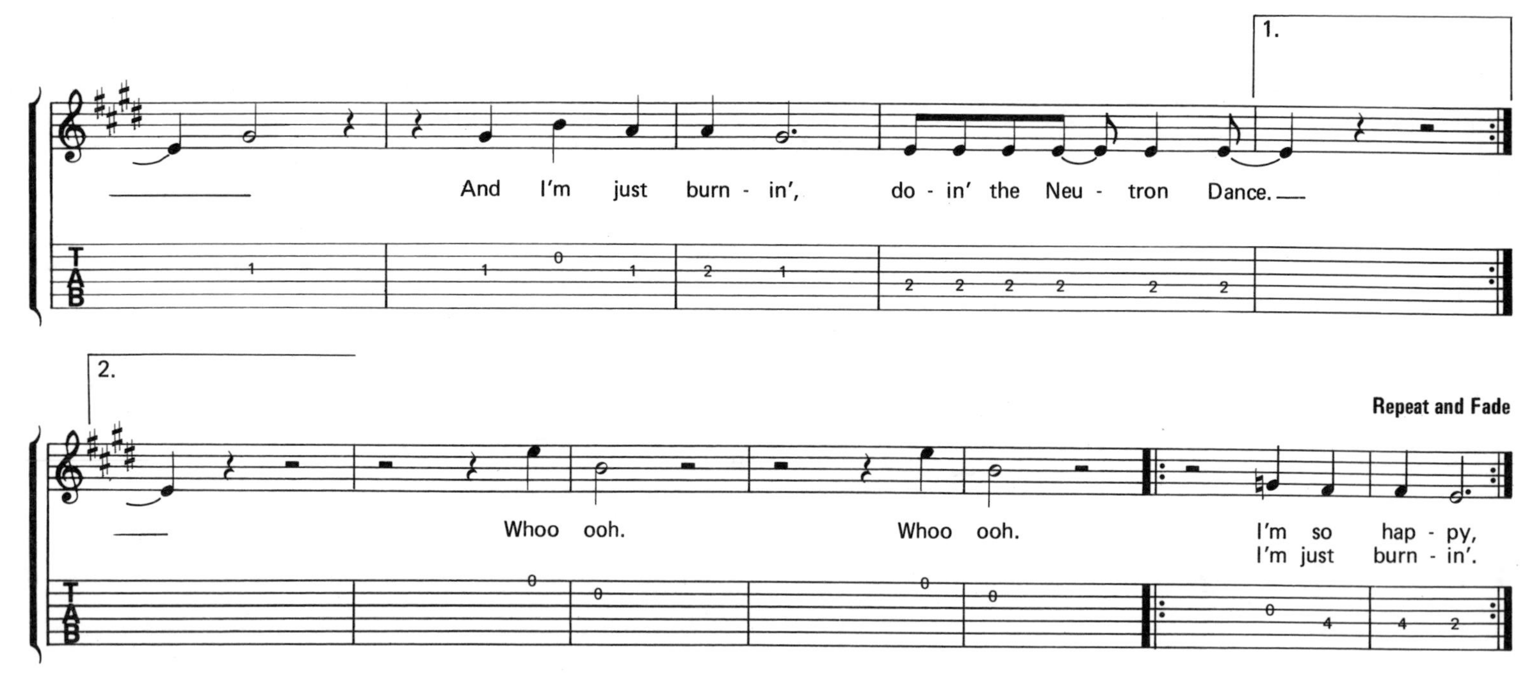

NIGHTSHIFT

Words and Music by
WALTER ORANGE, DENNIS LAMBERT and FRANNE GOLDE

Medium Funk
Strum Pattern: No. 4
Capo: Up Two Frets (Actual Key: A)

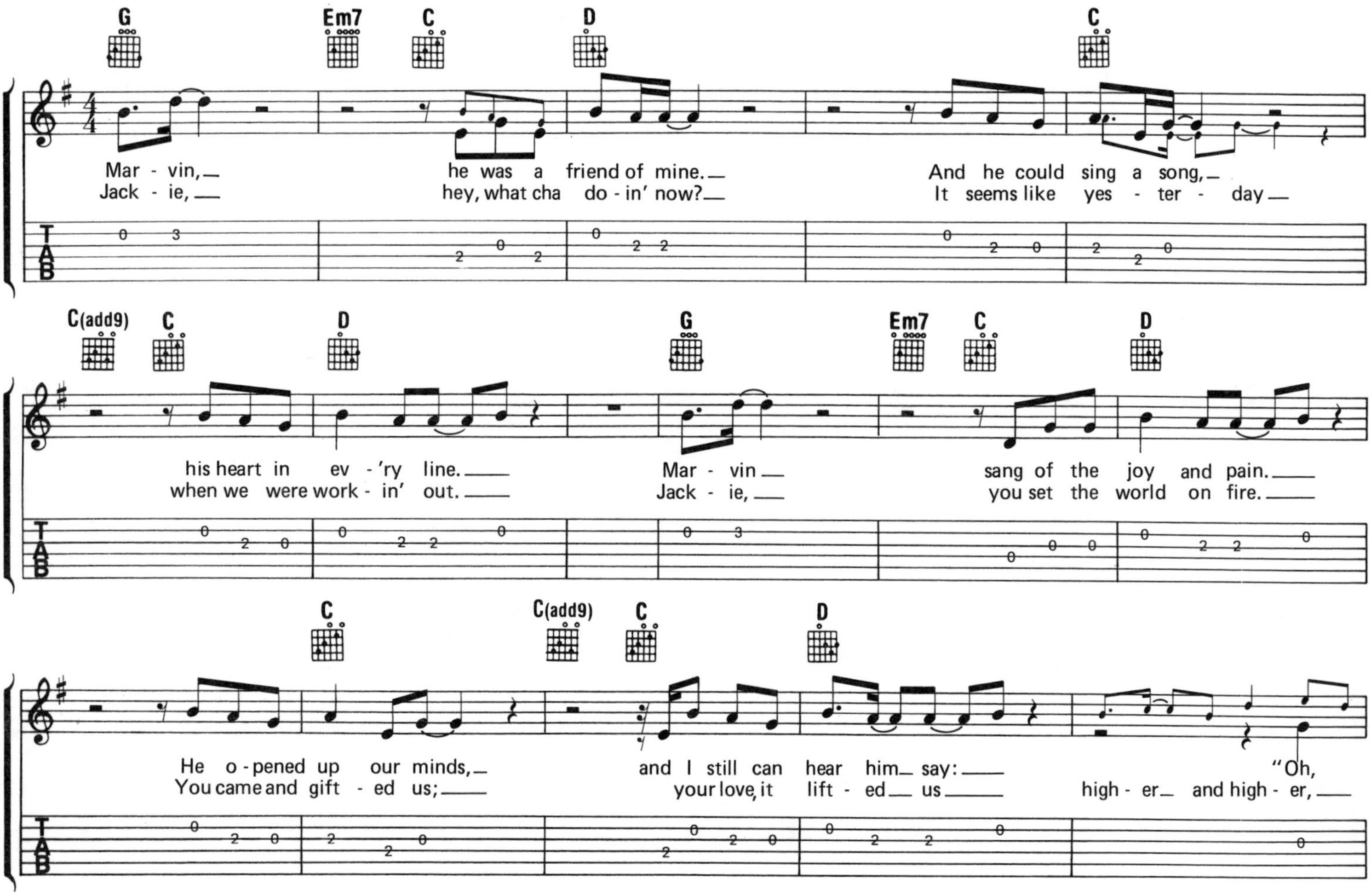

G Em7 C D C
Mar - vin, he was a friend of mine. And he could sing a song,
Jack - ie, hey, what cha do - in' now? It seems like yes - ter - day
C(add9) C D G Em7 C D
his heart in ev - 'ry line. Mar - vin sang of the joy and pain.
when we were work - in' out. Jack - ie, you set the world on fire.
C C(add9) C D
He o - pened up our minds, and I still can hear him say: "Oh,
You came and gift - ed us; your love, it lift - ed us high - er and high - er,

Em Am7 Am7/D Em Am7
talk to me so you can see what's go-in' on." Say you will sing your songs for-
Keep it up and we'll be there at your side.
Cmaj9 G Em C Am/D
ev-er-more (ev-er-more.) Gon-na be some sweet sounds com-in' down on the night shift.
C G Am7/D
I bet you're sing-in' proud, oh, I bet you pull a crowd. Gon-na be a
G Em C Am/D C
long night, it's gon-na be all-right on the night-shift. You found an-oth-er home, I know you're
D G Em C D
not a-lone on the night-shift. Oh, you found an-oth-er home, I know you're not a-lone on the
G Em7 C D D(add9) D D(add9) Em
night-shift. night-shift. Gon-na be some
Tacet
D.S. and Fade
TAB

NOT FADE AWAY

Words and Music by
CHARLES HARDIN and NORMAN PETTY

A D A D A

(Guitar solo)

E A E A E

2nd time, D.S. al Coda (3rd verse)

CODA

E A E

Repeat and Fade

fade a - way.

(Instrumental - same as Intro)

ONE NIGHT IN BANGKOK

Words and Music by BENNY ANDERSSON, TIM RICE and BJORN ULVAEUS

Moderate Funk/Disco Beat
Strum Pattern: No. 4

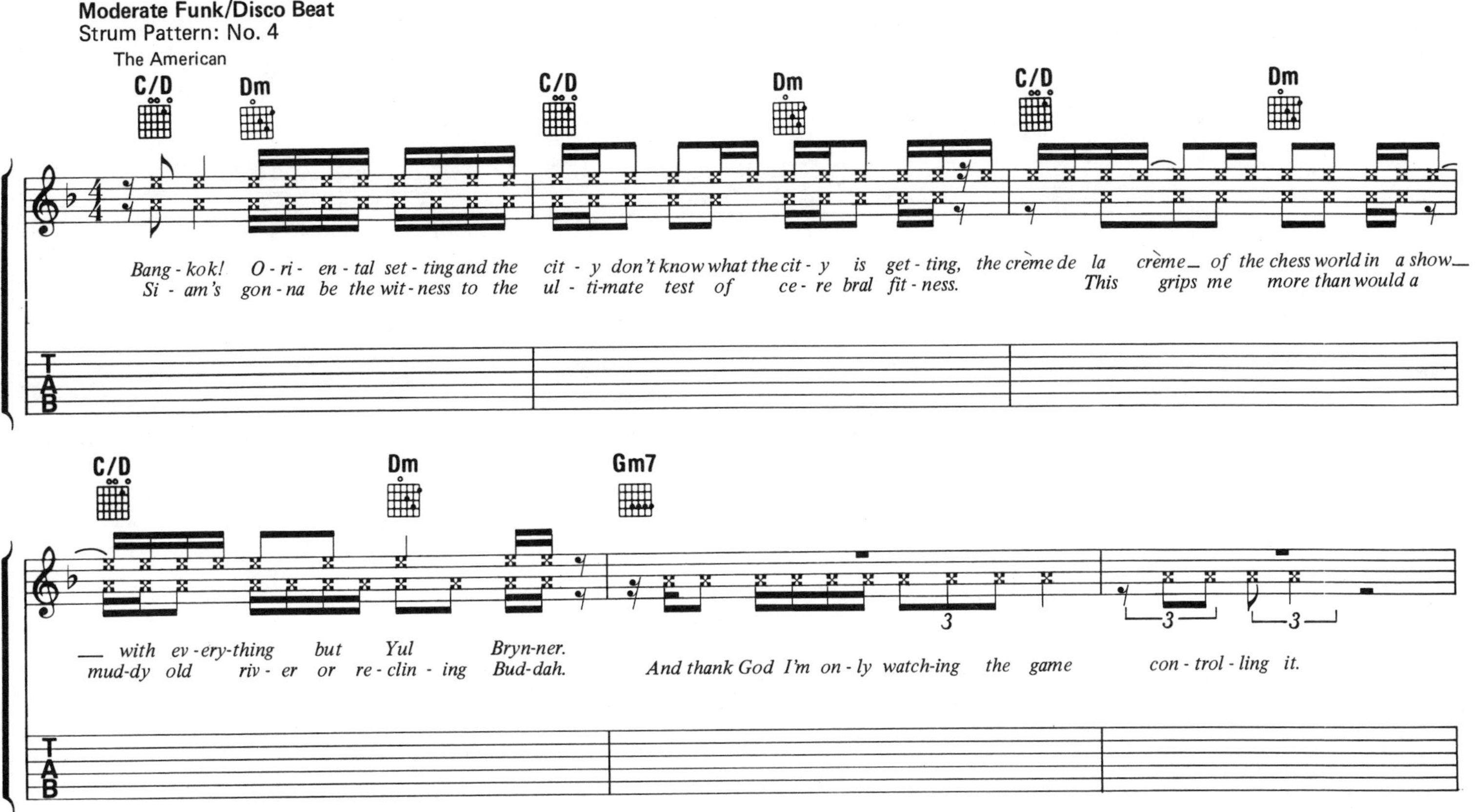

Dm7
C/D
Dm
C/D
Dm
Time flies does-n't seem a min-ute since the Ti-ro-le-an spa had the chess boys in it. All change don't you know that when you
I don't see you guys rat-ing the kind of mate I'm con-tem-plat-ing. I'd let you watch I would in-vite you but the
C/D
Dm
Gm7
play at this lev-el there's no or-di-na-ry ven-ue. It's Ice-land or the Phil-ip-pines or Has-tings
queens we use would not ex-cite you. So you'd bet-ter go back to your bars, your tem-ples, your mas-
Gm7
C#dim
CHORUS
Dm
Bb
F
C/E
Dm
Choir
or – or this place!
sage par-lours –
One night in Bang-kok and the world's your oys-ter, the bars are
Gm
Dm
Bb
F
C/E
Dm
tem-ples but the pearls ain't free. You'll find a god in ev-ery gold-en clois-ter and if you're a lit-tle
Gm
Second time to Chorus 2
Dm
The American
luck-y then the god's a she.
flesh, a lit-tle his-to-ry.
I can feel an an-gel slid-ing up to me. One town's ver-y like an-oth-er when your
Choir
head's down o-ver your piec-es broth-er. It's a drag, it's a bore, it's real-ly such a pit-y to be look-ing at the board, not look-ing at the cit-y.

The American
Gm7
Dm
Choir
Whad-dy - a mean? You've seen one crowd-ed, pol - lu - ted stink - ing town Tea, girls warm and sweet some are set up in the Som-er-set Maugh-am suite,
(warm, sweet)
The American
Gm7
Get Thai'd! You're talk-ing to a tour - ist whose ev - ery move's a - mong the pur - est. I get my kicks a -
CHORUS 2
Gm7 C#dim Dm Bb F C/E Dm
Choir
bove the waist- line, sun - shine! One night in Bang-kok makes a hard man hum-ble, not much be-tween
Gm Dm Bb F C/E Dm
de-spair and ec - sta - sy. One night in Bang-kok and the tough guys tum-ble, can't be too care -
Gm Dm Dm9
To Coda
D.C. al Coda
CODA
ful with your com-pa - ny. I can feel the dev - il walk - ing next to me.

OH SHEILA

Words and Music by MELVIN RILEY, JR., GORDON STROZIER and GERALD VALENTINE

Em11
Tacet
Oh ba - by, it's one - two - three, I love you ba - by, hon - est - ly.
I want to dee - dle - dee - dle - dee a dee - dle - dee - dle in.
C(add9)
C6/9
D.C. al Coda
Oh, oh Shei - la. Uh, uh, uh, Oh Shei - la. Shei - la.
CODA
Oh, oh Shei - la, let me love you 'til the morn-ing comes.
Oh, oh Shei - la, you know I want to be the on - ly one. Here we go: Oh.
Em7

PAPERBACK WRITER

Words and Music by
JOHN LENNON and PAUL McCARTNEY

Bright Rock
Strum Pattern: No. 1

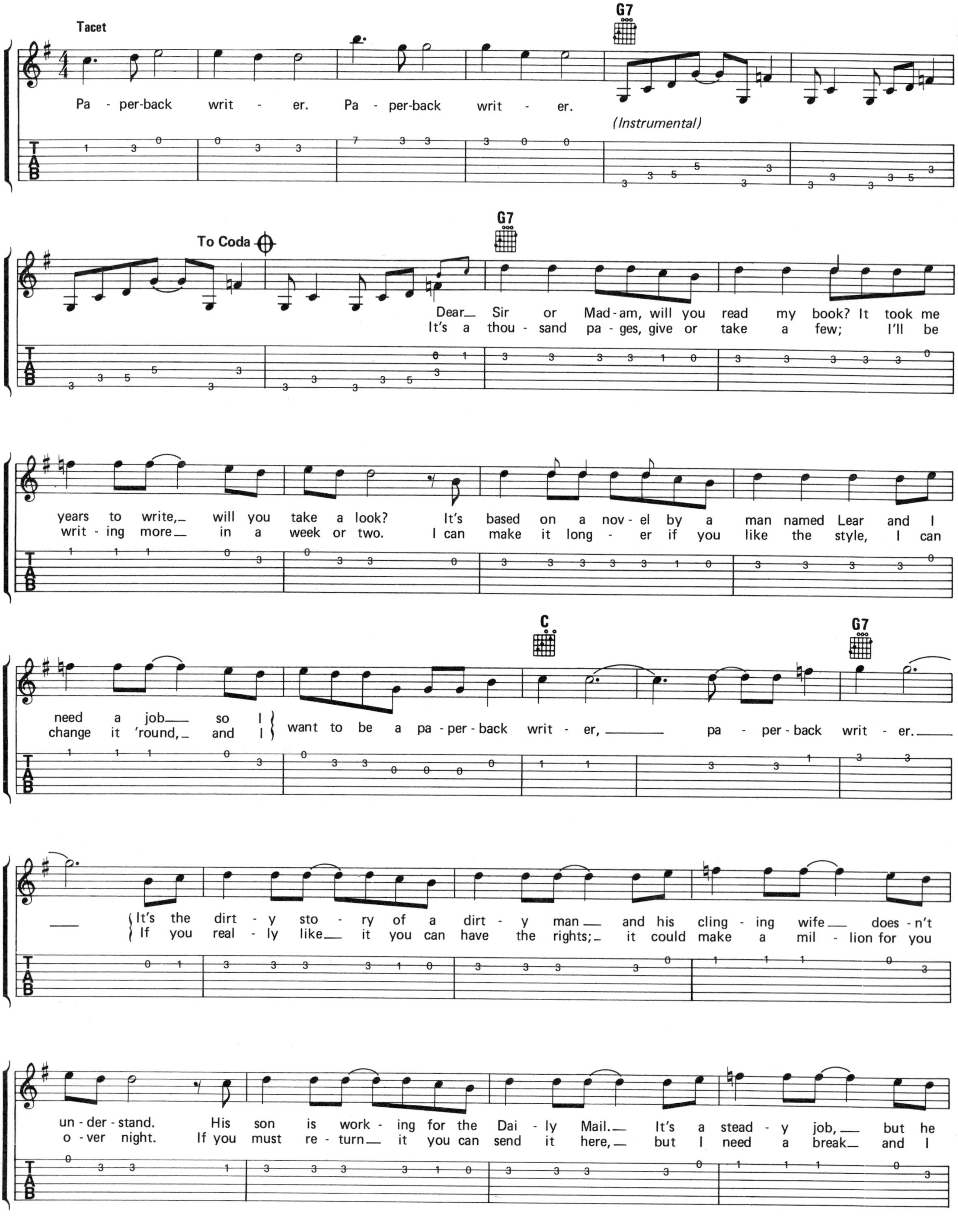

Tacet

G7

Pa - per-back writ - er. Pa - per-back writ - er.

(Instrumental)

To Coda

G7

Dear Sir or Mad-am, will you read my book? It took me
It's a thou - sand pa - ges, give or take a few; I'll be

years to write, will you take a look? It's based on a nov - el by a man named Lear and I
writ - ing more in a week or two. I can make it long - er if you like the style, I can

C G7

need a job so I / change it 'round, and I } want to be a pa - per - back writ - er, pa - per - back writ - er.

{It's the dirt - y sto - ry of a dirt - y man and his cling - ing wife does - n't
{If you real - ly like it you can have the rights; it could make a mil - lion for you

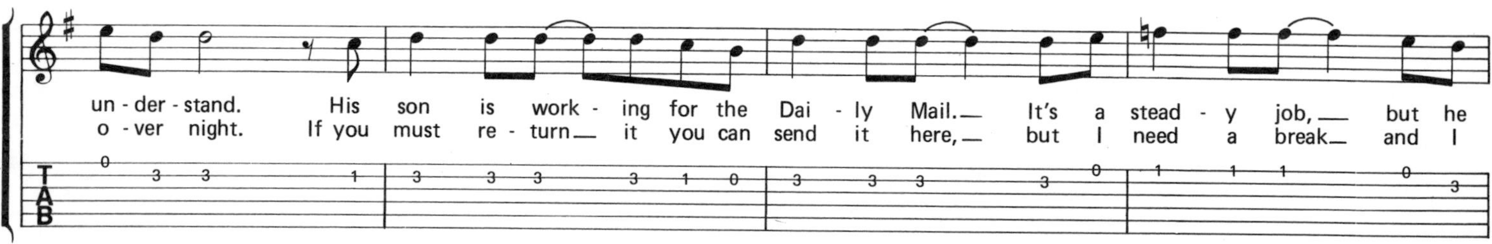

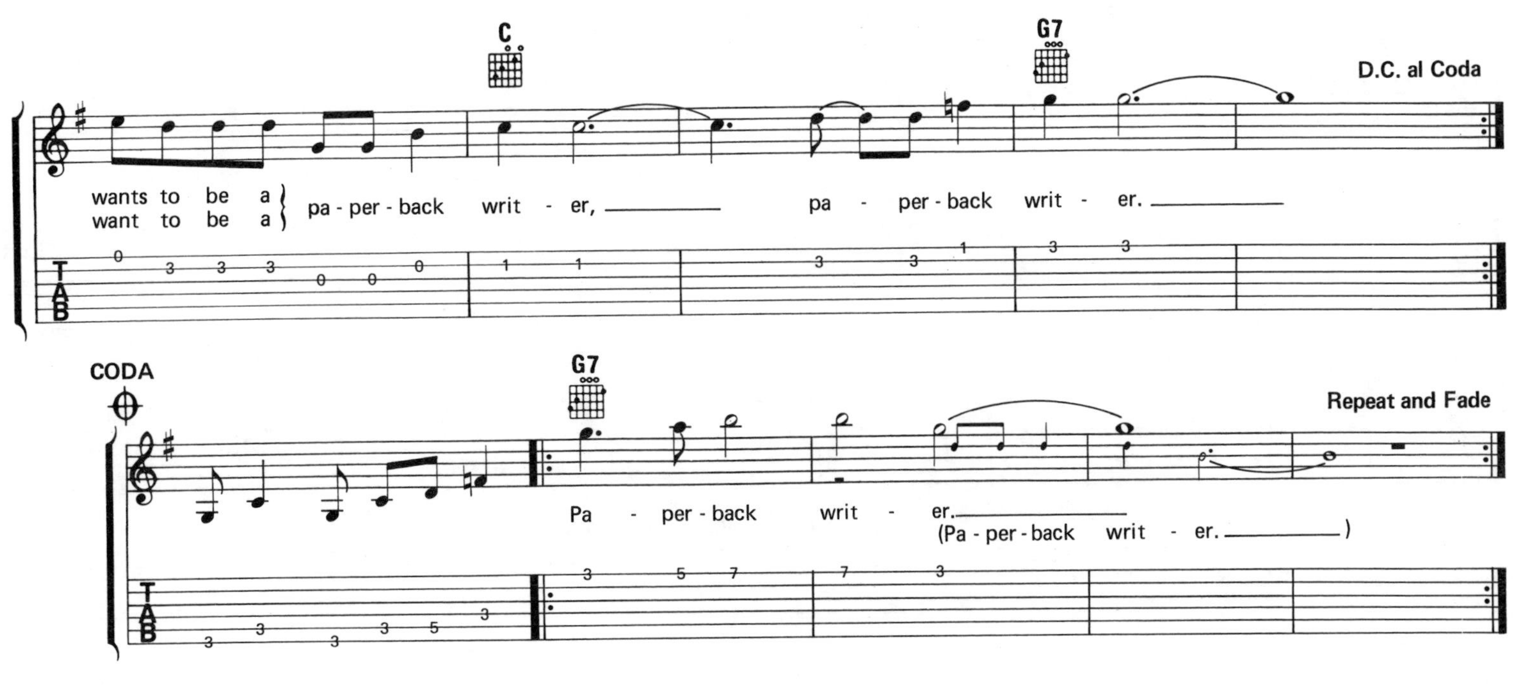

PEGGY SUE

Words and Music by
JERRY ALLISON, NORMAN PETTY and BUDDY HOLLY

Bright Rock Beat
Strum Pattern: No. 1

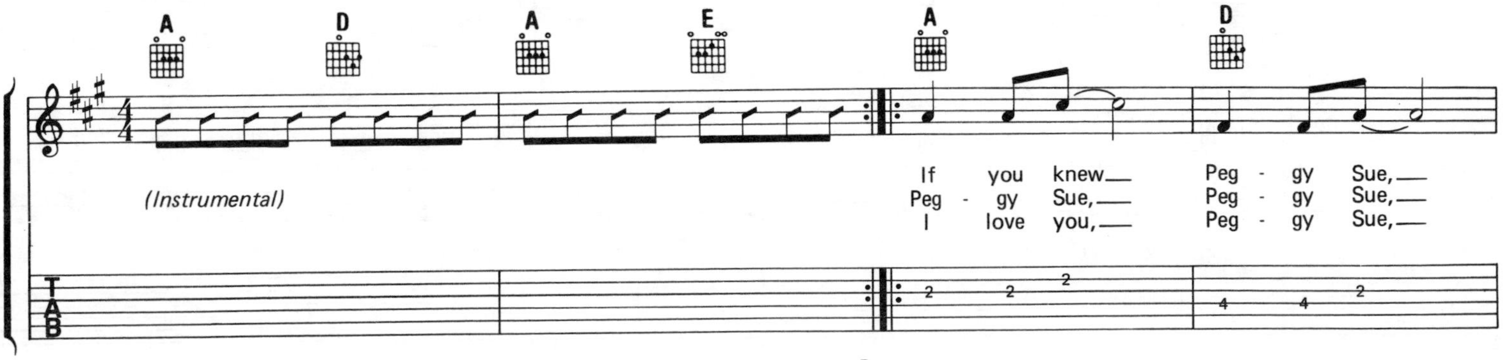

A D A E A D

(Instrumental)

If you knew Peg - gy Sue,
Peg - gy Sue, Peg - gy Sue,
I love you, Peg - gy Sue,

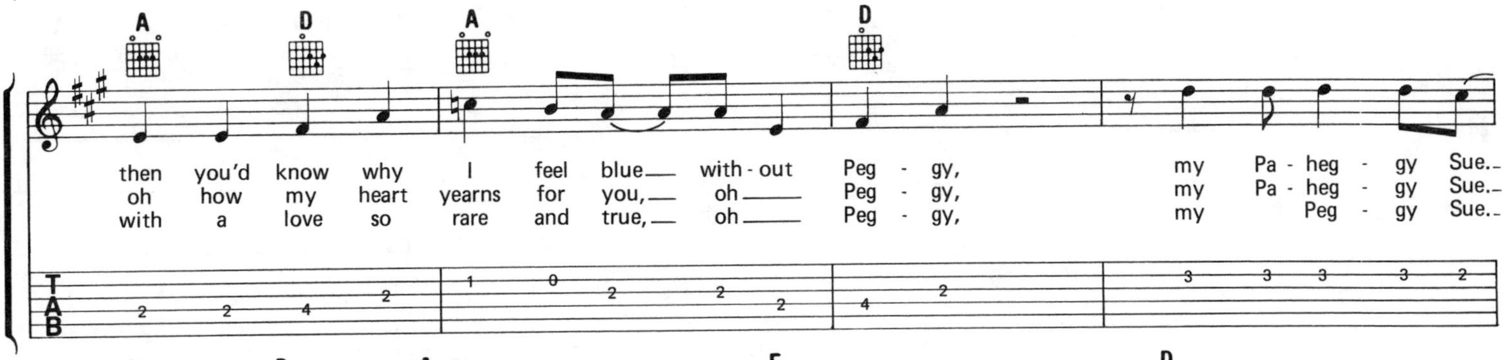

A D A D

then you'd know why I feel blue with - out Peg - gy, my Pa - heg - gy Sue.
oh how my heart yearns for you, oh Peg - gy, my Pa - heg - gy Sue.
with a love so rare and true, oh Peg - gy, my Peg - gy Sue.

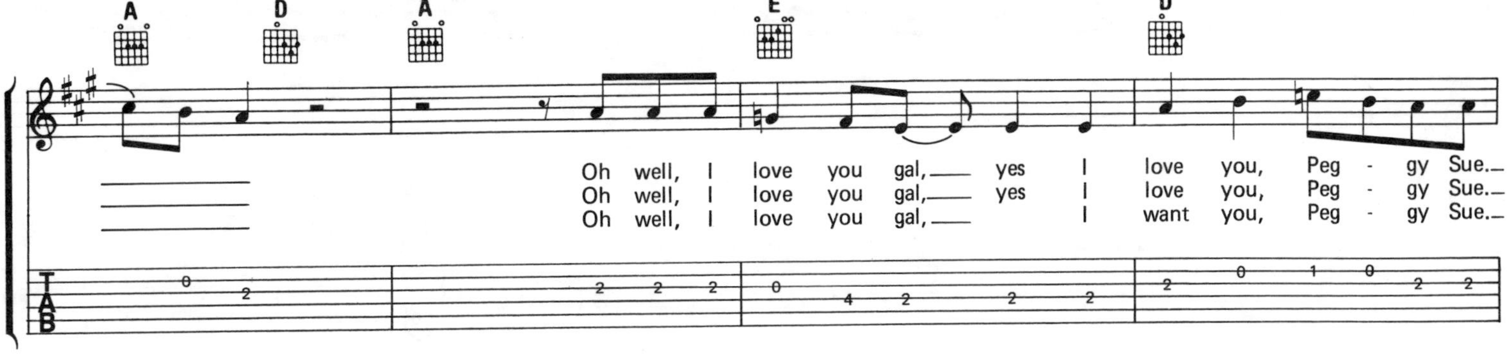

A D A E D

Oh well, I love you gal, yes I love you, Peg - gy Sue.
Oh well, I love you gal, yes I love you, Peg - gy Sue.
Oh well, I love you gal, I want you, Peg - gy Sue.

A
D
A
E
A
E
A
Peg - gy Sue,
Peg - gy Sue,
F
A
D
pret - ty, pret - ty, pret - ty, pret - ty
Peg - gy Sue, oh,
oh
Peg - gy,
my Peg - gy Sue.
Oh well, I love you, gal, and I need you Peg - gy Sue.
To Coda
(Guitar)
A(add9)
D.S. al Coda
CODA
Oh well, I love you gal, and I want you Peg - gy Sue.

PIPELINE

Words and Music by
BOB SPICKARD and BRIAN CARMAN

PRIDE IN THE NAME OF LOVE

Music by U2
Words by BONO

B(sus4)
E(sus2)
A
F♯m
of love what more in the name of love (In the name
Sung on fade only
(B bass)
(D bass)
(E bass)
(Instrumental)
Mmm mmm mmm
Ear - ly morn-ing Ap - ril four a shot rings out in the Mem-phis sky.
Free at last they took your life they could not take your pride in the name
D.S. and Fade
(repeat Chorus)

PURPLE HAZE

Words and Music by
JIMI HENDRIX

PRETTY IN PINK

Words and Music by TIM BUTLER, RICHARD BUTLER, VINCE ELY, JOHN ASHTON, DUNCAN KILBURN and ROGER MORRIS

2. She turns herself 'round
and she smiles and she says,
"This is it; that's the end of the joke."
And loses herself in her
dreaming and sleep, and her
lovers walk through in their coats. *(To Chorus:)*

3. All of her lovers all
talk of her notes and the
flowers that they never sent.
And wasn't she easy, and
isn't she pretty in pink?

4. The one who insists he was the
first in the line is the
last to remember her name.
He's walking around in this
dress that she wore.
She is gone, but the
joke's the same. *(To Chorus)*

5. Caroline talks to you
softly sometimes; she says,
"I love you" and "Too much."
She doesn't have anything
you want to steal.
Well, nothing you can touch.

6. She waves;
she buttons your shirt
The traffic is waiting outside.
She hands you this coat;
she gives you her clothes.
These car collide. *(To Chorus:)*

POISON IVY

Words and Music by
JERRY LIEBER and MIKE STOLLER

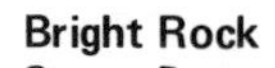

Bright Rock
Strum Pattern: No. 1
Capo: Up One Fret (Actual Key: A♭)

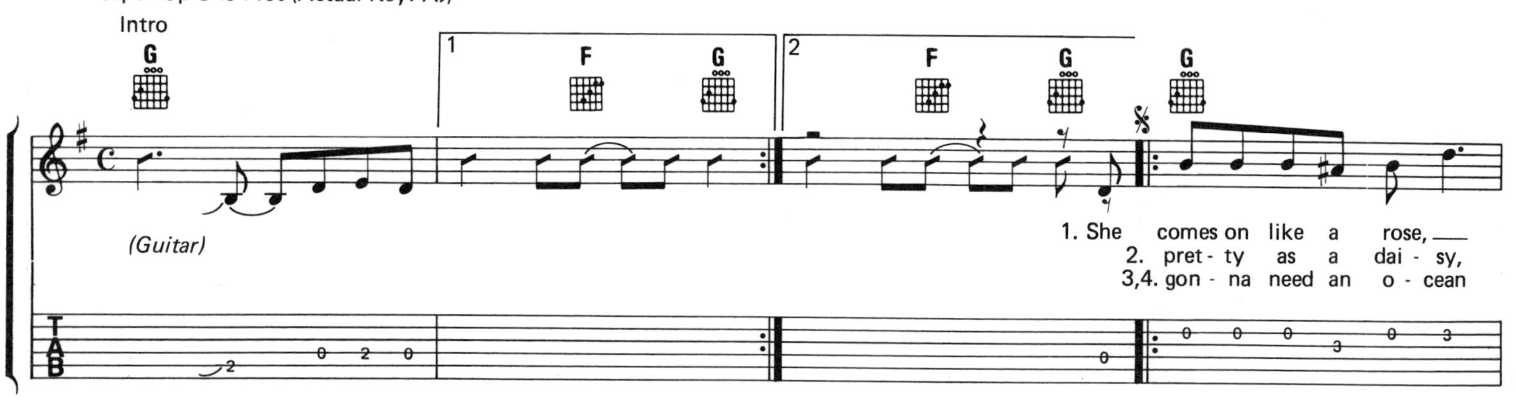

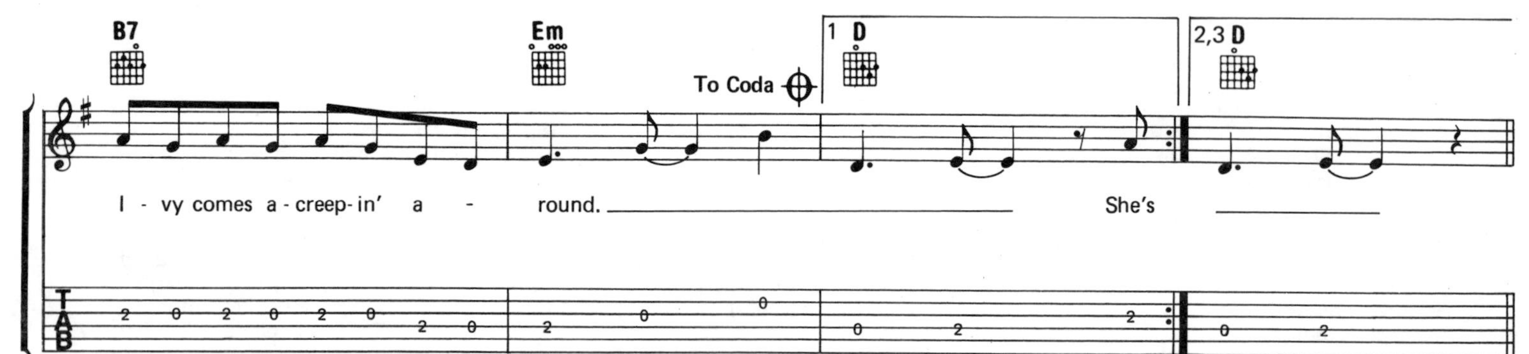

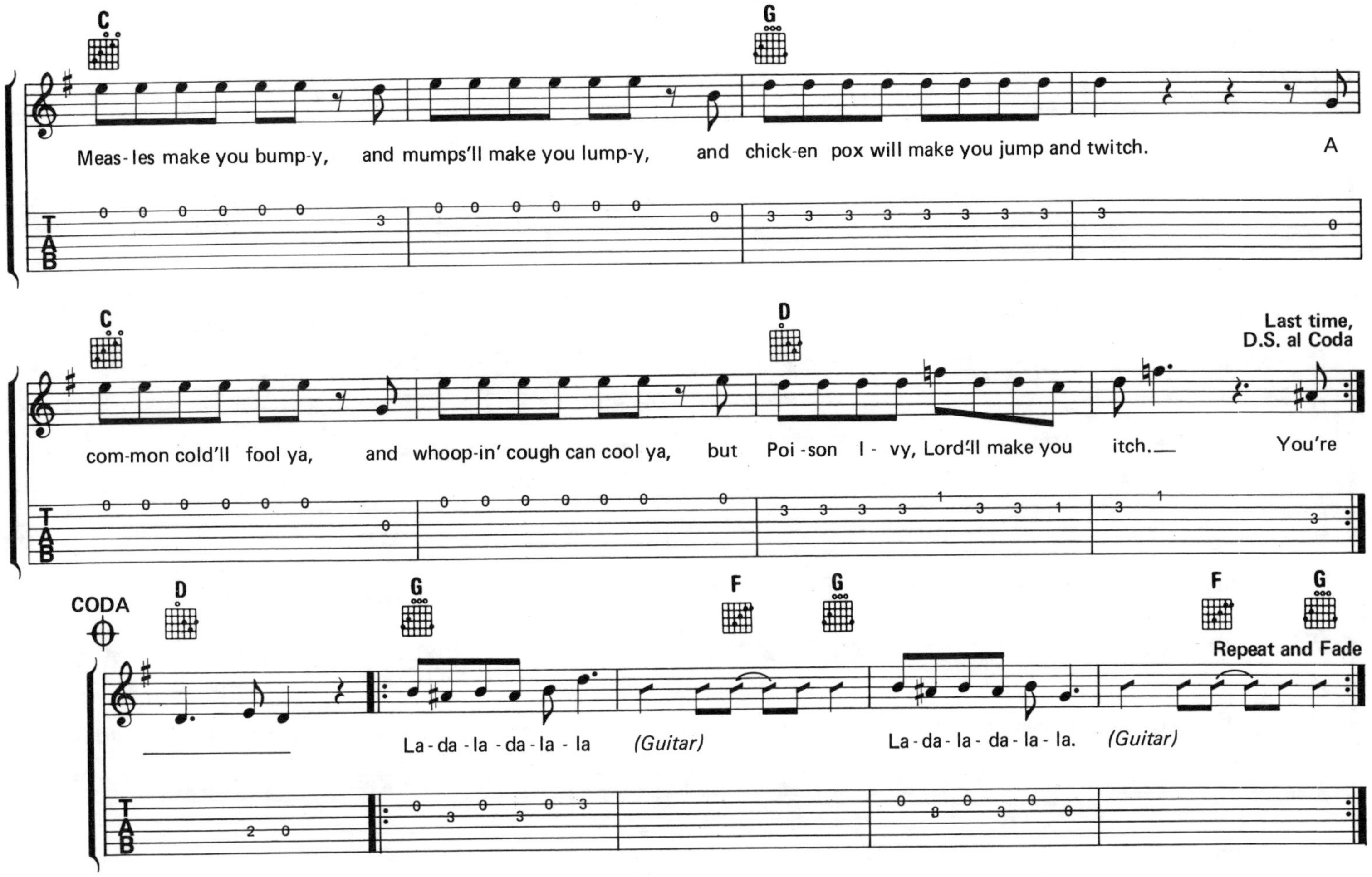

C
G
Meas-les make you bump-y, and mumps'll make you lump-y, and chick-en pox will make you jump and twitch.
A
C
D
Last time, D.S. al Coda
com-mon cold'll fool ya, and whoop-in' cough can cool ya, but Poi-son I-vy, Lord'll make you itch.
You're
CODA
D
G
F
G
F
G
Repeat and Fade
La-da-la-da-la-la
(Guitar)
La-da-la-da-la-la.
(Guitar)

QUEEN OF THE BROKEN HEARTS

Words and Music by
PAUL DEAN and MIKE RENO

Fast Rock
Strum Pattern: No. 11

E
A
E
(Guitar)
A
Ab
Db
1. Both sides are fight-in'; you don't know who to choose.
2. (See additional lyrics)

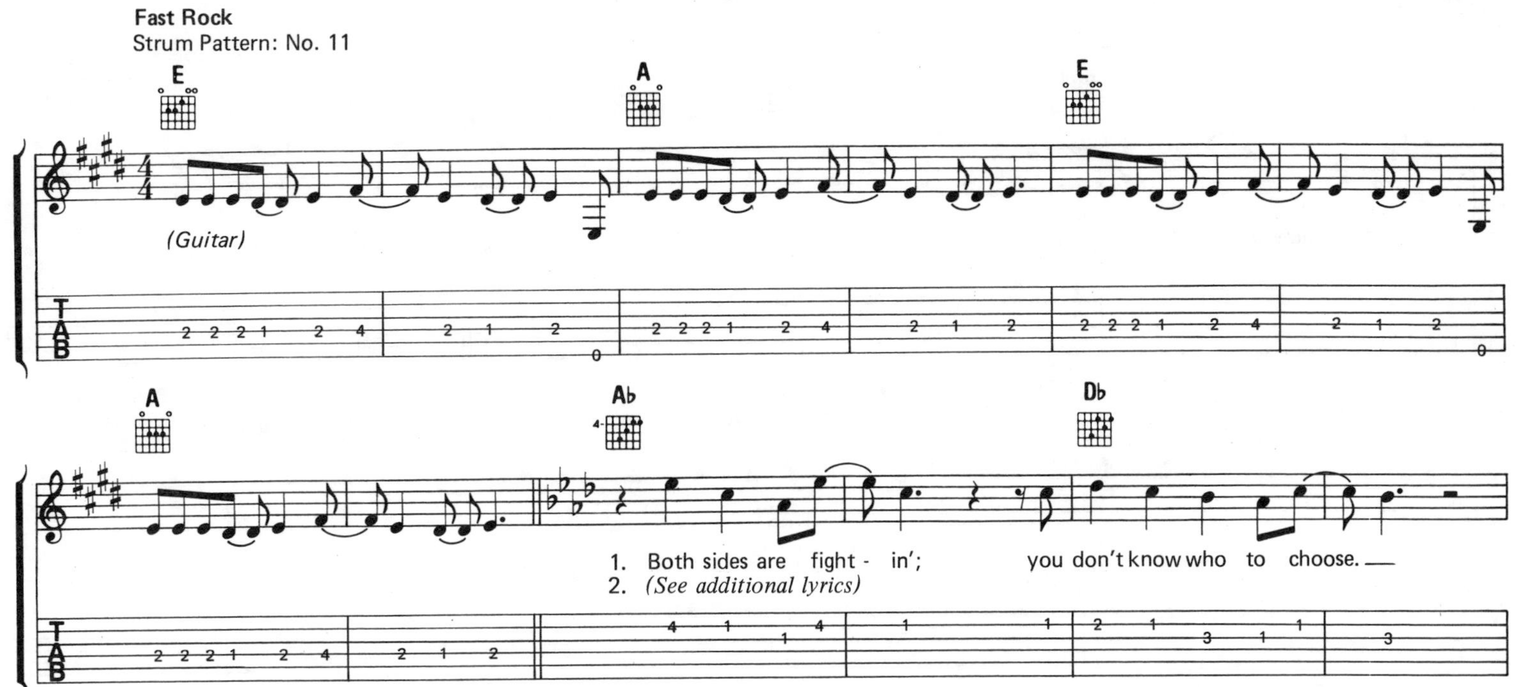

Ab
Db
Gb
Ab
You're stuck in the mid - dle and you can't lose.
Both sides are talk - in'; you've
Db
Bbm
Ab
Db
Gb
fi -n'lly seen the light.
You'll get it to - geth - er, but not to - night.
You were
B
F#/A#
G#m7
E
B
F#/A#
born with it and now you got it the way you want it.
And you don't care, 'cause noth-in's gon-na bring you down.
G#m7
E
F#
B
F#/A#
G#m7
E
You were born with it and now you got it and ooh, you flaunt it.
And
B
F#/A#
G#m7
E
F#
G#m
F#
you don't care 'cause noth-in's gon-na bring you down.
But she's not that kind of girl.
I'm
E
G#m
To Coda
E
F#
B
Bb(no3rd)
tell-in' all the world she was born the queen of the bro-ken hearts.

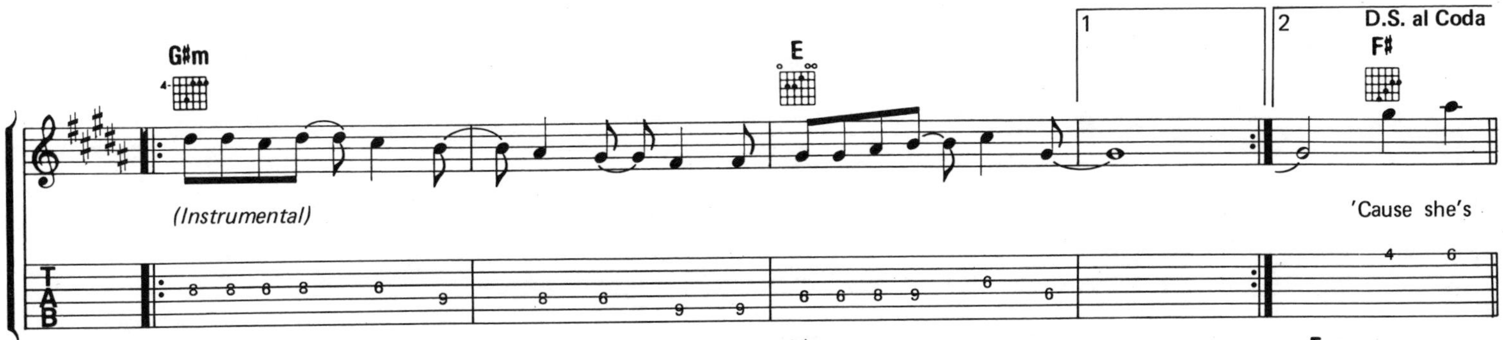

1
2
D.S. al Coda
G#m
E
F#
(Instrumental)
'Cause she's

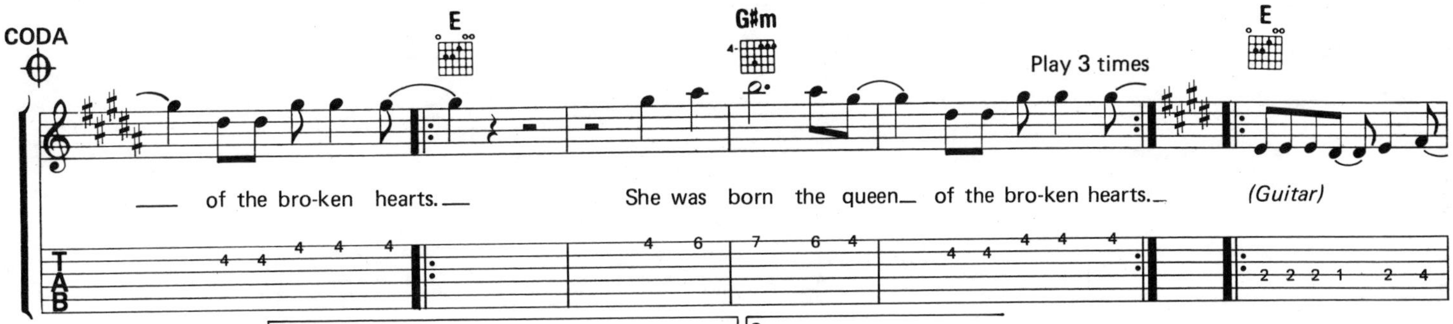

CODA
E
G#m
Play 3 times
E
___ of the bro-ken hearts.___
She was born the queen__ of the bro-ken hearts.__
(Guitar)

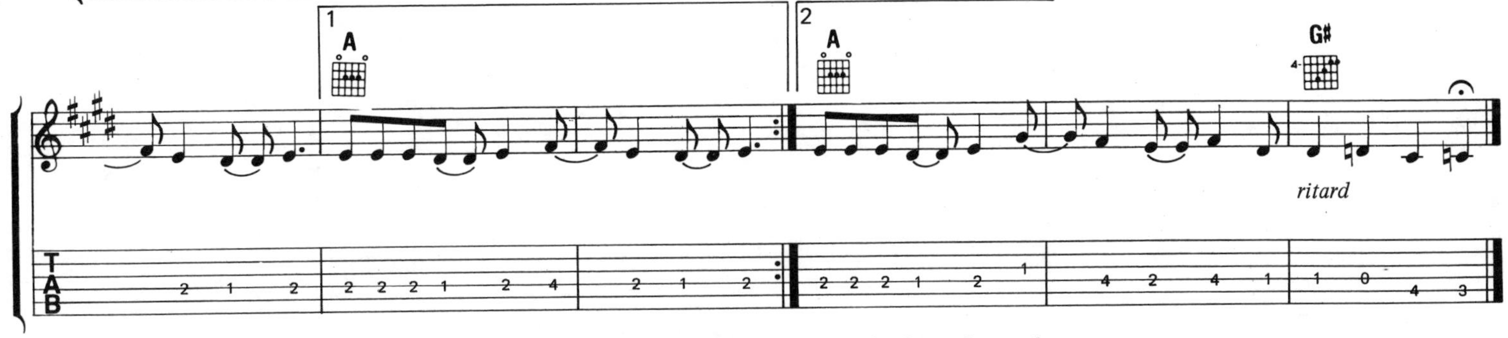

1
A
2
A
G#
ritard

2. She says she'll write you letters; but that's not face to face.
She'll give you a number, but it's not her place.
Don't keep her waiting; now see what you have done.
You look in the mirror; it ain't no fun.

RAUNCHY

Words and Music by
WILLIAM JUSTIS and SIDNEY MANKER

Medium Rockabilly Shuffle
Strum Pattern: No. 10

D
(Guitar)

To Coda
1,4
G7

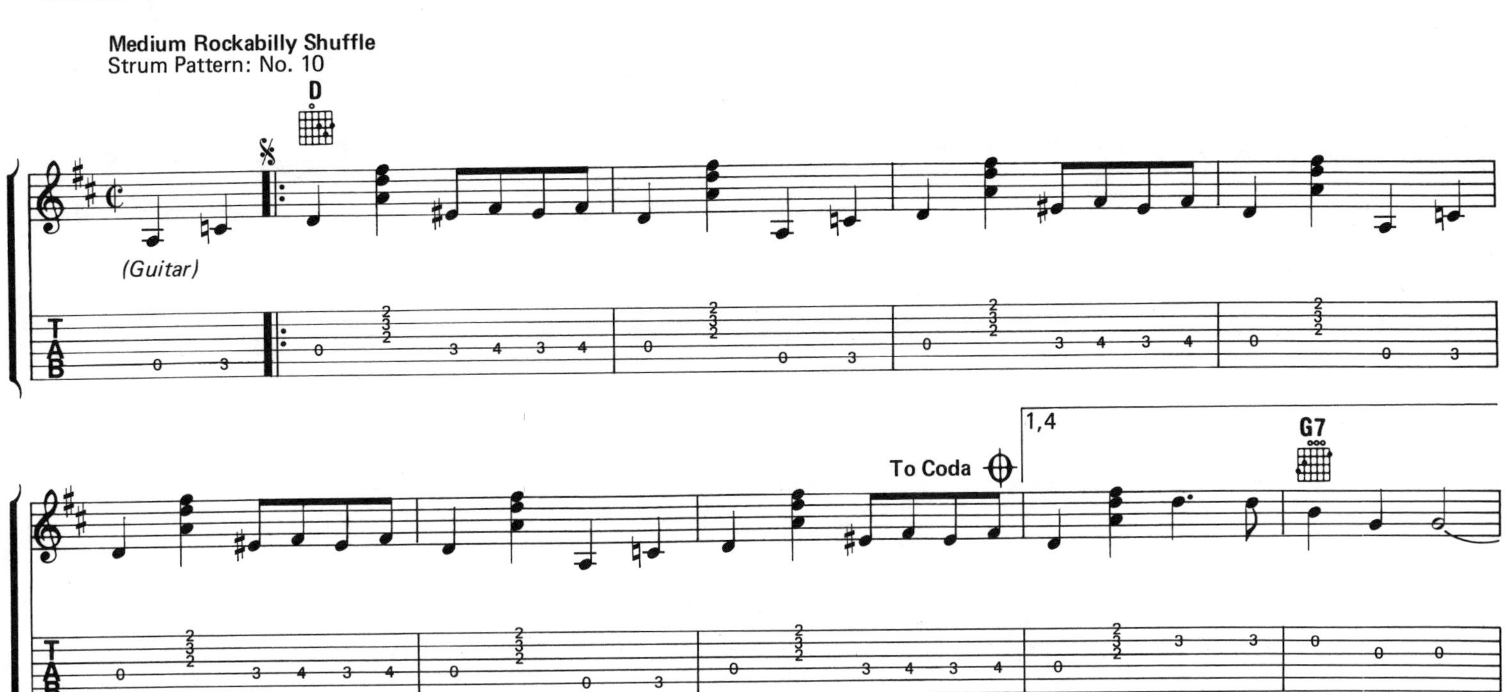

D
A7
G7
(Guitar)
(Instrumental)
Gsus
G6
G9
D.S. al Coda
CODA
Repeat and Fade

REELIN' AND ROCKIN'

Words and Music by
CHUCK BERRY

3. Well, I looked at my watch, it was nine forty-three,
and ev'ry time I'd spin, she'd spin with me,
we would reel, reelin' and a-rockin', etc.

4. Well, I looked at my watch, it was nine fifty-four,
I said, "Dance, ballerina girl, go go go!"
And we rolled, reelin' and a-rockin', etc.

5. Well, I looked at my watch, it was ten o' five.
Man, I didn't know wheth'r I was dead or alive,
and I's rollin', reelin' and a-rockin', etc.

6. Well, I looked at my watch, it was ten twenty-six,
but I'm-a keep on dancin' 'til I get my kicks,
we were reelin', reelin' and a-rockin', etc.

7. Well, I looked at my watch, it was ten twenty-eight,
I gotta get my kicks before it gets too late.
We were reelin', reelin' and a-rockin', etc.

8. Well, I looked at my watch, it was ten twenty-nine,
I had to hold her hand; she was still holdin' mine,
we were reelin', reelin' and a-rockin', etc.

9. Well, I looked at my watch, and to my surprise,
I was dancin' with a woman that was twice my size,
I was reelin', reelin' and a-rockin', etc.

10. Well, I looked at my watch, and it was time to go.
The band leader said, "We ain't playin' no mo'!"
And we was reelin', reelin' and a-rockin', etc.

REBEL ROUSER

Words and Music by
DUANE EDDY and LEE HAZLEWOOD

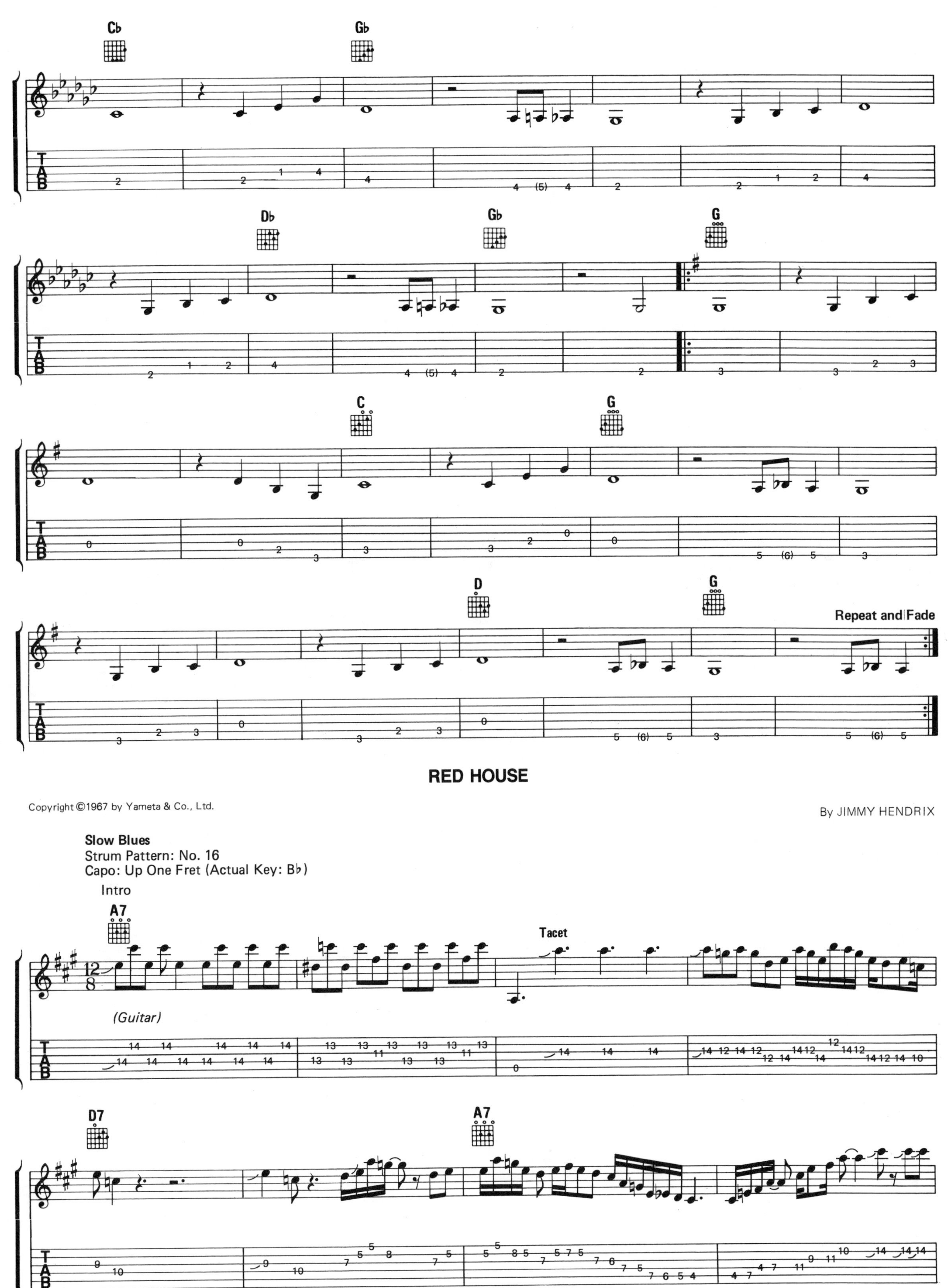
Cb
Gb
Db
Gb
G
C
G
D
G
Repeat and Fade
RED HOUSE
Copyright ©1967 by Yameta & Co., Ltd.
By JIMMY HENDRIX
Slow Blues
Strum Pattern: No. 16
Capo: Up One Fret (Actual Key: B♭)
Intro
A7
Tacet
(Guitar)
D7
A7

E7
D7
A7
E7
There's a
A7
D7
A7
red house o - ver yon - der;
that's where my ba - by stays.
min - ute, some-thing's wrong here:
the key won't un-lock this door.
(Guitar solo)
go back o - ver yon - der,
'way back up on the hill.
Lord, I
D7
A7
Lord, there's a red house o - ver yon - der;
Lord, that's where my ba - by stays.
Wait a min - ute there's some-thing wrong;
Lord, have mer - cy, this key won't un - lock this door.
(Spoken: Something's gone wrong here.)
might as well go back o - ver yon - der,
'way back yon - der 'cross the hill.
E7
1,2,3
D7
A7
E7
I ain't been home to see my ba - by
in nine - ty nine 'n' one-half days.
Wait a
I have a bad, bad feel - ing
that my ba - by don't live here no more.
(Guitar solo)
Guess if my ba - by don't love me no more,
Well, I might as well, uh,
4
D7
Tacet
A7
A/C♯
D
D♯dim7
A/E
B♭7
A7
I know her sis - ter will,
(Guitar)

REELIN' IN THE YEARS

Words and Music by
WALTER BECKER and DONALD FAGEN

Brisk Shuffle
Strum Pattern: No. 7

D A/C# Bm7 A D A/C#

Your ev-er-last-ing sum-mer, you can see it fad-ing fast, so you grab a piece of some-thing that you think is
You've been tell-in' me you're a gen-ius since you were sev-en-teen. In all the time I've known you I still don't know
I've spent a lot of mon-ey and I've spent a lot of time. The trip we made to Hol-ly-wood is etched up-

Bm7 A A7/E D#dim7 Dm6 A/C#

gon-na last. Well, you would-n't e-ven know a dia-mond if you held it in your hand. The
what you mean. The week-end at the col-lege did-n't turn out like you planned. The
on my mind. Af-ter all the things we've done and seen, you find an-oth-er man. The

D A/C# Bm7

things you think are pre-cious
things that pass for know-ledge } I can't un-der-stand.
things you think are use-less

CHORUS

A

Are you reel-in' in the

Gmaj9 A

years, stow-in' a-way the time?

Tacet

Are you gath-er-in' up the

Gmaj9 A

tears? Have you had e-nough of mine?

Tacet

Are you reel-in' in the

Gmaj9
A
years,
stow - in' a - way the time?
Are you gath - er - in' up the
Gmaj9
F♯m
To Coda
1
A
2
tears?
Have you had e - nough of mine?
G
A
(Guitar Solo)
1
2
G
A

G
A
slow bend
C
D.C. (To 3rd Verse) al Coda
dim.
CODA
F#m
Gmaj9
Repeat and Fade
(Ad lib. guitar)

RIGHT TIME OF THE NIGHT

Words and Music by
PETER McCANN

Moderate Rock Ballad
Strum Pattern: No. 5
Capo: Up Three Frets (Actual Key: B♭)

G C G C G C G

Sun goes down on a silk - y day. Quar - ter moon walk - in' through the Milk - y Way.
No use talk - ing when the shad - ows fall. Night birds call - ing and he says it all.

Oh,

C G/B Am7 D7sus

you and me, ba - by, we could think of some-thing to do.

CHORUS

G Bm7 C D7sus G Bm7 C D7sus G Bm7 C D7sus

It's the right time of the night. The stars are wink - in' a - bove. It's the right time of the night for mak - in' love.

To Coda

1. G C/G G D7sus
2. G F/G C G D7

I got you, and you got me. Tell you

Bm7 B7 Em A7

that's the way my mom - ma al - ways said it should be. I'll be good. You be kind.

C D7sus

We'll be bad if you don't mind. It's the

D.S. al Coda

CODA

G C Bm7 E7

It's the

Repeat Chorus (in Key of A) and Fade

RIP IT UP

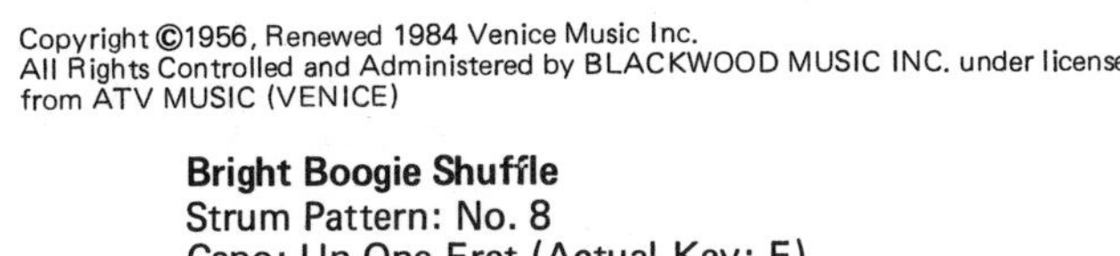

Words and Music by
ROBERT A. BLACKWELL and JOHN S. MARASCALCO

Bright Boogie Shuffle
Strum Pattern: No. 8
Capo: Up One Fret (Actual Key: F)

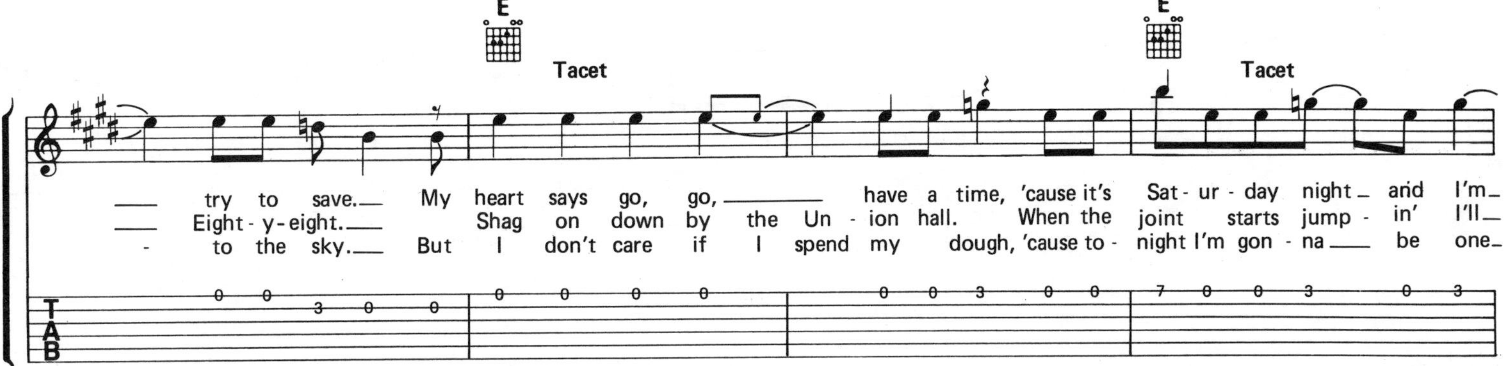

ROCK AROUND THE CLOCK

By MAX C. FREEDMAN and JIMMY DeKNIGHT

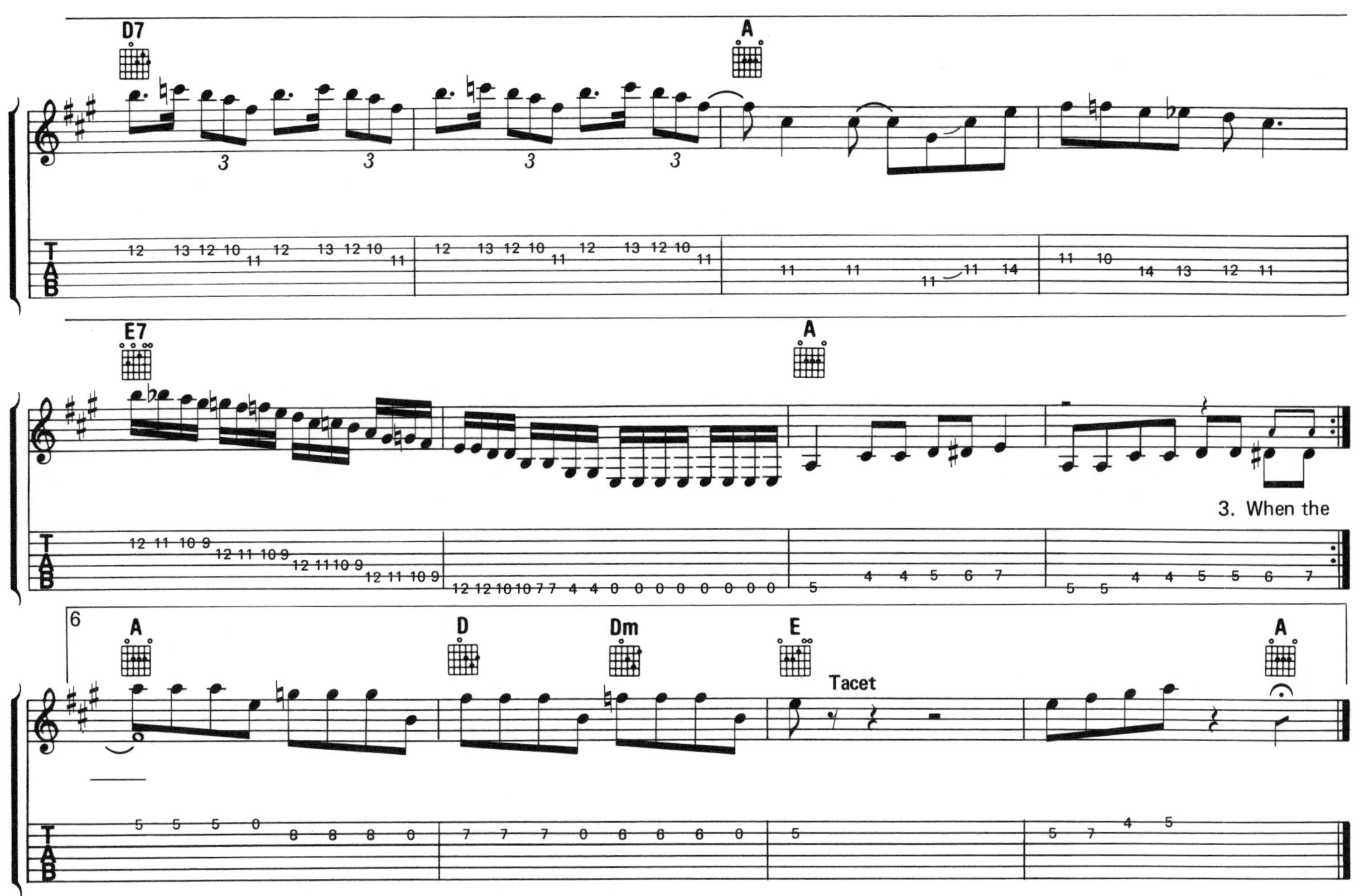

2. When the clock strikes two, and three and four,
If the band slows down we'll yell for more,
We're gonna rock around the clock tonight,
We're gonna rock, rock, rock, 'til broad daylight,
We're gonna rock, gonna rock around the clock tonight.

3. *Instrumental solo*

4. When the chimes ring five and six and seven,
We'll be rockin' up in seventh heav'n,
We're gonna rock around the clock tonight,
We're gonna rock, rock, rock, 'til broad daylight,
We're gonna rock, gonna rock around the clock tonight.

5. When it's eight, nine, ten, eleven, too,
I'll be goin' strong and so will you,
We're gonna rock around the clock tonight,
We're gonna rock, rock, rock, 'til broad daylight,
We're gonna rock, gonna rock around the clock tonight.

6. When the clock strikes twelve, we'll cool off, then,
Start a rockin' 'round the clock again.
We're gonna rock around the clock tonight,
We're gonna rock, rock, rock, 'til broad daylight,
We're gonna rock, gonna rock around the clock tonight.

ROUND AND ROUND

Words and Music by ROBBIN LANTZ CROSBY, WARREN DeMARTINI and STEPHEN E. PEARCY

Medium Rock
Strum Pattern: No. 1
Capo: Up One Fret (Actual Key: E m)

Intro

D(no3rd) F6 F C Bb(b5) Bb Bb(b5) | 1 Bb Csus C Dsus D F6 | 2 Bb Csus C D

(Instrumental)

D(no3rd) F G D(no3rd) F To Coda G D(no3rd) F G D(no3rd) F G C G D C G A

1. Out on the streets, that's where we meet. You make the night. I always cross the lines. tighten our belts, abuse ourselves. Get in our way, we'll put you on your shelf. Another day, some other way, we're gonna go, but then we'll see you again. I've had enough, we've had enough. Call it vain.
2. Lookin' at you, lookin' at me, the way you move, you know it's easy to see. The neon lights in me tonight. I've got a way, we're gonna prove it tonight, like Romeo to Juliet, time and time, I'm gonna make you mine. I've had enough, we've had enough. It's all the same.

She said, "I knew it right from the beginning that you would end up winning. I knew right from the start you'd put an arrow through my heart."

CHORUS
D F C Bb Bb(b5) Bb Csus C D
'Round and 'round, well love will find a way, just give it time. 'Round
F Csus C Bb(b5) Bb Bb(b5)
and 'round, what comes a-round goes a-round. I'll tell you why.
1 Bb Csus C
Dig!
2 Bb C
D.S. al Coda
Yeah!
CODA
F G A G A
we'll put you on your shelf. 'Round and
D F C Bb Bb(b5) Bb Csus C D
'round well love will find a way just give it time. 'Round
and 'round,
F Csus C Bb(b5) Bb Bb(b5) Bb Csus C D
Repeat and Fade
and 'round, what comes a-round goes a-round, I'll tell you why. 'Round

ROCKIN' ROBIN

Words and Music by
J. THOMAS

Bright Shuffle
Strum Pattern: No. 7

Intro

Tacet

Play 3 times

Tweedle-e deedle-e-dee, tweedle-e deedle-e-dee. Tweet, tweet, tweet, tweet. 1.,3. He

G

rocks in the treetop all the day long. Hoppin' and a-boppin' and a-singin' his song.
2. Ev'ry little swallow, ev'ry chickadee, ev'ry little bird in the tall oak tree. The

All the little birds on Jaybird Street love to hear the robin goin' tweet, tweet, tweet.
wise old owl, the big black crow, flap their wings singin' go, bird, go.
Rockin'

C7 G

Robin, rock, rock, Rockin' Robin.

D7 C7 G To Coda 1 2

Blow, Rockin' Robin, 'cause we're really gonna rock tonight. A

C G

pretty little raven at the bird bandstand taught him how to do the bop and it was grand. They

C
D7
Tacet
D.S. al Coda
(1st verse)
start - ed go - in' stead - y and, bless my soul, he out - bopped the buz-zard and the or - i - ole. He
CODA
Tacet
Play 3 times
Twee-dle - e dee-dle - e dee, twee-dle - e dee-dle e - dee. Tweet, Tweet. (Whistle)
ROCK ON
©1974 SBK SONGS LTD.
All Rights in the U.S.A. Controlled and Administered by APRIL MUSIC INC.
Words and Music by
DAVID ESSEX
Slowly, but with a Funky Double-time Feeling - Bo Diddley Beat
Strum Pattern: No. 12
Capo: Up One Fret (Actual Key: C♯m)
C7
Hey, did y'rock 'n' roll? Rock on! Oh, my soul! Hey, did y'boog-ie, too? Did ya?
Hey, shout sum-mer-time blues, jump up an'down in the blue suede shoes. Hey, did y' rock 'n' roll? Rock on! And
where do we go from here? Which is the way that's clear? Still look - in' for that
To Coda
Tacet
D.S. al Coda
blue jean' ba-by queen, pret-ti-est girl I ev-er seen. See her shake on the mov-ie screen, Jim-my Dean! James Dean. And

CODA
Tacet
C7
Repeat and Fade
Jim - my Dean! Rock on! Rock

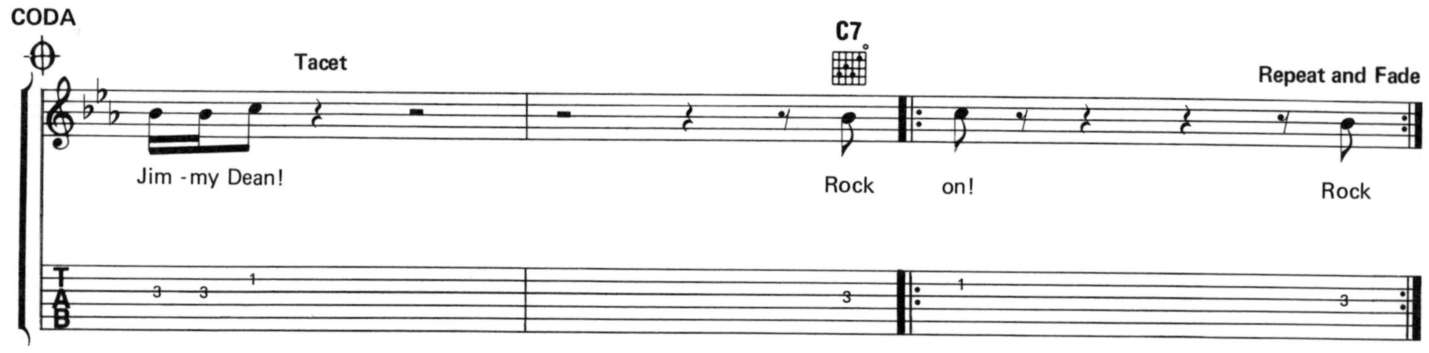

RUNAWAY

Words and Music by
DEL SHANNON and MAX CROOK

Moderately Bright Rock
Strum Pattern: No. 2
Capo: Up One Fret (Actual Key B♭m)
Intro

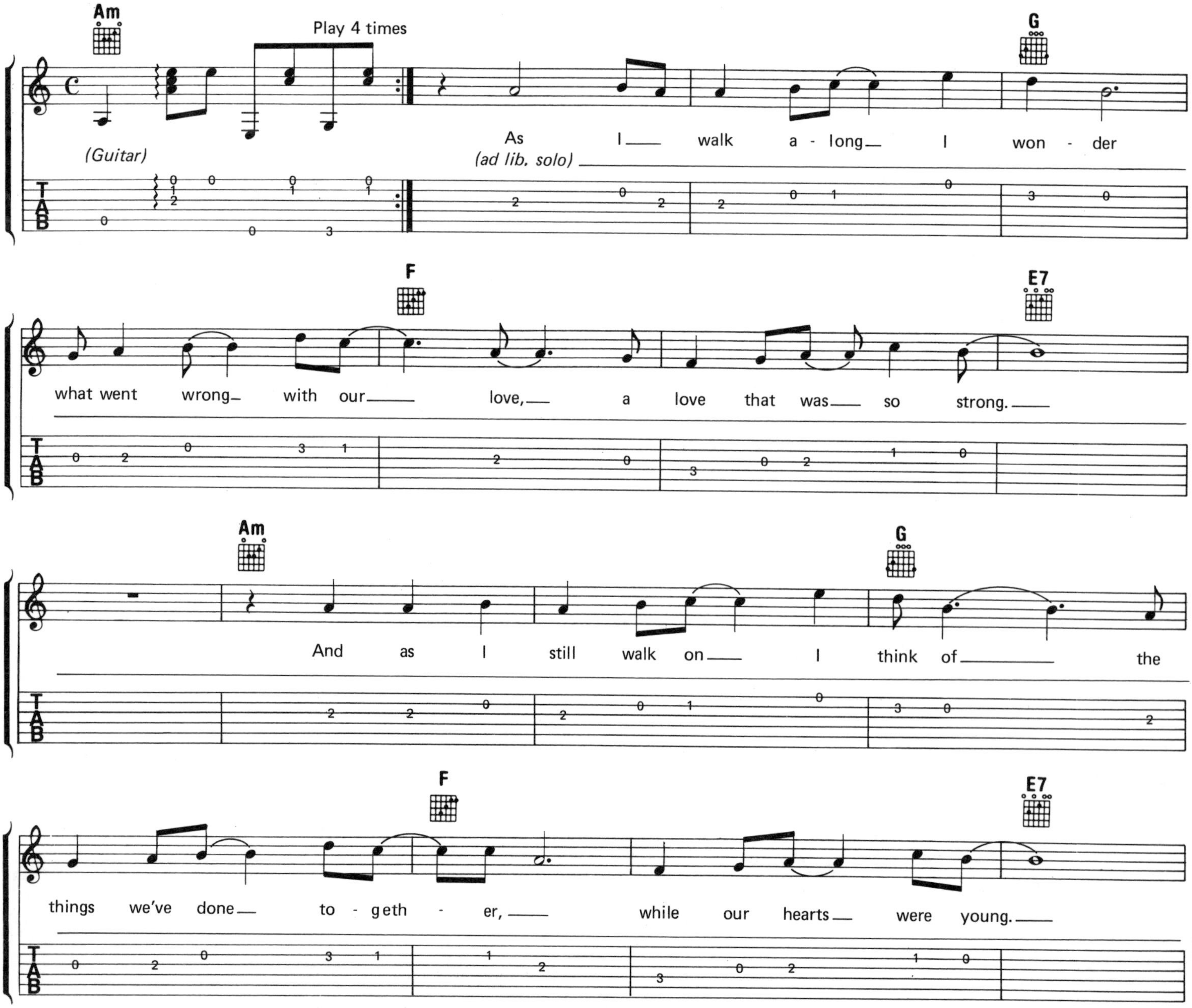

Am
Play 4 times
G
(Guitar)
As I walk a - long I won - der
(ad lib. solo)
F
E7
what went wrong with our love, a love that was so strong.
Am
G
And as I still walk on I think of the
F
E7
things we've done to - geth - er, while our hearts were young.

A
F♯m
I'm a - walk - in' in the rain.
Tears are fall - in' and I
feel a pain.
A - wish - in' you were here with me,
to end this
mis - er - y, and I won - der,
I wa - wa - wa - wa won - der
why,
a - why why why why why she ran a - way,
and I won - der
D
E7
where she will stay,
my lit - tle run - a - way,
a - run - run - run - run -
run - a - way.
run - a - way,
a - run - run - run - run -
Repeat and Fade

SARA

Copyright 1985 by Petwolf Music and Kikiko Music.
All rights for the world controlled by Chappell & Co., Inc. and Unichappell Music, Inc.
Music by PETER WOLF and INA WOLF
Words by INA WOLF
Bright Rock Ballad
Strum Pattern: No. 5
Capo: Up Three Frets (Actual Key: B♭)
D/G G F♯m7 D/G G
Go now, don't look back, we've drawn the line. Move on,
Dan - ger in the game when the stakes are high. Brand - ed,
Instrumental
F♯m B Em7 Cmaj7
it's no good to go back in time.
a heart was brand - ed while my sens - es stood by.
Instrumental ends
I'll nev - er find an-oth-er girl like you, for hap - pi -
Em7 Cmaj7 Em/B A7sus 1 Bsus B 2,3 Bsus To Coda
- ness it takes two. We're fi - re and ice, the dream won't come true. true.
D/G G Bm7 C Bm7/E D/G G
Sa - ra, Sa - ra, the storms are brew-in' in your eyes. Sa - ra,
Bm7 C D/C F C/B♭ 1 Dsus D 2 Dsus D
Sa - ra, no time is a good time for good-byes ('Cause Sa - ra)

C
C/D
D
C
C/D
D
Love me like no one has ev - er loved me be - fore. (and Sa - ra) Hurt me, no one could ev - er hurt me more. (and Sa - ra)
C
C/D
D
C
C/D
D7sus
D.C. al Coda
Sa - ra (and Sa - ra) No - bod - y love me an - y - more.
CODA
Gmaj7
G
Bm7(♯5)
Bm7
Cmaj7
Bm7/E
D/G
G
Sa - ra,
Bm7
C
D/C
B♭/A♭
C/D
D/C
CHORUS
D/G
G
Bm7
Sa - ra, no time is a good time. Oh Sa - ra, Sa - ra, the
C
Bm7/E
D/G
G
Bm7
storms are brew-in' in your eyes. Sa - ra, Sa - ra,
C
D/C
B♭
C/B♭
Dsus
D
B♭
C/D
Repeat Chorus with 2nd ending and Fade
no time is a good time for good - byes. good time. Oh,

SECRET AGENT MAN

Words and Music by
P. F. SLOAN and STEVE BARRI

Em
Bm
Em
C7
B7
— se - cret a - gent man, — they've giv - en you — a num - ber and
Em
Em
Play 3 times
tak - en 'way — your name. (Guitar)
Se - cret a - gent man. —
SEA OF LOVE
Copyright ©1957, 1959 by Fort Knox Music Inc. and Trio Music Company, Inc.
All rights administered by Hudson Bay Music, Inc.
Words and Music by
GEORGE KHOURY and PHILIP BASTISTE
Medium Slow Fifties Rock
Strum Pattern: No. 7
Intro
G
B7
C
A7
G
C
G
Hmm, hmm, hmm, —— hmm ——
G
B7
C
A7
1. Come with me, — my love, — to — the sea, — the sea of — love. —
2.,3.,4. Do you re - mem - ber when — we met? That's — the day — I knew you were my pet.
I —
G
A7
G
C
To Coda
1 G
2,3 G
— want to tell you how —— much I love you. ——
D
C
D
C
B7
D
D.S. al Coda (4th verse)
CODA
G
Come — with — me to — the — sea of love.
Oooh.

SAY, SAY, SAY

Words and Music by
McCARTNEY/JACKSON

D Dm7
1 Am Am7
2 Am
(Instrumental)
G Am G Am
You nev - er ev - er wor - ry and you nev - er shed a tear. You're
G Am E7(#9)
D.C., repeat Instrumental and Fade
say-ing that my love ain't real. Just look at my face; these tears ain't dry-ing.
SEARCHIN'
Copyright ©1957 by Tiger Music, Inc., Copyright renewed, assigned to Chappell & Co., Inc.
(Intersong Music, Publisher), Quintet Music, Inc. and Bienstock Publishing Co.
All rights administered by Chappell & Co., Inc.
Words and Music by
JERRY LEIBER and MIKE STOLLER
Moderate Country Shuffle
Strum Pattern: No. 10
Capo: Up One Fret (Actual Key: D♭)
C G9 C Play 3 times C G9 C
Gon - na find her. Gon - na find her. Well, I been
G9 C G9 C G9
search - in'. And I'm search - in'. Oh yeah, search - in' ev - 'ry
C G9 C
CHORUS
F9
which a - way, yay yay. Oh yes, search - in', uh I'm
search - in', oh yeah,

C G9 C G9
search - in', search - in', my good - ness, search - in' ev - 'ry which a - way, yay yay.
C G7 Tacet
But I'm like that North - west Moun - tie; you know I'll bring her in some day. (Gon - na find her.)
C G9 C G9 C G9 C
To Coda
Gon-na find her.
Well, now if I have to swim a riv - er, you know I will.
Well, Sher - lock Holmes, Sam Spade got noth - in', child, on me;
G9 C G9 C G9
And if I have to climb a moun - tain, you know I will.
Sar - geant Fri - day, Char - lie Chan and Bos - ton Black - ie.
C G9 C G9 C
And if she's hid - in' up on a blue - ber - ry hill,
No mat - ter where she's hid - in' she's gon - na hear me a - com - in', I'm gon - na
C7
1 2
D.S. al Coda
am I gon - na find her? Child, you know I will. 'Cause I've been
walk right down that street like Bull - Dog Drum - mond, 'cause I've been
CODA
C G7
Fade
Tacet
But I'm like that North - west Moun - tie; you know I'll...

SLEEPWALK

Words and Music by SANTO FARINA,
JOHN FARINA and ANN FARINA

Slowly
Strum Pattern: No. 16
Capo: Up One Fret (Actual Key: D♭)

SGT. PEPPER'S LONELY HEARTS CLUB BAND

Words and Music by
JOHN LENNON and PAUL McCARTNEY

Slow, Heavy Rock/Funk
Strum Pattern: No. 3

Intro

A7 C7 G

(Guitar solo)

It was

G A C G

twen - ty years a - go to - day that Ser - geant Pep - per taught the band to play. They've been
real - ly want to stop the show, but I thought you might like to know that the

A C G A

go - ing in and out of style, but they're guar - an - teed to raise a smile. So may I in - tro - duce to you the
sing - er's going to sing a song and he wants you all to sing a - long. So let me in - tro - duce to you the

C G7 C7 G

act you've known for all these years, Ser - geant Pep - per's Lone - ly Heart's Club Band.
one and on - ly Bil - ly Shears,

To Coda

C7 F C7 D7

(Instrumental interlude)

CHORUS
Strum Pattern: No. 1

G B♭ C7 G C7

We're Ser - geant Pep - per's Lone - ly Heart's Club Band. We hope you will en - joy the show.

G
Bb
C7
G
A
We're Ser-geant Pep-per's Lone - ly Heart's Club Band. Sit back and let the eve - ning go.
D7
C
G
Ser - geant Pep-per's Lone - ly, Ser - geant Pep-per's Lone - ly, Ser - geant Pep - per's Lone - ly Heart's
C G
C7
F7
C7
Club Band. It's won-der - ful to be here, it's cer -tain - ly a thrill. You're such a love - ly au - di - ence we'd
D
D7
D.S. al Coda
CODA
C
like to take you home with us, we'd love to take you home. I don't
(Instrumental)

SHAKE, RATTLE AND ROLL

Words and Music by
CHARLES CALHOUN

3. I'm a one-eyed cat, peepin' in a seafood store.
I'm a one-eyed cat, peepin' in a seafood store.
I can look at you, tell you don't love me no more.

4. I believe you're doin' me wrong and now I know.
I believe you're doin' me wrong and now I know.
The more I work, the faster my money goes.

SHE BOP

Words and Music by C. LAUPER,
S. LUNT, G. CORBETT and R. CHERTOFF

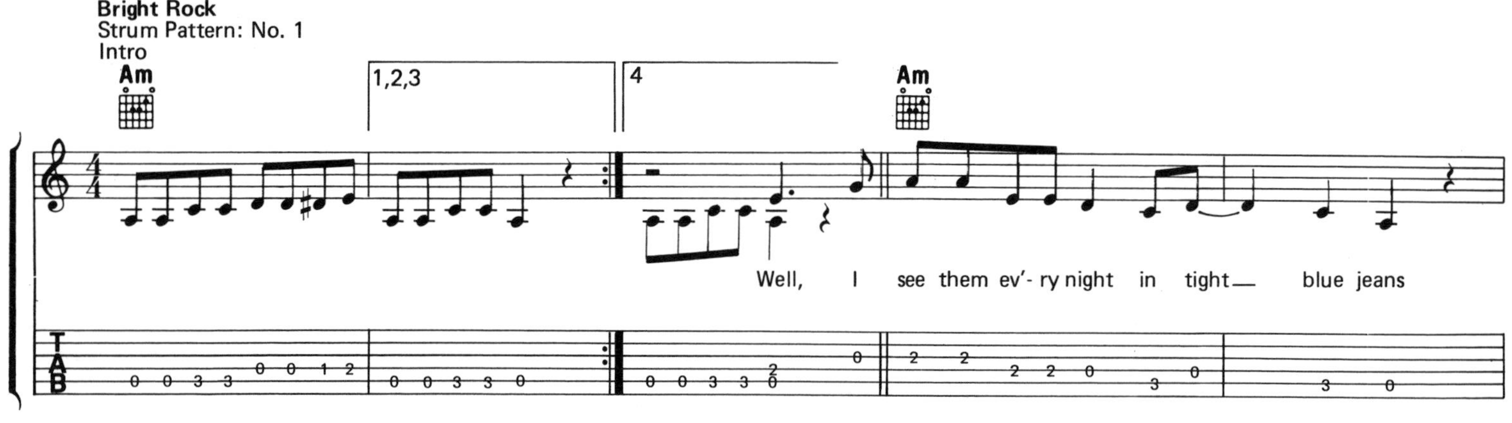

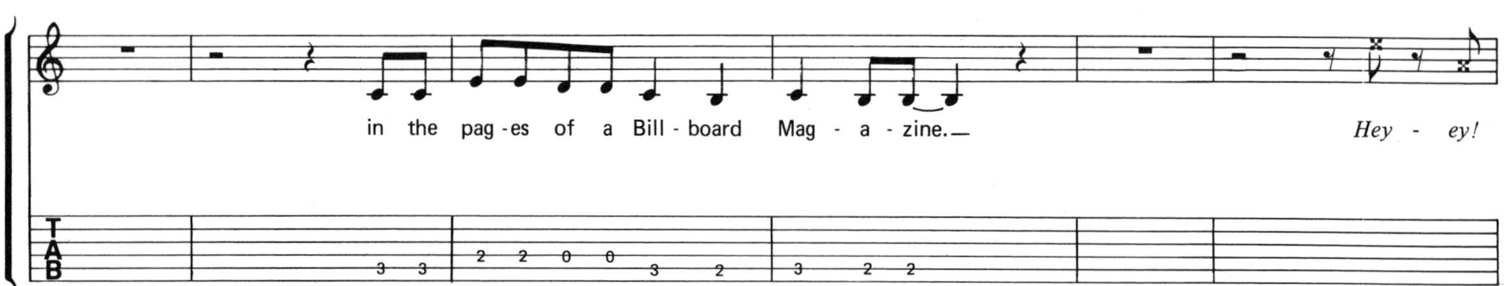

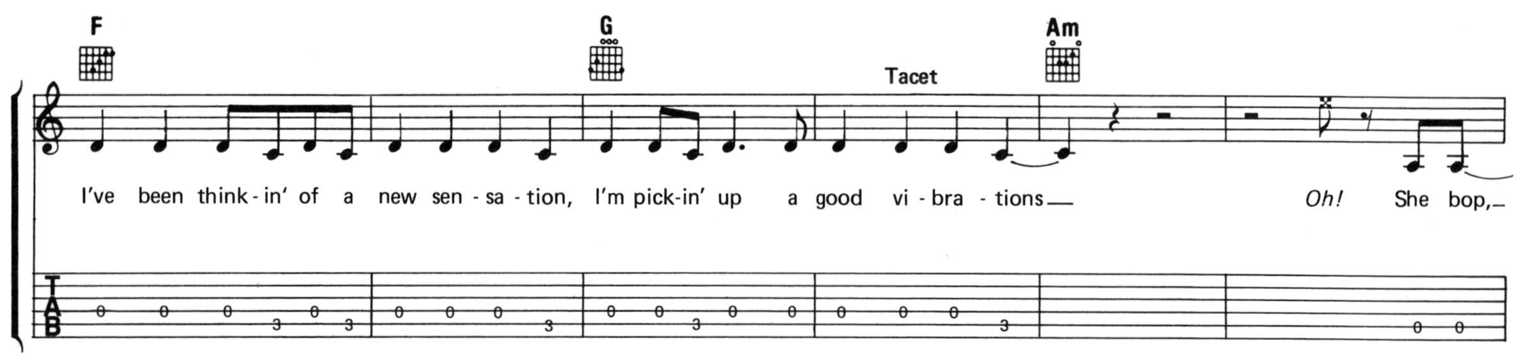

G
Tacet
Am
say I'd bet-ter stop or I'll go blind.
Ain't no law a-gainst it yet.
Oh! She bop, she bop.
Dm7
C
F
G
E7
She bop, he bop-a we bop. I bop, you bop-a they bop, be-bop be-bop-a-lu-bop.
Am
Dm7
C
F
She bop, he bop-a we bop, I bop, you bop-a they bop,
(I don't e-ven un-der-stand.)
G
Em
Tacet
Am
To Coda
D.S. al Coda
be-bop be-bop-a-lu she bop. Oh she does, She bop.
CODA
Oh she does, she bop. Oh she does,
(Guitar)

SHE'S A WOMAN

Words and Music by
JOHN LENNON and PAUL McCARTNEY

E7
A7
D7
(Guitar solo)
A7
E7
D7
A7
C#m
F#7
C#m
D
E
D.S. al Coda
She's a wom - an who un-der - stands.
She's a wom - an who loves her man.
CODA
A7
Repeat and Fade
She's a wom - an.
She's a wom -

SISTER CHRISTIAN

Words and Music by
KELLY KEAGY

C/E
F/E♭
B♭/D
G
D.S. al Coda
8va
CODA
C
F
C
F
G
C
Sis- ter Chris- tian, oh the
F
G
C
F
G
F
C
Dm
G11
time has come
and you know that you're the
on - ly one
to say,
"O. K."
C
F
C
F
C
F
G
C
But you're mo-tor - ing,
you're
mo - tor - ing.

SOLITARY MAN

Words and Music by
NEIL DIAMOND

Em D Em D
To Coda
I'll be what I am: sol - i - tar - y man, sol - i - tar - y
Em 1 2 Em7
man.
(Instrumental)
Am Em Am
D.S. al Coda
CODA
Em D Em D Em
Repeat and Fade
man. sol - i - tar - y man. Mm, mm,

(SHE'S) SOME KIND OF WONDERFUL

Words and Music by
JOHN ELLISON

D G D
She's, she's some kind of won-der-ful, yeah, yeah, yeah, yeah. When I
D
Now is there an-y-bod-y got a sweet lit-tle wom-an like mine?
D Bm
There got to be some Yeah. Now can I get a wit-ness, yeah? Can I get a wit-ness?
D Bm
Well can I get a wit-ness? Can I get a wit-ness? I'm talk-in,' talk-in' 'bout my
D G D
Repeat and Fade
ba-by, she's some kind of won-der-ful, talk-in' 'bout my ba-by, she's some kind of won-der-ful. Talk-in' 'bout my

SOME LIKE IT HOT

Words and Music by ROBERT PALMER,
ANDY TAYLOR and JOHN TAYLOR

C
D
Em
C
Dsus
D
Em
cide that — they can't go on. —
some like it hot. —
Some like — it hot, but — you
(Guitar solo to D.S.)
can't tell — how hot till — you try, —
Some like — it hot, so — let's
To Coda
D.S. al Coda
turn up — the heat 'til — we fry. —
The girl is
CODA
Am7
Bm
fry. —
Some like — it hot,
some like it hot. —
Bm7
Tacet
Some like — it hot,
some like it hot. —

SOMETHING ABOUT YOU

Words and Music by M. KING, P. GOULD, R. GOULD, M. LINDUP and W. BADAROU

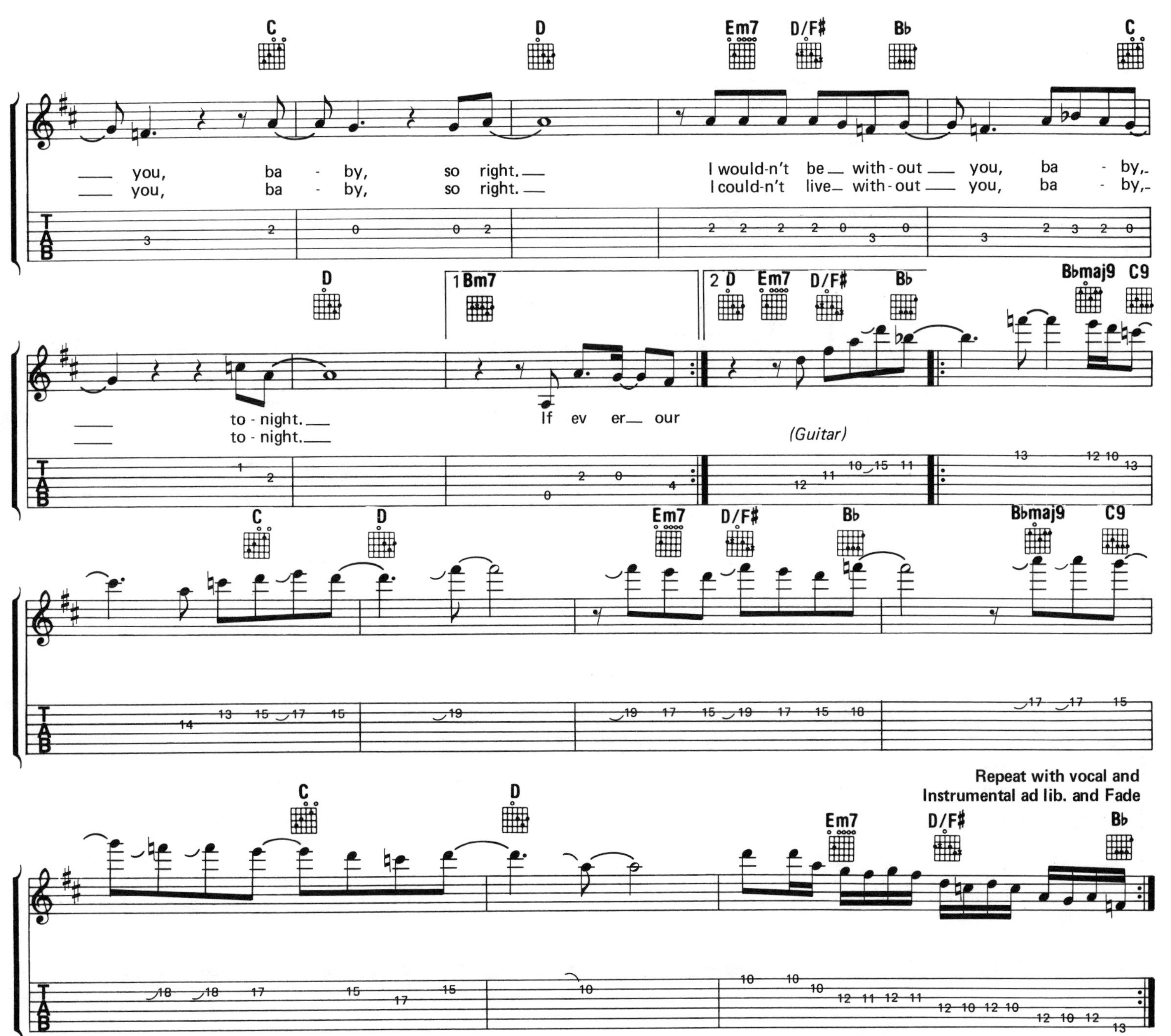
C D Em7 D/F♯ B♭ C
— you, ba - by, so right. — I would-n't be — with-out — you, ba - by,-
— you, ba - by, so right. — I could-n't live — with-out — you, ba - by,-
D 1 Bm7 2 D Em7 D/F♯ B♭ B♭maj9 C9
— to - night. — If ev er — our
— to - night. —
(Guitar)
C D Em7 D/F♯ B♭ B♭maj9 C9
C D Em7 D/F♯ B♭
Repeat with vocal and
Instrumental ad lib. and Fade

STAYIN' ALIVE

Words and Music by
BARRY GIBB, ROBIN GIBB and MAURICE GIBB

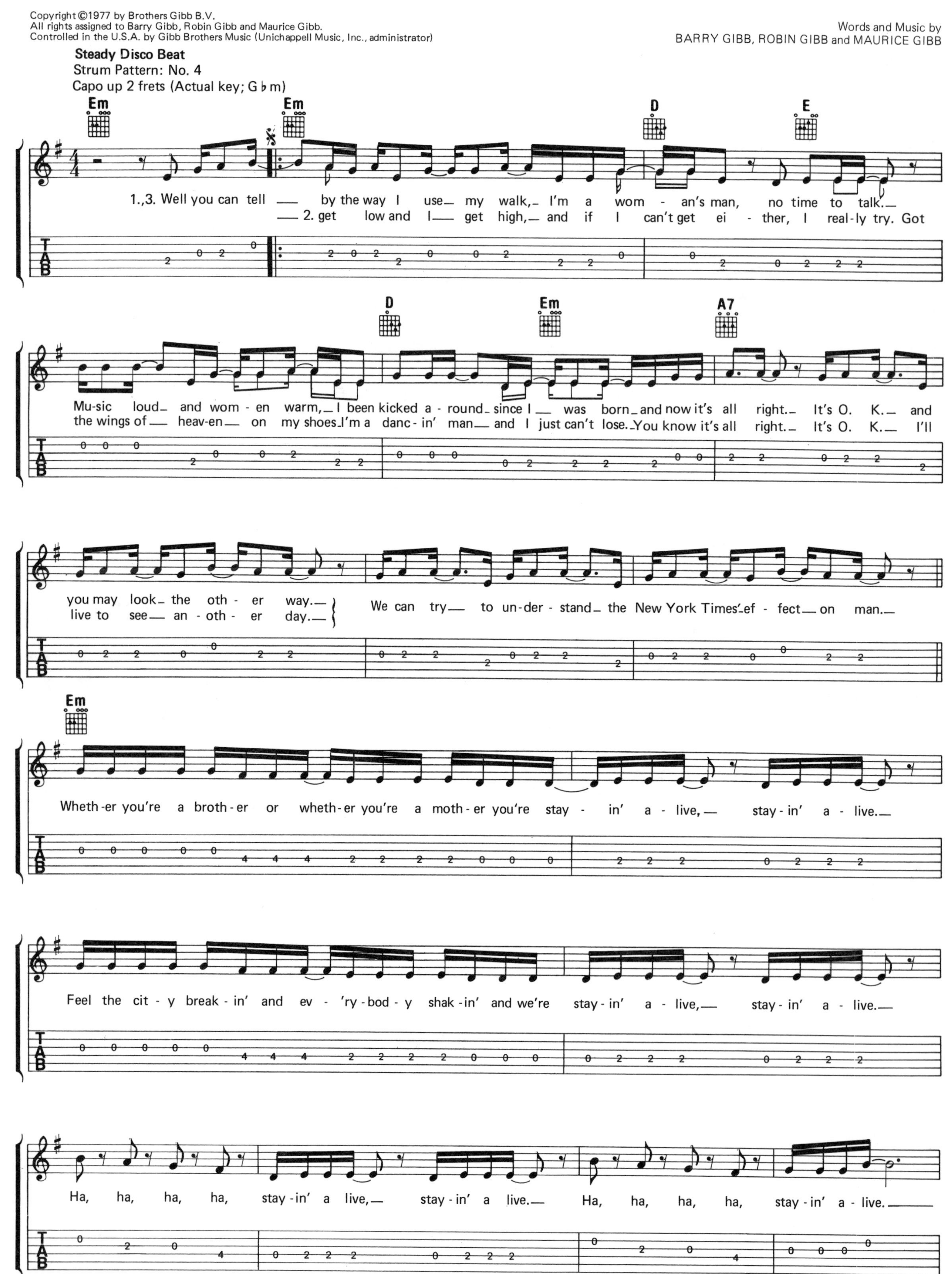

D
Em
Bm7
Em
To Coda
1
2
2. Well, now I
A7
Em
Life go-in' no-where, some-bod-y help me, some-bod-y help me, yeah.
A7
Em
D.S. (3rd verse) al Coda
Life go-in' no-where, some-bod-y help me, yeah. Stay-in' a-live. 3. Well, you can tell
CODA
Em
A7
Life go-in' no-where, some-bod-y help me. Some-bod-y help me, yeah.
Em
A7
Life go-in' no-where, some-bod-y help me, yeah.
Em
Repeat and Fade
I'm stay-in' a live.

STEAL AWAY (THE NIGHT)

Words and Music by
JOHN OSBOURNE, ROBERT DAISLEY & RANDY RHOADS

E
CHORUS
Steal a - way, steal a - way, steal a
- way the night.
B
To Coda
1 A
You got - ta steal it,
come on ba - by.
2 E(no3rd)
C(no3rd)
F♯(no3rd)
B(no3rd)
E
B
A
G
(Guitar rhythm)
1 A
E
2 A
Gm
Gdim
(Guitar solo)
(bend)

B
a.h.
8va
(bend)
sounds
a.h.
muted
8va
loco
bend
release bend
bend
release bend
A
8va
8va
D.C. al Coda
CODA
E
Steal a - way,
steal a - way,
B
E7#9
steal a - way the night.

STAND BY ME

Words and Music by BEN E. KING, JERRY LEIBER and MIKE STOLLER

Moderately Slow Rock
Strum Pattern: No. 2

STUCK IN THE MIDDLE WITH YOU

Words and Music by
JOE EGAN and GERRY RAFFERTY

STRAY CAT STRUT

Words and Music by
BRIAN SETZER

Dm Tacet Am G F E Am Tacet
Get my din-ner from a gar - bage can.____ (Instrumental)
Dm Dm7 Am
I don't both-er chas - ing mice a - round.__ I
Dm B7 E7+5 Am G
slink down the al - ley, look - in' for a fight, Howl - in' to the moon-light on a hot sum-mer night,__ Sing - in' the blues__ while the
F E7 Am G F7 E7 Am G F7 E7
la - dy cats cry. Wild__ stray cat, you're a real gone guy. I wish I could be as care-free and wild__ but I
Am Tacet To Coda Am G F7 E7 Am Tacet D.S. al Coda
got cat class and I got cat style.____ (Guitar)
CODA Am G F E Am Tacet Am9
(Guitar)

THE STROLL

Words and Music by
CLYDE OTIS and NANCY LEE

SUMMER IN THE CITY

Words and Music by JOHN SEBASTIAN, STEVE BOONE and MARK SEBASTIAN

Moderate Funk Beat
Strum Pattern: No. 3
Capo: Up Three Frets (Actual Keys: Cm and F)

Intro Play 3 times

Am Am/G F♯m7(♭5) Fmaj7 E7

1.,3. Hot town, sum - mer in the ci - ty, back o' my neck get - tin' dirt and grit - ty.
2. Cool town, eve - nin' in the ci - ty, dressed so fine and look - in' so pret - ty.
4. *(Instrumental)*

Am Am/G F♯m7(♭5) Fmaj7 E E7

Been down. Is - n't it a pi - ty, does-n't seem to be a shad-ow in the ci - ty. All a-round, peo-ple look-in' half dead,
Cool cat, look-in' for a kit - ty, gon-na look in ev - 'ry cor-ner of the ci - ty. 'Til I'm wheez-in' like a bus stop;

Am A D G

walk - in' on the side - walk hot - ter than a match, yeah.
run - nin' up the stairs, gonna meet you on the roof - top.
But at night it's a diff - 'rent world.

D G D G D G

Go out and find a girl. Come on, come on and dance all night. De-spite the heat, it - 'll be all right, and

Bm E Bm E Bm E

babe, don't you know it's a pi - ty the days can't be like the nights in the sum - mer, in the ci - ty, in the

1 Bm E

sum-mer, in the ci - ty.

2,3,4 Bm E

sum-mer, in the ci - ty.

Tacet

(Guitar)

D.S. to 3rd verse, use 2nd ending,
D.S. again to 4th verse, Fade

Am Am/G F♯m7(♭5) Fmaj7 E7 Am Am/G F♯m7(♭5) Fmaj7 E7

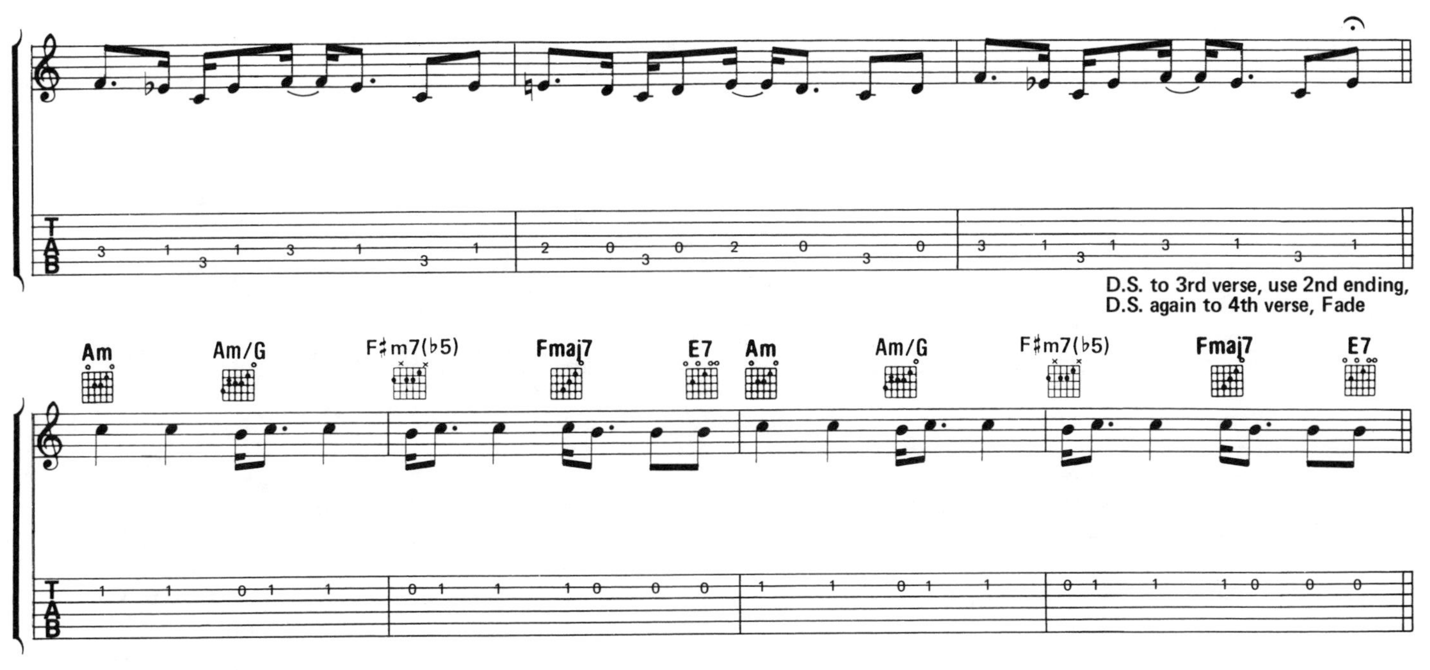

SPINNING WHEEL

Words and Music by
DAVID CLAYTON THOMAS

Funky, Moderate Rock
Strum Pattern: No. 3

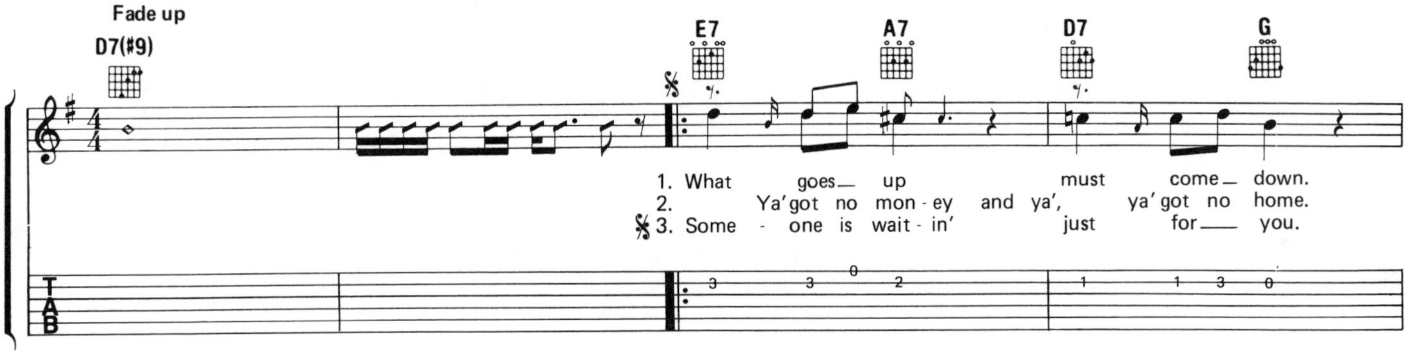

Fade up
D7(♯9) E7 A7 D7 G
1. What goes — up must come — down.
2. Ya' got no mon - ey and ya', ya' got no home.
3. Some - one is wait - in' just for — you.

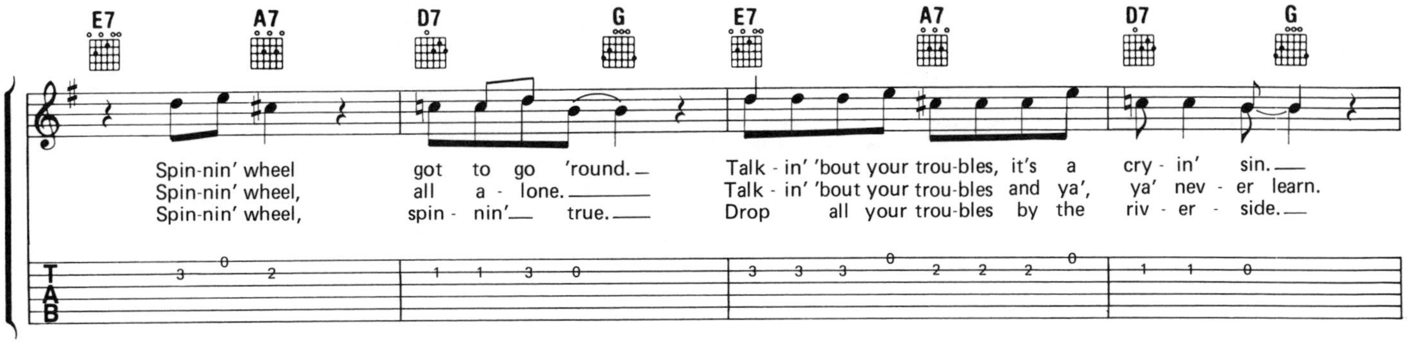

E7 A7 D7 G E7 A7 D7 G
Spin-nin' wheel got to go 'round. — Talk - in' 'bout your trou-bles, it's a cry - in' sin. —
Spin-nin' wheel, all a - lone. — Talk - in' 'bout your trou-bles and ya', ya' nev - er learn.
Spin-nin' wheel, spin - nin' — true. — Drop all your trou-bles by the riv - er - side. —

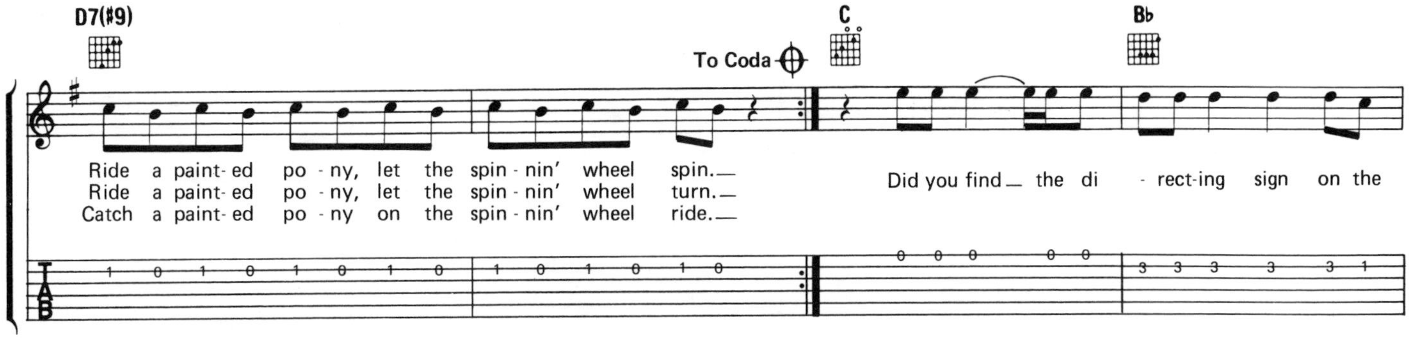

D7(♯9) To Coda C B♭
Ride a paint-ed po - ny, let the spin - nin' wheel spin. —
Ride a paint-ed po - ny, let the spin - nin' wheel turn. —
Catch a paint-ed po - ny on the spin - nin' wheel ride. —
Did you find — the di - rect-ing sign on the

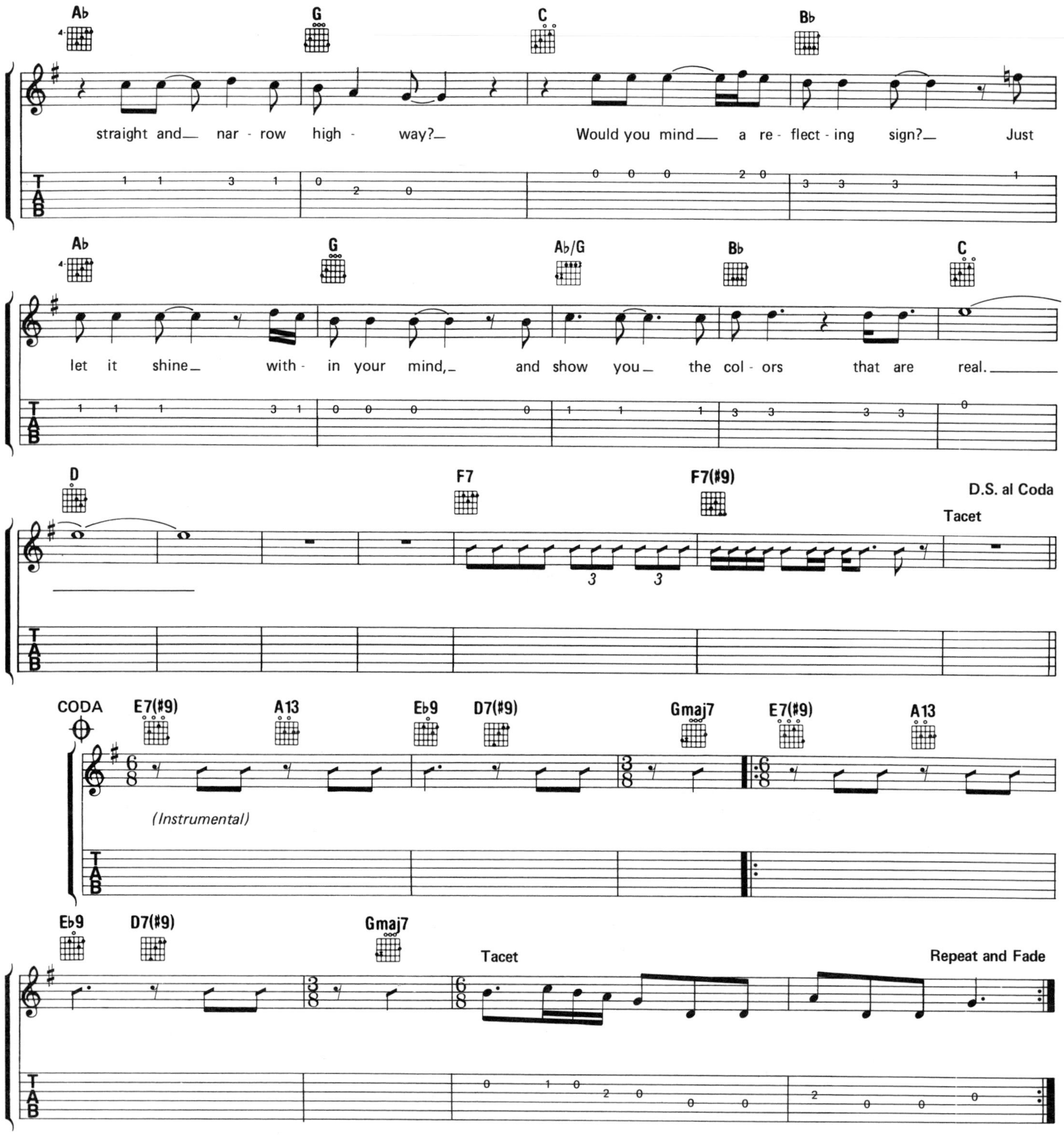

Ab G C Bb
straight and__ nar - row high - way?__ Would you mind__ a re - flect - ing sign?__ Just
Ab G Ab/G Bb C
let it shine__ with - in your mind,__ and show you__ the col - ors that are real.______
D F7 F7(#9)
D.S. al Coda
Tacet
CODA
E7(#9) A13 Eb9 D7(#9) Gmaj7 E7(#9) A13
(Instrumental)
Eb9 D7(#9) Gmaj7
Tacet
Repeat and Fade

SUMMERTIME BLUES

Words and Music by
EDDIE COCHRAN and JERRY CAPEHART

Medium Rock
Strum Pattern: No. 1

Intro
E A B7 E
(6-string bass)
(Guitar)

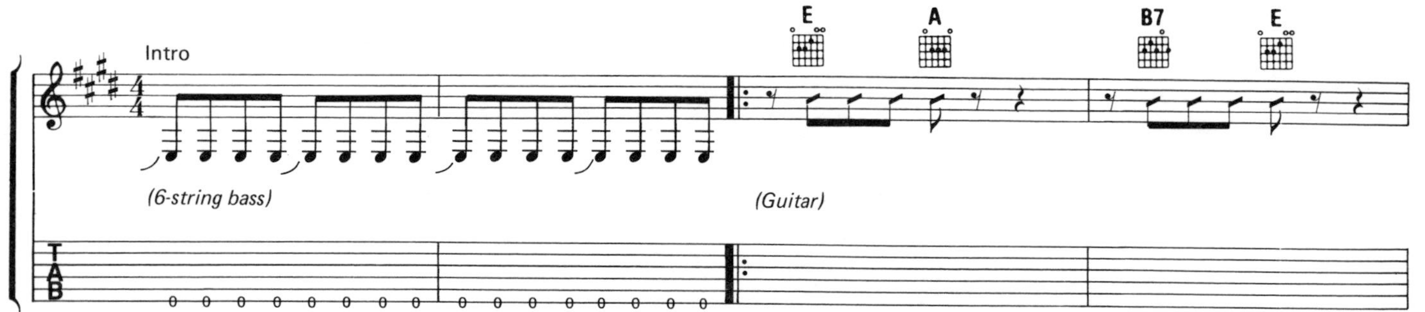

A
B7
E
Well I'm a - gon - na raise a fuss,— I'm a - gon - na raise a hol - ler.
A - well my mom and pa - pa told me, "Son you got-ta make some mon - ey,
I'm gon - na take two weeks, gon-na have a fine va - ca - tion.
A-bout a - work - in' all summer just to try to earn a dol - lar.
a - if you wan - na use the car to go a - rid - in' next Sun - day."
I'm gon-na take my prob - lem to the U - nit - ed Na - tions.
(Spoken:)
Ev - 'ry time I call my ba - by, try to get a date, my
- well I did - n't go to work, told the boss I was sick "Now you
Well, I called my Con - gress - man and he said, quote, "I'd
Tacet
boss says, "No dice, son, you got - ta work late."
can't use the car 'cause you did - n't work a lick."
like to help you, son, but you're too young to vote."
Some - times I won - der what
I'm a - gon - na do, but there ain't no cure— for the sum - mer - time— blues.
(6-string bass figure)
1,2
3
Repeat and Fade

THE SUNSHINE OF YOUR LOVE

Words and Music by JACK BRUCE,
PETE BROWN and ERIC CLAPTON

Moderate Rock
Strum Pattern: No. 1
Intro

D C D | 1,2,3 | 4 | D C D

It's get-ting near dawn, when
I'm with you my love. The

C D C D

lights close their tired eyes. I'll soon be with you, my love,
lights shin - ing through on you. Yes, I'm with you my love, it's the

C D G F G

give you my dawn sur - prise. I'll be with you dar - ling, soon. I'll
morn-ing and just we two. I'll stay with you dar - ling, now. I'll

F G D C D D C D

be with you when the stars start fall - ing.
stay with you 'til my seas are dried up.

A C G A C G A

I've been wait - ing so long, to be where I'm go - ing, in the sun-

C G A To Coda 1 D C D 2

- shine of your love. I'm (Guitar)

D.C. (2nd verse) al Coda
CODA
Repeat and Fade
(Guitar)

SURFIN' U.S.A.

Music by CHUCK BERRY
Lyric by BRIAN WILSON

Bright Rock
Strum Pattern: No. 1
Capo: Up One Fret (Actual Key: E♭)

Intro

Tacet A7 **Tacet**

If ev - 'ry - bod - y had an o - cean, a - cross the U. S. A.
route we're gon - na take real soon.

D **Tacet** A7 **Tacet** D

then ev - 'ry - bod - y'd be surf - in' like Cal - i - for - ni - a.
We're wax - in' down our surf - boards, we can't wait for June.

Tacet G **Tacet** D **Tacet**

You'd see 'em wear - in' their bag - gies, huar - a - chi san - dals too. A bush - y, bush - y blonde
We'll all be gone for the sum - mer, we're on sa - fa - ri to stay. Tell the teach - er we're

A7 G **Tacet** D A7

hair - do, surf - in' U. S. A. You'll catch 'em surf - in' at Del Mar,
surf - in', surf - in' U. S. A. At Hag - gar - ty's and Swam - i's,
(Instrumental)

D A7

Ven - tu - ra Coun - ty line, San - ta Cruz and Tres - sels, Aus - tra - lia's Nar - a - bine,
Pac - if - ic Pal - i - sades, San O - nofre and Sun - set, Re - don - do Beach, L. A.,

D G D

all o - ver Man - hat - tan, and down Do - he - ny way,
all o - ver La Jol - la, at Wai - a - me - a Bay,

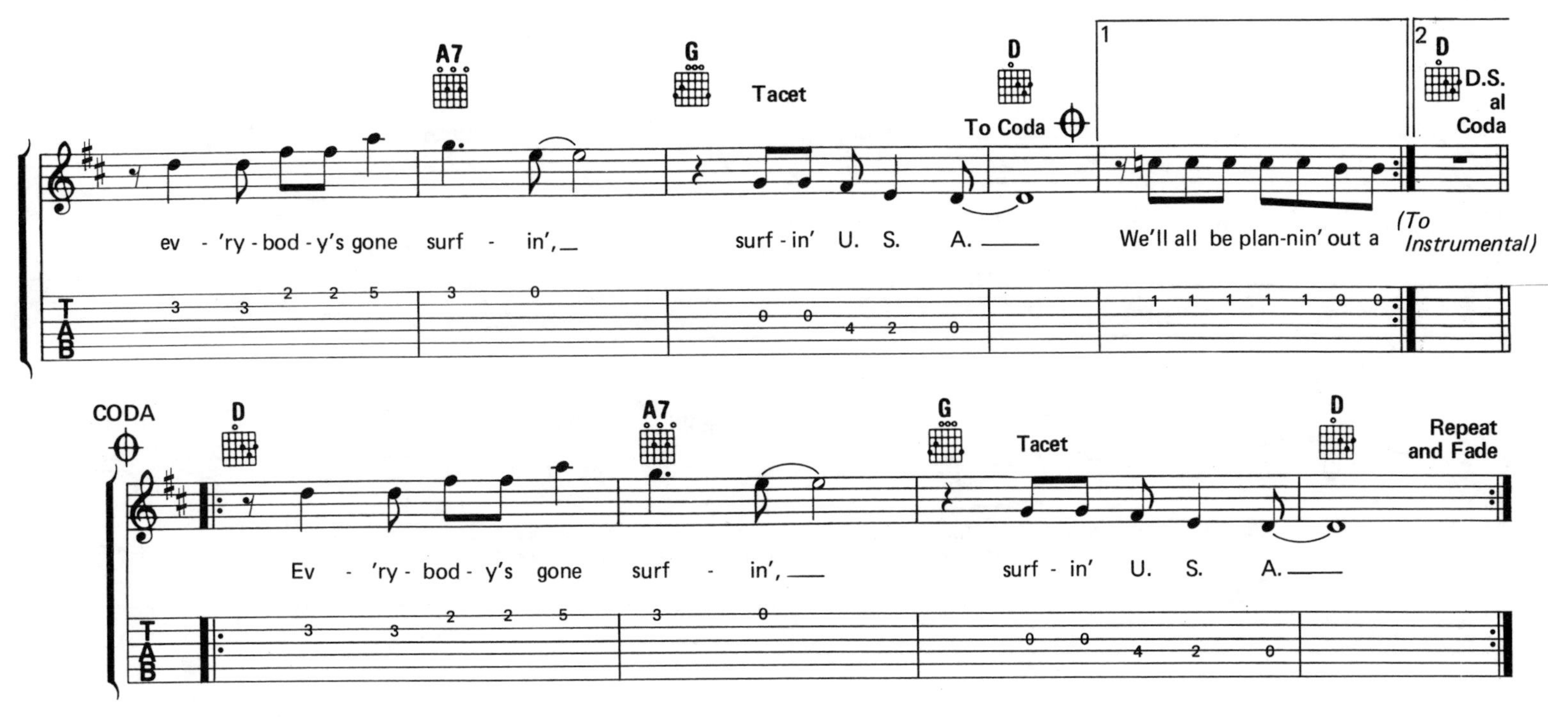

SUSIE Q

Words and Music by D. HAWKINS, S. J. LEWIS and E. BROADWATER

E
I like the way you walk.
Well, say that you'll be true.
I like the way you talk.
Well, say that you'll be true.
A7
C7
B7
E
I like the way you walk, I like the way you talk, my Su - sie Q.
Well, say the you'll be true and nev - er leave me blue, my Su - sie Q.
(Guitar solo)
A7
E7
B7
E
2nd time, D.S.
(to 1st verse)
and Fade

SYNCHRONICITY II

Words and Music by
STING

G
C/G
C#dim7/G
G
C/G
Moth - er chants_ her lit - an - y___ of bore - dom and___ frus - tra - tion, but
sec - re - tar - ies pout___ and preen_ like cheap___ tarts in___ a red___ light street, but
Dad - dy grips___ the wheel___ and stares_ a - lone___ in - to___ the dis - tance. He
G
C/G
C#m7-5
Am7/G
we know all___ her su - i - cides_ are ___ fake.
all he ev - er thinks___ to do___ is ___ watch. And
knows that some - thing some - where has___ to ___ break. He
Cm7
Cm6
Cm7
Cm6
Dad - dy on - ly stares___ in - to___ the dis - tance, there's
ev - ery sin - gle meet - ing with his___ so - called su - per - i - or is a hu -
sees the fam - 'ly home___ now ___ loom - ing in his head - lights. The
Cm7
Cm6
D7sus
Gm(add 9)
on - ly so___ much more___ that he can ___ take._ Man - y miles___ a - way___
mil - i - at - ing kick in the crotch. Man - y miles___ a - way___
pain up - stairs_ that makes_ his eye - balls ___ ache._ Man - y miles___ a - way___
Eb/G
F
Cm/Eb
D7
To Coda
some - thing crawls from the slime ___ at the bot - tom of a dark
some - thing crawls to the sur - face ___ of a dark___ Scot - tish lake.
there's a shad - ow on the door ___ of a cot - tage on the shore

1
D7sus
D7
F
C/G
2
F9
D7
F
C
D.S. al Coda
Scot - tish lake.
CODA
Cm6/D
D7
Cm6/D
Cm7
D
of a dark
Scot - tish lake.
Cm7
Dm7
Cm7
D
Repeat and Fade
Man - y miles a - way.

SWEET HOME ALABAMA

Words and Music by RONNIE VAN ZANT, ED KING and GARY ROSSINGTON

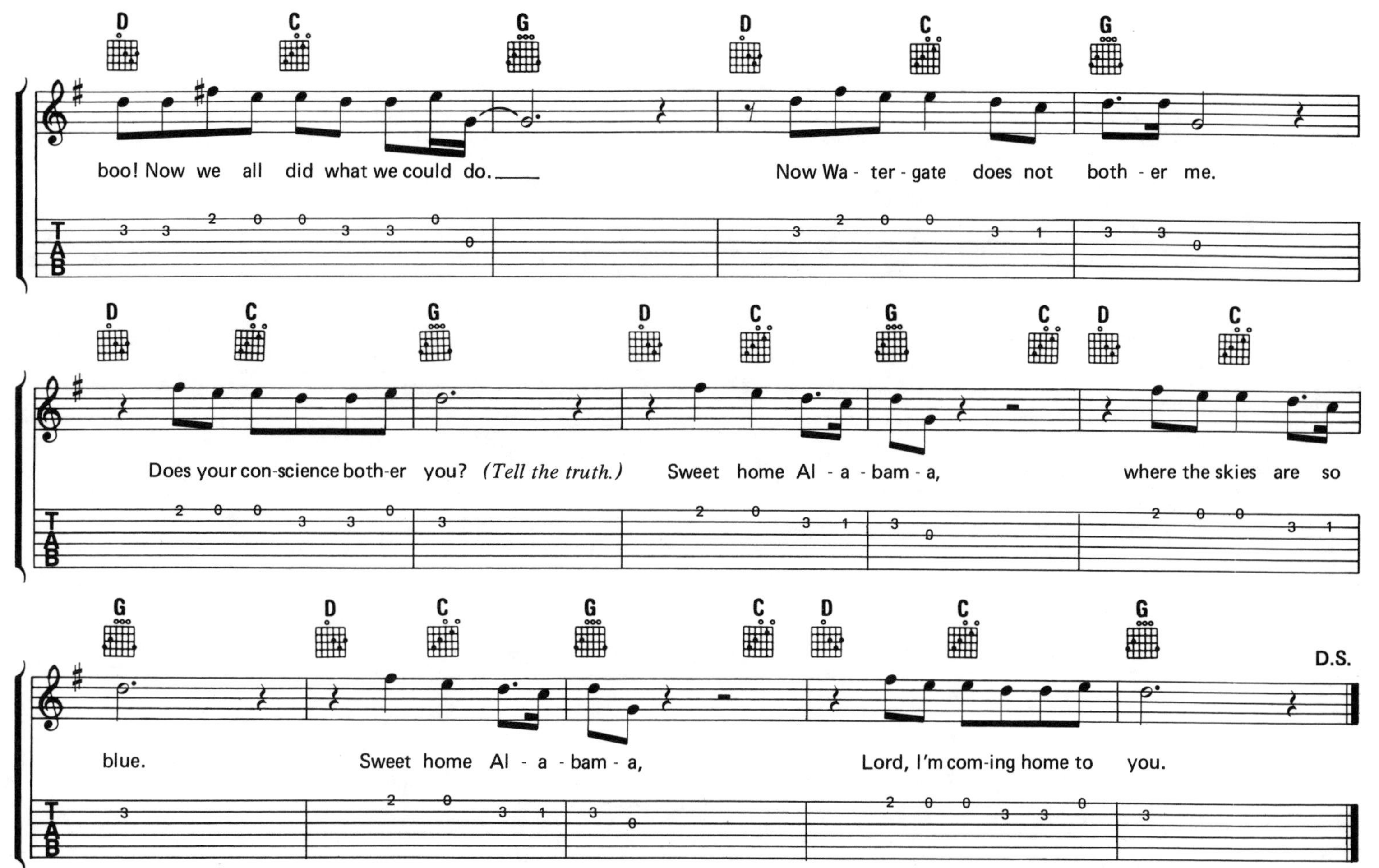

4. Now Muscle Shoals has got the Swampers
and they've been known to pick a song or two
Lord they get me off so much
they pick me up when I'm feeling blue
(Now how about you.)

SWEET LITTLE SIXTEEN

Words and Music by
CHUCK BERRY

Bright Rock Beat
Strum Pattern: No. 1
Capo: Up One Fret (Actual Key D♭)
Intro

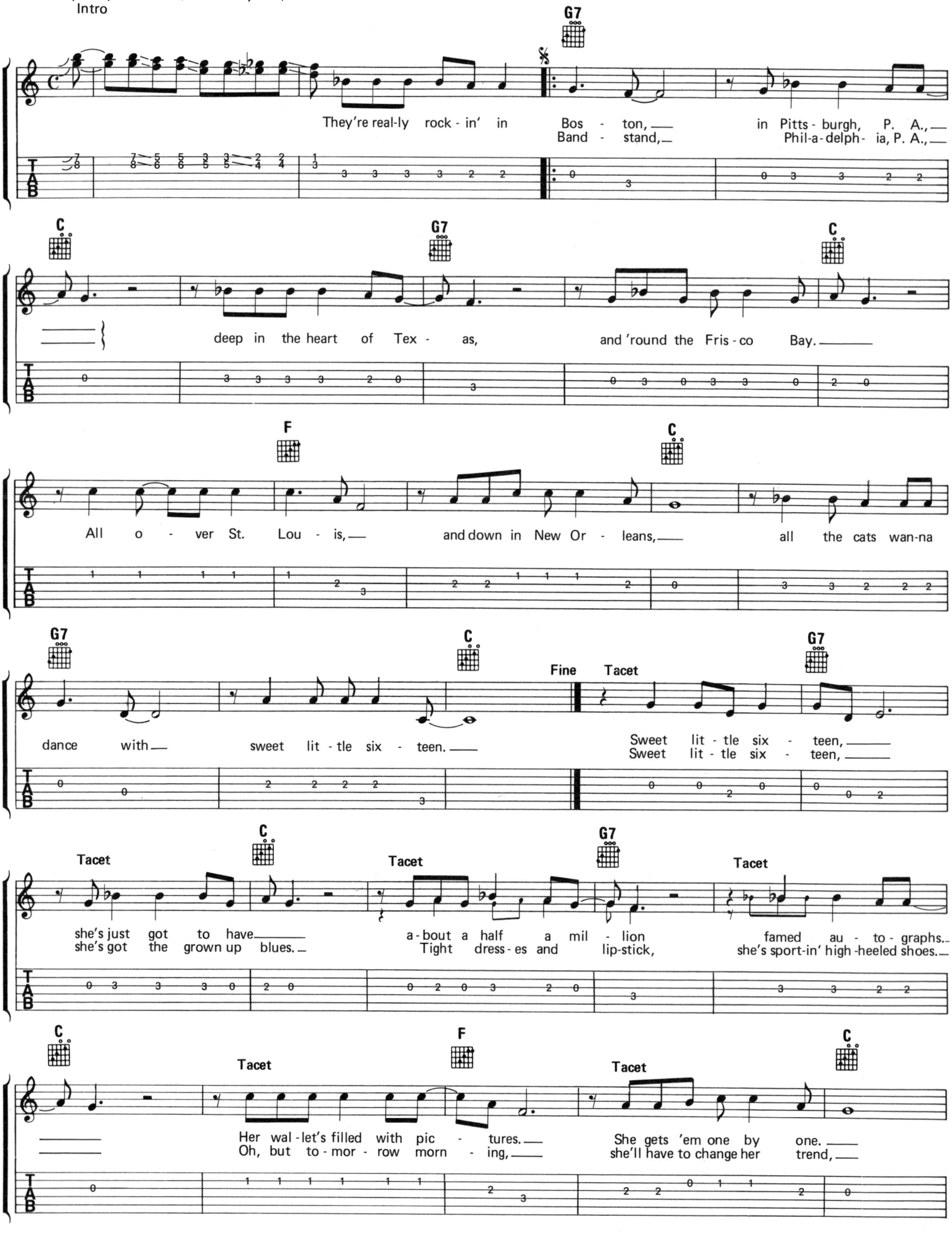
G7
They're real-ly rock-in' in Bos-ton, in Pitts-burgh, P. A.,
Band-stand, Phil-a-delph-ia, P. A.,
C G7 C
deep in the heart of Tex-as, and 'round the Fris-co Bay.
F C
All o-ver St. Lou-is, and down in New Or-leans, all the cats wan-na
G7 C
dance with sweet lit-tle six-teen.
Fine
Tacet
G7
Sweet lit-tle six-teen,
Sweet lit-tle six-teen,
Tacet
C
she's just got to have
she's got the grown up blues.
Tacet
G7
a-bout a half a mil-lion
Tight dress-es and lip-stick,
Tacet
famed au-to-graphs.
she's sport-in' high-heeled shoes.
C
Tacet
F
Her wal-let's filled with pic-tures.
Oh, but to-mor-row morn-ing,
Tacet
C
She gets 'em one by one.
she'll have to change her trend,

Second time to next phrase
Tacet
G7
Tacet
C
Be-comes so ex - cit - ed,
and be sweet six - teen,
watch her, look at her run.
"Oh, Mom-my, Mom-
F
C
G7
- my, please may I go?"
It's such a sight to see
C
F
some-bod - y steal the show.
"Oh, dad - dy, dad - dy,
I beg of you,
C
G7
C
D.S. (first verse) al Fine
whis - per to Mom - my
it's all right with you."
and back in class a - gain.
'Cause they'll be rock-in' on
But they'll be rock-in' in

THAT'LL BE THE DAY

Words and Music by JERRY ALLISON, NORMAN PETTY and BUDDY HOLLY

Moderate Shuffle
Strum Pattern: No. 7

A E D

(Instrumental) Well, that-'ll be the day, when you say good-bye, yes

A D

that-'ll be the day, when you make me cry. You say you're gon-na leave; you know it's a lie, 'cause

A E A D A

that-'ll be the day when I die. Well, { you give me all your lov-in' and your tur-tle dov-in', a- / when Cu-pid shot his dart, he shot it at your heart,

D A D A

all your hugs and kiss-es and your mon-ey too. Well, a, you know you love me ba-by, still you tell me, may-be,
so if we ev-er part then I'll leave you. You sit and hold me and you tell me bold-ly,

B7 E7 D A

that some day, well, I'll be blue. { Well, that-'ll be the day, when you say good-bye, yes, that-'ll be the day, when
that some day, well, I'll be through. }

D A E A

you make me cry. You say you're gon-na leave; you know it's a lie 'cause that-'ll be the day when I die. *(Guitar)*

To Coda

A
D
A
E7
D7
A7
E7
D.S. al Coda
Well,
CODA
E
A
D
A
when I die. Well, that-'ll be the day,
ooh, that-'ll be the day,
D
A
ooh. That-'ll be the day,
ooh, that-'ll be the day.
(Instrumental)

THESE DREAMS

Words and Music by
MARTIN PAGE and TAUPIN

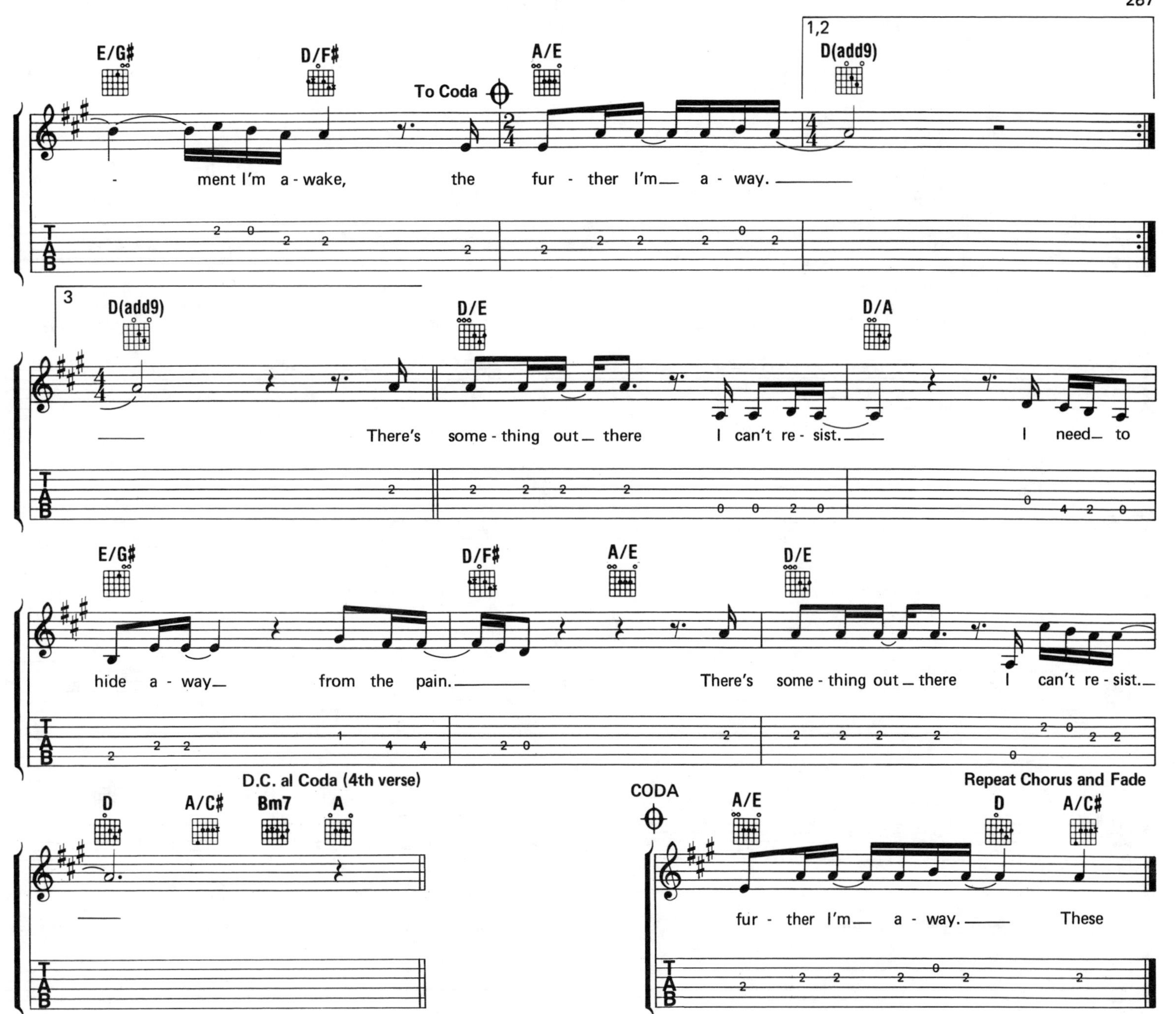

The sweetest song is silence that I've ever heard.
Funny how your feet in dreams never touch the earth,
In a wood full of princes, freedom is a kiss,
But the prince hides his face from dreams in the mist.

TAKE ON ME

Music by PAL WAAKTAAR and MAGS FURUHOLMEN
Words by PAL WAAKTAAR, MAGS FURUHOLMEN and MORTON HARKET

A
E/G#
D
1 E
2 E
(8va)
D.S. al Coda
two.
So,
Oh, the
CODA
D
A
E/G#
F#m
D
8va
D.S.S. and Fade
in a day.
(Take on me.)
TICKET TO RIDE
Copyright ©1965 NORTHERN SONGS LIMITED
All Rights Controlled and Administered by BLACKWOOD MUSIC INC. under license from ATV MUSIC (MACLEN) & SBK UNART CATALOG INC.
Words and Music by
JOHN LENNON and PAUL McCARTNEY
Moderate Rock
Strum Pattern: No. 2
Tuned down a Fret Low (Actual Key: A♭)
Play 3 times
1.,3. I think I'm gon - na be sad. I think it's to - day, yeah. The girl that's driv - in' me mad is go - in' a - way.
2.,4. said that liv - in' with me is bring - in' her down, yeah. For she would nev - er be free when I was a - round.
Bm7
E7
F#m
D7
She's got a tick - et to ride, she's got a tick - et to ri - hi - hide, she's got a tick - et to ride, but she don't care.
G
Last time To Coda
1 A
2. She

2,3
A
D7
I don't know why she's rid - in' so high.
She ought-ta
E7
D7
think twice, she ought-ta do right by me.
Be - fore she gets through say - in' good - bye,
D.S. (3rd and 4th verse) alCoda
E7
she ought-ta think twice, she ought-ta do right by me.
(Guitar)
She
CODA
A
Repeat and Fade
My ba - by don't care.

TOBACCO ROAD

Words and Music by
JOHN D. LOUDERMILK

TOTAL ECLIPSE OF THE HEART

Words and Music by
JIM STEINMAN

MIDDLE

G
Em
C
D7
part and I need you now to-night; and I need you more than ev-er. And if you on-ly hold me tight
we'll be hold-ing on for-ev-er. And we'll on-ly be mak-ing it
D
right, 'cause we'll nev-er be wrong to-geth-er we can take it to the end of the line. Your
A
love is like a shad-ow on me all of the time; I
D/F♯
don't know what to do and I'm al-ways in the dark. We're liv-ing in a pow-der keg and giv-ing off sparks.
Tacet
G/B
D/A
I real-ly need you to-night. For-ev-er's gon-na start to-night.

C
D7
G
Em
For-ev - er's gon-na start to - night.
Once up-on a time I was fall-ing in love, but
B
C
G/B
Am7
D7♭9
now I'm on-ly fall-ing a-part.
There's noth-ing I can do, a tot-al e-clipse of the heart.
G
Em
C
D7
D/F♯
G
Em
Once up-on a time there was light in my life, but
B
C
G/B
Am
D7♭9
now there's on-ly love in the dark.
Noth-ing I can say, a tot-al e-clipse of the heart.
G
Em
To Coda
C
D7
D/F♯
G
D.C. al Coda (take 2nd ending)
CODA
C
D7
D/F♯
G
Repeat with vocal ad lib. and Fade

(SO) TIRED OF WAITING FOR YOU

Words and Music by
RAY DAVIES

Medium Rock
Strum Pattern: No. 2

Intro Play 4 times

F G F G F G F G F G F G F

(Continue this riff throughout song)

So tired, tired of wait- ing, tired of wait-ing for you.

G F G F G F G F G F C

To Coda

So tired, tired of wait - ing, tired of wait-ing for you. I was a lone - ly soul;

F C F C F F♯ G D7 G D7 G D7

I had no - bod - y 'til I met you, but you keep - a me wait - ing all of the time. What can I do?

G Bm F D G Bm

It's your life, and you can do what you want. Do what you like, but

F D F 1 D 2 D D.S. al Coda

please don't keep - a me wait - in', please don't keep - a me wait - in'. 'Cause I'm - in'. 'Cause I'm

CODA

G F G F G F G F G F G

For you, for you.

TUESDAY AFTERNOON

Words and Music by
JUSTIN HAYWARD

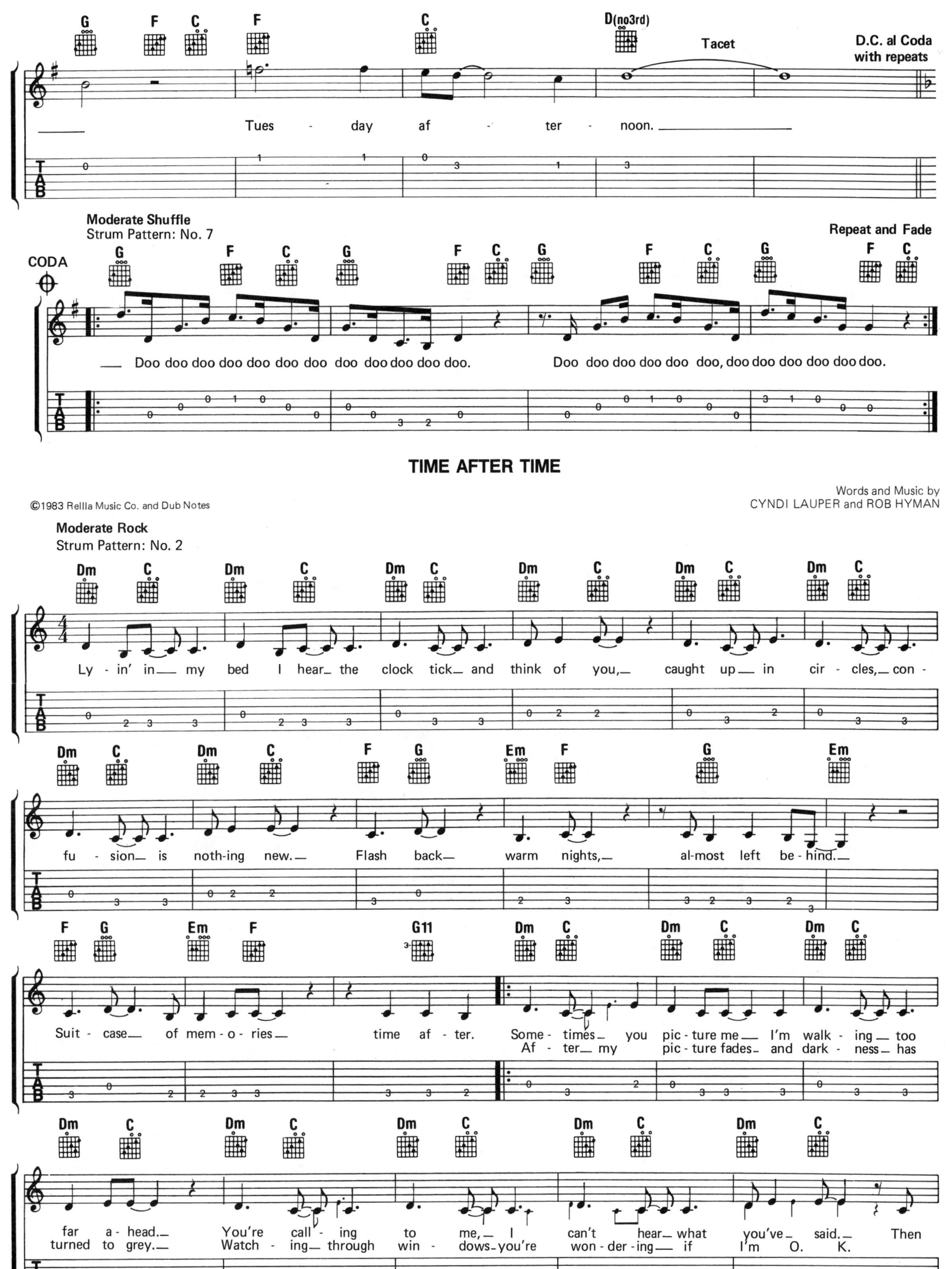
G F C F C D(no3rd)
Tacet
D.C. al Coda with repeats
Tues - day af - ter - noon.
Moderate Shuffle
Strum Pattern: No. 7
CODA
G F C G F C G F C G F C
Repeat and Fade
Doo doo doo doo doo doo doo doo doo doo doo doo.
Doo doo doo doo doo doo, doo doo doo doo doo doo.
TIME AFTER TIME
Words and Music by
CYNDI LAUPER and ROB HYMAN
©1983 Rellla Music Co. and Dub Notes
Moderate Rock
Strum Pattern: No. 2
Dm C Dm C Dm C Dm C Dm C Dm C
Ly - in' in my bed I hear the clock tick and think of you, caught up in cir - cles, con -
Dm C Dm C F G Em F G Em
fu - sion is noth-ing new. Flash back warm nights, al-most left be - hind.
F G Em F G11 Dm C Dm C Dm C
Suit - case of mem - o - ries time af - ter. Some - times you pic - ture me I'm walk - ing too
Af - ter my pic - ture fades and dark - ness has
Dm C Dm C Dm C Dm C Dm C
far a - head. You're call - ing to me, I can't hear what you've said. Then
turned to grey. Watch - ing through win - dows you're won - der - ing if I'm O. K.

F G Em F G Em F G
you say go slow. I fall be - hind. The sec - ond hand
Sec - rets sto - len from deep in - side. The drum beats out
Em F G Am F G C
un - winds. / of time. If you're lost you can look and you will find me time af - ter time. If you fall
G Am F G C G
I will catch you I'll be wait - ing time af - ter time. If you're lost you can look and you will
(Instrumental)
Am F G C G Am
find me time af - ter time. If you fall I will I catch you I'll be wait - ing
F G To Coda 1 C F G Em
time af - ter time.
(Guitar)
F 2 C D.S. al Coda (verse 1)
CODA C F G C Repeat and Fade
time af - ter time.

TUTTI FRUTTI

Words and Music by
R. PENNIMAN and D. LA BOSTRIE

Bb7
F
C7
frut - ti au rut - ti, tut - ti frut - ti au_ rut - ti, tut - ti frut - ti, au rut - ti, a -
F
Tacet
To Coda
1
2
D.S. al Coda
wop - bop - a - loom-op - a - lop - bomp - bom! I got a *ow!* Tut - ti
CODA
lop - bam boom.

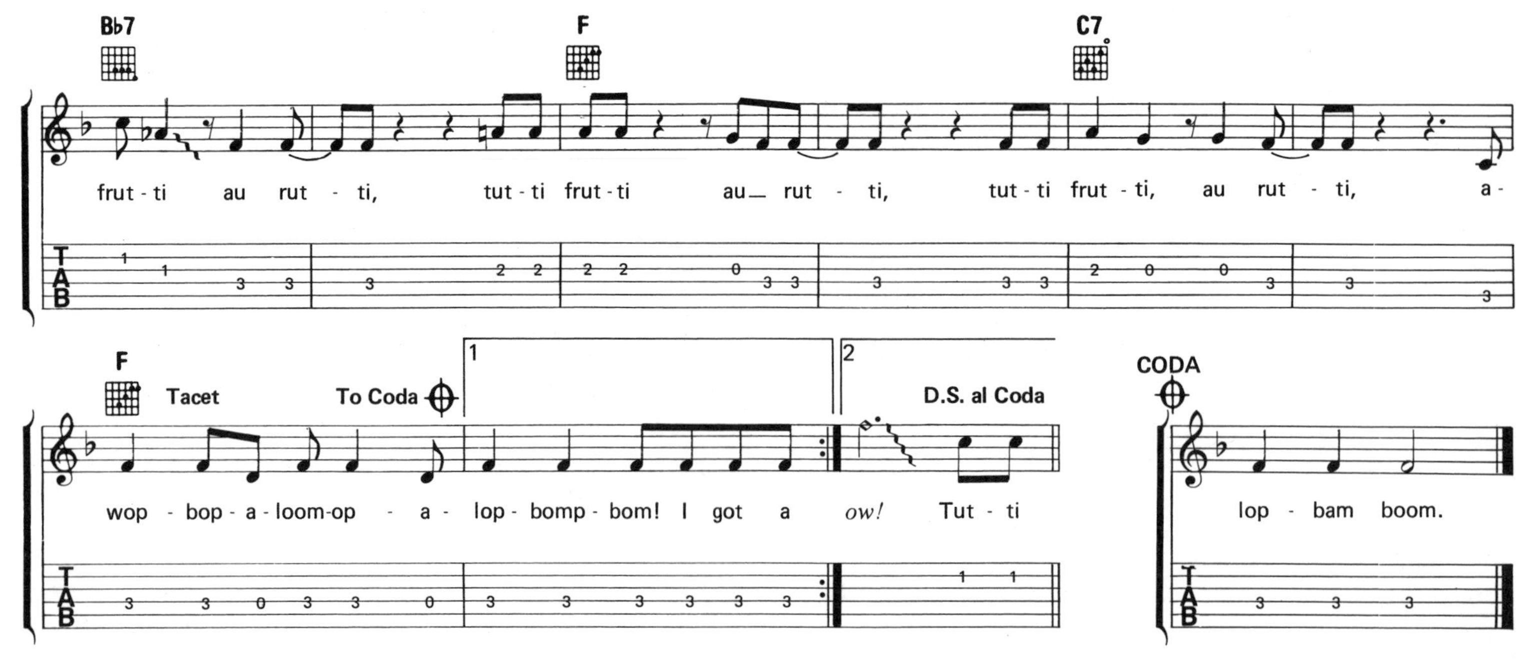

WAKE ME UP BEFORE YOU GO-GO

Words and Music by
GEORGE MICHAEL

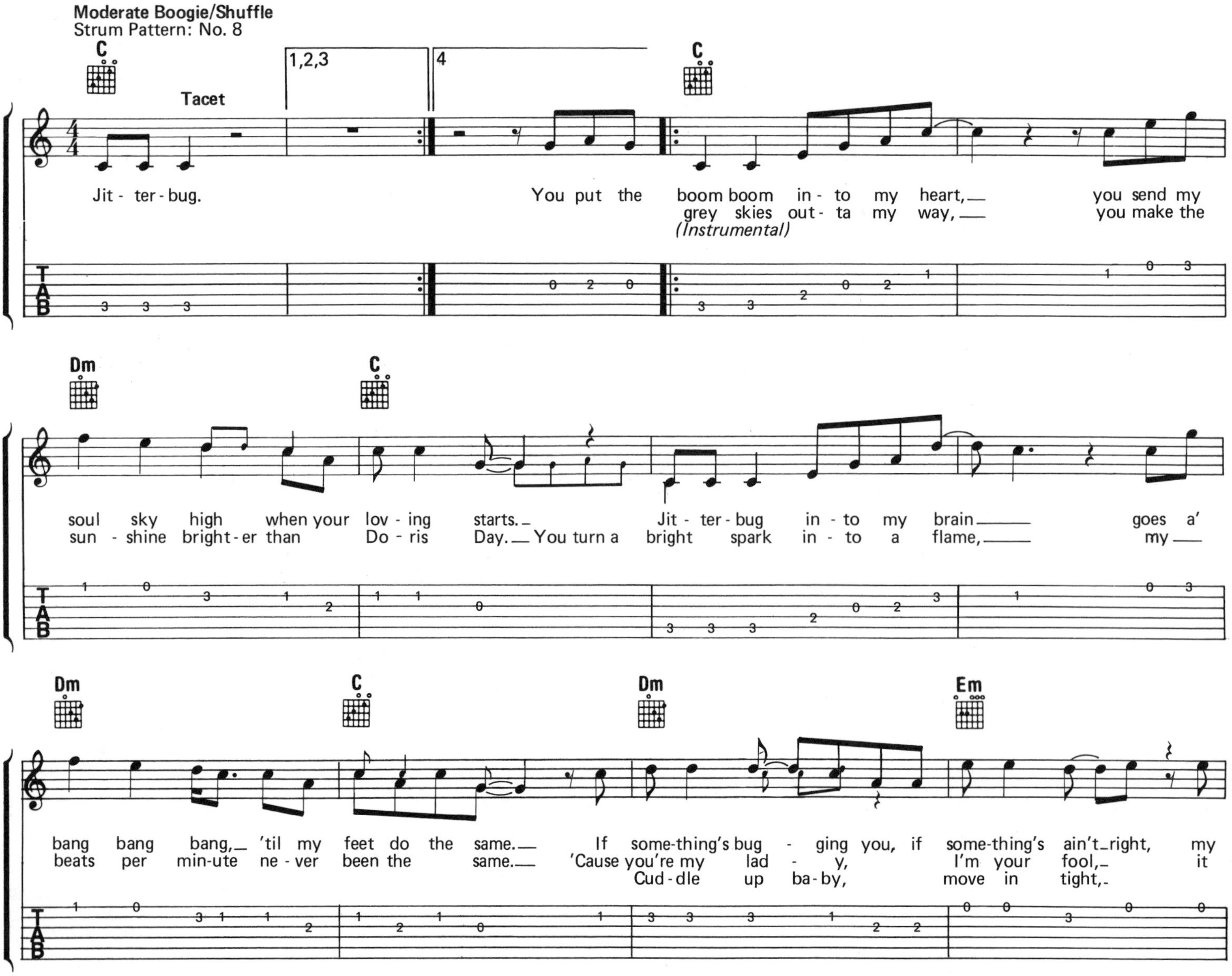

Moderate Boogie/Shuffle
Strum Pattern: No. 8
C
Tacet
1,2,3
4
C
Jit - ter - bug. You put the boom boom in - to my heart,_ you send my
grey skies out - ta my way,_ you make the
(Instrumental)
Dm
C
soul sky high when your lov - ing starts._ Jit - ter - bug in - to my brain___ goes a'
sun - shine bright - er than Do - ris Day._ You turn a bright spark in - to a flame,___ my__
Dm
C
Dm
Em
bang bang bang,_ 'til my feet do the same._ If some-thing's bug - ging you, if some-thing's ain't_right, my
beats per min-ute ne - ver been the same._ 'Cause you're my lad - y, I'm your fool,_ it
Cud - dle up ba - by, move in tight,_

F
Em
A11
Dm
Em
best friend told — me what you — did last — night, left me sleep - ing in my bed. —
makes me cra - zy when you — act so — cruel, come on ba - by, let's not fight, —
we'll go danc - ing to - mor - row night. — It's cold out there — but it's warm in bed, —
F
G
Tacet
C
I was dream-ing but I should have been with you in - stead. —
we'll go danc - ing, ev' - ry - thing will be al - right. —
they can dance — we'll stay home in - stead. —
Wake me up — be-fore you go — go, don't leave me hang -
Dm
C
Dm
- ing on — like a yo - yo. Wake me up — be-fore you go — go, I don't wan-na miss — it when you hit that high —
C
Dm
C
— Wake me up — be-fore you go — go 'cause I'm not plan - ning on — go - ing so - lo. Wake me up —
Em
Dm
1,2
C7
F/C
C7
— be-fore — you go — go, take me danc - ing to - night. —
F/C
C7
3
C
D.S. and Fade
I wan-na hit that high. — Yeah — yeah. — You put the — Wake me up —

WAKE UP, LITTLE SUSIE

Words and Music by
BOUDLEAUX BRYANT and FELICE BRYANT

Straight Rock
Strum Pattern: No. 1
Intro

D F D G D F

Moderate Shuffle
Strum Pattern: No. 9

D F D G

Wake up, lit-tle Su - sie, wake up.

1. D F D 2. D F D G D7 G D7

We've both been sound a - sleep. Wake up lit-tle Su - sie and
The mov - ie was-n't so hot. It did-n't have much of a

G D7 G D7 G D7 G

weep. The mov - ie's o - ver. it's four o - clock, and we're in trou-ble deep. Wake up, lit-tle
plot. We fell a - sleep, our goose is cooked, our rep - u - ta - tion is shot.

A G A E7

Su - sie, wake up lit - tle Su - sie. Well, what-'re we gon - na tell your ma -

A E7 A E7 A

- ma? What-'re we gon - na tell your pa? What-'re we gon - na tell our friends when they say,

A7 D A7 D

"Ooh la la." Wake up, lit - tle Su - sie. Wake up, lit - tle Su - sie.

To Coda

D7

Well, I told your ma-ma that you'd be in by ten. Well,

G A

Su-sie ba-by, looks like we goofed a-gain. Wake up, lit-tle Su-sie.

G A A7 D F D G D F

D.S. al Coda

Wake up, lit-tle Su-sie. We got-ta go home.

CODA

A7 D D F D G D F D G D F

Play 4 times

Repeat and Fade

WALK THIS WAY

Words and Music by
STEVEN TYLER and JOE PERRY

Moderate Disco/Funk Beat
Strum Pattern: No. 4

A
B
C
1. Back seat lov - er al - ways hot 'neath the cov - ers 'til I
2.,4. See - saw swing - er with the boys in the school, and your
3. School girl sweet - ies with a class - y, kind - a sass - y lit - tle
talked to my dad - dy, he say, ___ he said, "You ain't seen noth - in' 'til you're
feet fly - in' up in the air, ___ sing - in' "Hey did - dle did - dle" with your
skirts climb - in' way up their knees; ___ there was ___ three young la - dies in the
down on a muf - fin, and you're sure to be chang - in' your ways." ___ I met a
kit - ty in the mid - dle of the swing ___ like you did - n't care. ___ So I
school gym ___ lock - er when I no - ticed they was look - in' at me. ___ I was a
cheer - lead - er was a real big bleed - er; oh, the times I could rem - i - nisce, ___
took a big chance at the high school dance with a miss - y who was read - y to play. ___
high school los - er, nev - er made it with a la - dy 'til the boys told me some - thin' I missed. ___
on the best things of lov - in' with her sis - ter and her cou - sin, and they
It was - n't me she was fool - in', 'cause she knew what she was do - in' and I
Then my next door neigh - bor with a daugh - ter had a fav - or. So I
(4.) when she
1,3
A(no3rd)
2,4
start - ed with a lit - tle kiss ___ like this...
knowed love was here to stay ___ ___ when she told me to
gave her just a lit - tle kiss ___ like this...
told me how to walk this way. ___ ___ she told ___ me to

C
8va
walk this way,
F7
talk this way.
C
Walk this way,
F7
talk this way.
She told me to
Just give me a
C
(Guitar)
kiss.
bend
release
bend
bend
D.C. al Coda (with repeats)
A(no3rd)
To Coda
like this!
bend
CODA
Tacet
A(no3rd)
Repeat and Fade

WE BUILT THIS CITY

Words and Music by TAUPIN, MARTIN PAGE, PETER WOLF and DENNIS LAMBERT

Medium Rock
Strum Pattern: No. 1
Capo: Up Three Frets (Actual Key: F)

G/D
C/D
A/D
sink - ing in your fight, too man - y run - a-ways
some - one stole the stage, they call us ir - res- pon - si - ble,
'cause we're the ship of fools, look - ing for A - mer - i - ca
D
A/C♯
Bm
Gmaj7/B
F/C
A
eat - ing up the night.
write us off the page.
call - ing through our schools.
Mar - con - i plays the mam - ba, lis - ten to the ra - di - o.
D
G(add 9)
F♯m
Em7
Don't you re - mem - ber? We built this cit - y, we built this cit - y on
Gmaj7
D/F♯
rock and roll. We built this cit - y, we built this cit - y on
rock and roll, Built this cit-y, we built this cit-y on rock and roll.
G
To Coda
1
2

A/G G A D/F# G/D D/F# G A/C# D D/F# D G A D

It's just an - oth - er Sun- day in a tired old street. Po - lice have

D.S. al Coda

D/F# G/D D/F# Gmaj9 A/E D D/F# G/D G A/C# A D

got the choke-hold, oh, oh-oh-oh, but we just lost the beat. Who

CODA

Gmaj7

Built this cit - y

Repeat and Fade

We built, we built this cit-y, now, we built, we built this cit - y.

WALK ON THE WILD SIDE

By LOU REED

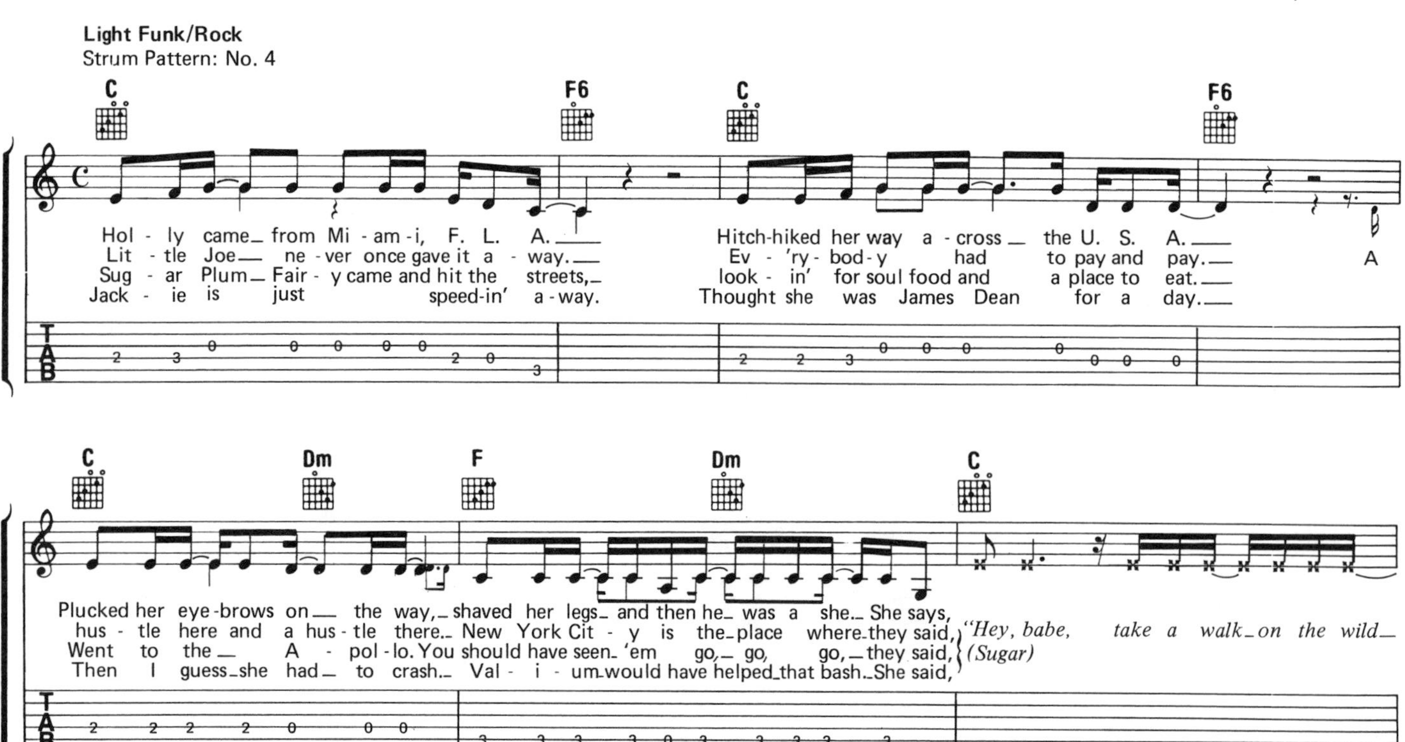

F6 C F6 C F6 C F6 C F6 C F6 C F6 C F6 C F6 C F6 C F6 F6 C F6 C F6 C F6
1
2,3
4
side." I said, "Hey, (babe,) take a walk on the wild side." And the colored girls go: "Doo doo doo doo doo doo, doo doo
(Joe,)
(honey,)
doo doo doo doo doo doo, doo doo doo doo doo doo doo doo, doo doo doo doo doo doo doo doo, doo doo
doo doo doo doo doo doo, doo doo doo doo doo doo doo doo, doo doo doo doo doo doo doo doo, doo doo
doo doo doo doo doo doo, doo doo doo."
wild side."
wild side." And the colored girls say:
"Doo doo doo doo doo doo, doo doo doo doo doo doo doo doo, doo doo doo."
Play 6 times
T
A
B

WE'RE NOT GONNA TAKE IT

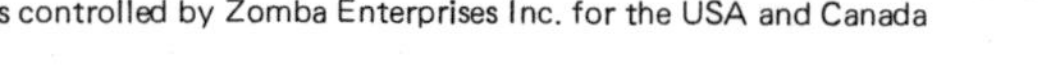

Words and Music by
D. SNIDER

Fast Rock
Strum Pattern: No. 1

Tacet

We're not gon - na take — it. No, we ain't gon-na take — it. We're not gon - na take — it an - y - more. —

(Guitar)

E B E A E

We've got the right to choose and there ain't no way we'll lose — it. — This is our life; —
Oh, you're so con - de-scend - ing, your gall is nev - er - end - ing. — We don't want

B E B E B

— this is — our song. — *(Guitar)* We'll fight the powers that be — just.
noth - in', not a thing — from you. — Your life is trite and ja - ded,

E A E B To Coda E

Don't pick our des - tin - y — 'cause — you don't know us, — you don't be - long. —
bor - ing and con - fis - ca - ted. — If that's your best, — your best won't do. —

B E B E A

(Guitar) We're not gon - na take — it. No, we ain't gon - na take — it.

E
B
E
B/D♯
C♯m
B
D.S. al Coda
We're not gon - na take it any - y - more.
(Guitar)
CODA
D
Bm
Oh,
Oh,
We're
right, yeah! We're free, yeah! We'll fight, yeah! You'll see.
Oh
F
F♯
CHORUS
A
We're not gon - na take it.
No, we ain't gon-na take it.
We're not gon - na take
it an - y - more.
Repeat Chorus with 1st ending and Fade

WHAT'D I SAY

Words and Music by
RAY CHARLES

When you see me in misery,
Come on, baby see about me now, yeah,
Hey, hey. All right.

See the girl with the red dress on.
She can do the birdland all night long. Oh yeah, yeah.
What'd I say? All right.

WHAT'S LOVE GOT TO DO WITH IT

Words and Music by
TERRY BRITTEN and GRAHAM LYLE

Moderate Funk-rock
Strum Pattern: No. 3
Capo: Up One Fret (Actual Key: A♭m)

Gm7 F 1 E♭maj7 F 2 E♭maj7 F C G F G
Who needs_a heart when_a heart can_ be bro - ken?_ It heart can_ be bro - ken?_ Oh. Oh._
C G 1,2 F G 3 F B♭/C C B♭/C
(Instrumental) I've been tak - ing on a new di - rec - tion,_ but I have_ to say,_
C A♭ B♭/A♭ Gm7 C7
I been think-ing a - bout my own pro - tec-tion. It scares me to feel this way._ Oh,_
Am G/A G Fmaj7 G Am G Fmaj7 G
oh, what's / bro - ken? love_ got to do,_ got to do_with it? What's love_ but a sec - ond hand e - mo - tion?_ / sweet old fash-ioned no - tion?_
Am G/A G Fmaj7 G Am G Fmaj7
What's love_ got to do,_ got to do_with it? Who needs_ a heart when_ a heart can_ be
Repeat and Fade

WHAT YOU NEED

Words and Music by
ANDREW FARRISS and MICHAEL HUTCHENCE

2. Don't you get sad and lonely.
   You need a change from what you do all day.
   Ain't no sense in all your crying,
   Just pick it up and throw it into shape. (To CHORUS)

3. Hey you, won't you listen?
   This is not the end of it all.
   Don't you see there is a rhythm?
   I'll take you where you really need to be. (To CODA)

WHEN THE GOING GETS TOUGH THE TOUGH GET GOING

Words and Music by
WAYNE BRATHWAITE, BARRY J. EASTMOND,
ROBERT JOHN "MUTT" LANGE and BILLY OCEAN

Moderate Rock Shuffle
Strum Pattern: No. 7

E C#m B E C#m B E C#m
do the things that lov-ers do?
Ooh (ooh) wan-na hold ya (wan-na hold ya.) I got to get it through to you.
B E C#m B A
Oh, when the go-ing gets tough
('cause)
(the tough get going)
When the go - ing gets rough
(the tough get rough.)
Hey
Hey
D/A A E C#m B E C#m B
To Coda
D.S. al Coda
hey hey hey hey.
hey hey hey.
Oh ba - by.
I'm gon-na
CODA
Bsus
Woh woh oh oh oh
Yeah yeah yeah
E C#m E A B C#m A
(Saxophone solo)
Dar - lin', I'll climb an - y moun - tain;
B C#m A B C#m A B C#m A
dar - lin', I'll swim ev-'ry sea.
Dar - lin', I'll reach for the heav - en;
dar - lin', with you

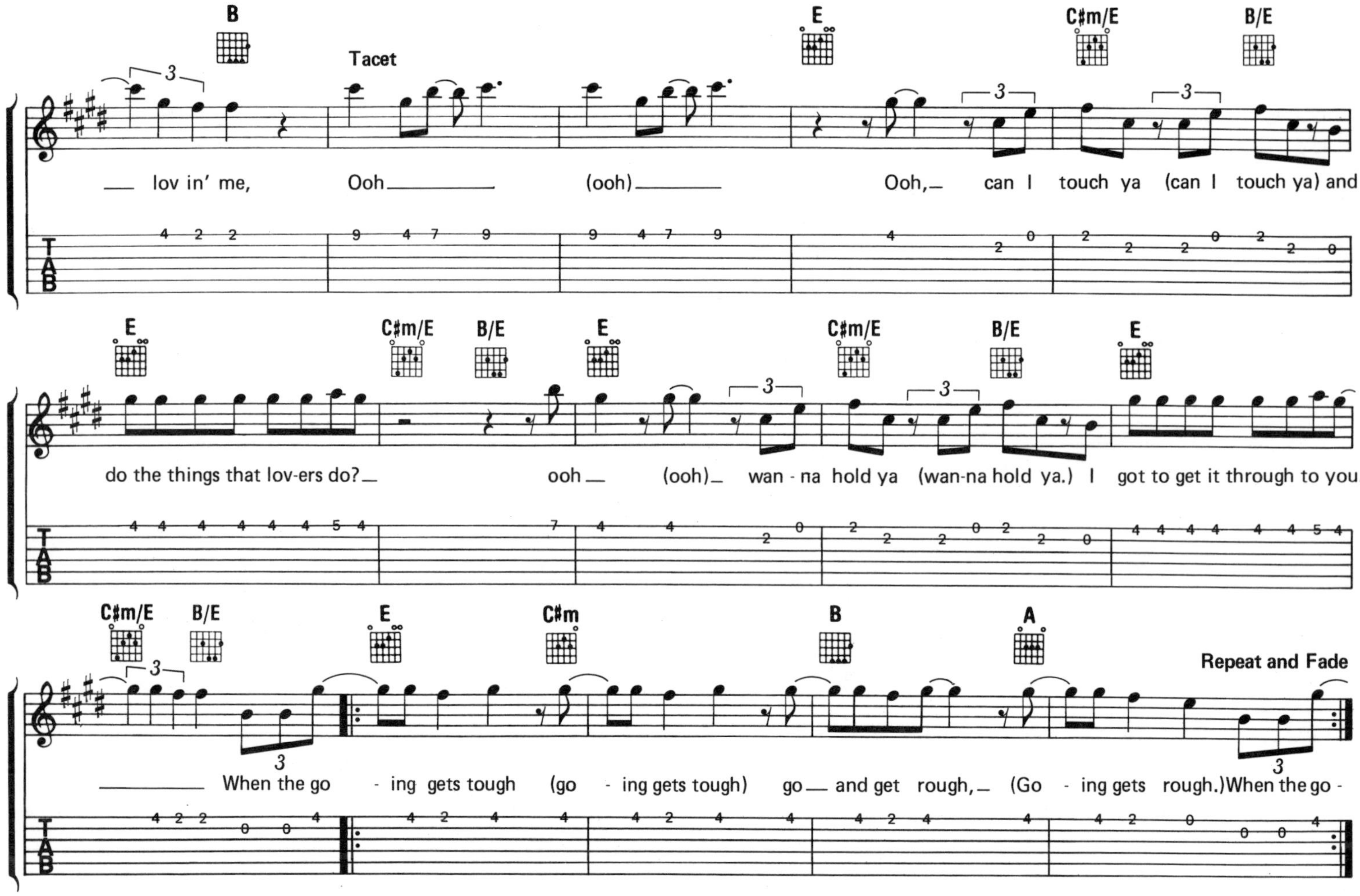

B
Tacet
E
C#m/E
B/E
lov in' me, Ooh (ooh) Ooh, can I touch ya (can I touch ya) and
E
C#m/E
B/E
E
C#m/E
B/E
E
do the things that lov-ers do? ooh (ooh) wan - na hold ya (wan-na hold ya.) I got to get it through to you.
C#m/E
B/E
E
C#m
B
A
Repeat and Fade
When the go - ing gets tough (go - ing gets tough) go and get rough, (Go - ing gets rough.) When the go -

A WHITER SHADE OF PALE

Words and Music by
KEITH REID and GARY BROOKER

Slow Rock Beat
Strum Pattern: No. 5

C
Em
Am
C/G
F
Am
Dm
F/C
G
G/F
Em
G7
C
F
To Coda
G
F
G7

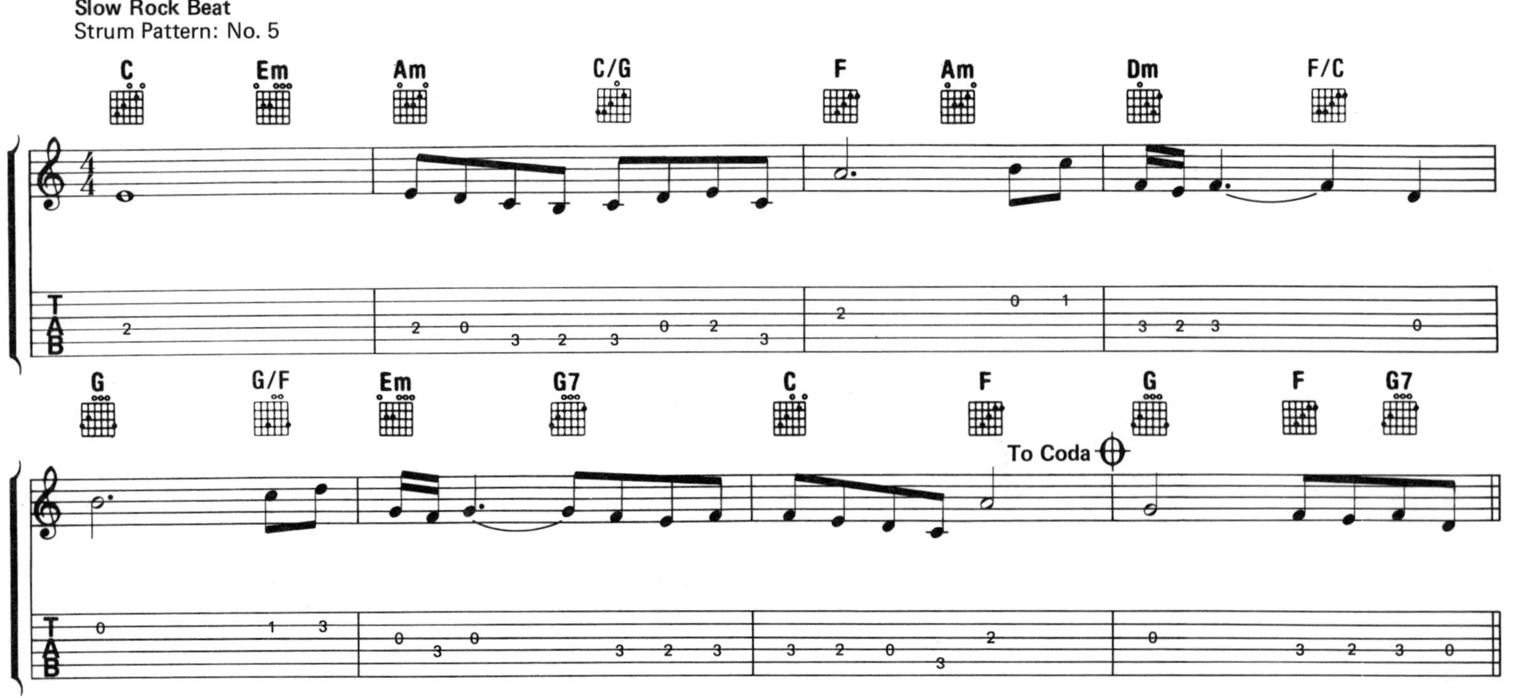

C
Em
Am
C/G
F
Dm
F/C
G
G/F
G7
We skipped the light fan - dan - go, turned cart-wheels 'cross the floor. I was feel - ing kind of
She said there is no rea - son, and the truth is plain to see. But I wan-dered through my
sea - sick. The crowd called out for more. The room was hum-ming hard - er,
play-ing cards, and would not let her be one of six - teen ves - tal vir - gins,
as the ceil - ing flew a - way. When we called out for an - oth - er drink,
who were leav-ing for the coast. And al - though my eyes were o - pen,
CHORUS
the wait - er brought a tray.
they might just as well have been closed.
And so it was that la - ter,
as the mil-ler told his tale, that her face at first just ghost - ly, turned a
whit - er shade of pale. pale.
D.C. al Coda
CODA
Repeat Chorus and Fade
And so we

WHEN YOU CLOSE YOUR EYES

Words and Music by JACK BLADES,
ALAN FRANCIS FITZGERALD and BRADLEY GILLIS

Bb F Eb
I re-mem-ber we learned a-bout love in the back of a Chev-ro-let. Well, it felt
I re-mem-ber I held you so tight and we danced the night a-way with the moves
I re-mem-ber we learned a-bout love in the back of a Chev-ro-let. No good
Bb F G
CHORUS
so good to be young, it feels like yes-ter-day.
of two wide-eyed kids. I need you so much to-day.
for an old mem-ory to mean so much to-day.
When you
G/B C Em D/C C
close your eyes do you dream a-bout me? When you
G/B C 1Dsus D
close your eyes do you dream a-bout me? Do you still dream a-bout
G C D 2Dsus
me? I me?

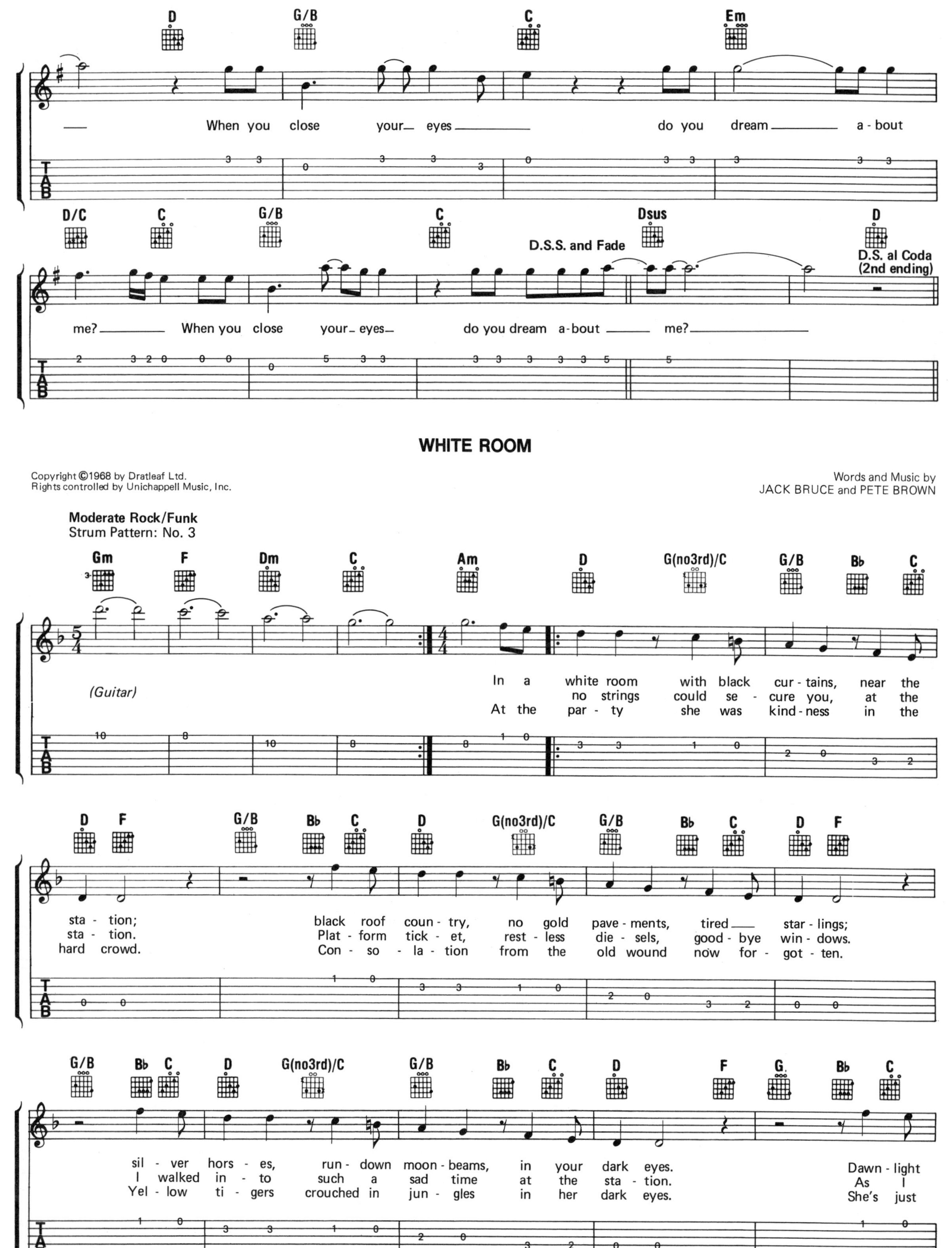

WHITE ROOM

Words and Music by
JACK BRUCE and PETE BROWN

D
G(no3rd)/C
G/B
B♭
C
F
G
smiles on your leav - ing, my con - tent - ment. I'll wait in this
walked out, felt my own need just be - gin - ning. I'll wait in this
dress - ing good - bye win - dows, tired star - lings. I'll sleep in this
A
place where the sun nev - er shines, wait in this place
queue when the trains come back; lie with you where the shad - ows
place with the lone - ly crowd; lie in the dark
To Coda
Tacet
D.C. al Coda
run from them - selves. You said - selves.
CODA
Gm
Dm
Am
- selves.
(Guitar)
(Guitar solo)
Repeat with guitar ad lib. and Fade
8va

WHO'S JOHNNY

Words and Music by
PETER WOLF and INA WOLF

Am C C/D Ab Bb Ab/C Bb/D Eb Ab Fm7 Ab/C Ab/Bb
To Coda
tried to look the oth-er way. her eyes gave her a - way.
Eb Ab Fm7 Ab/C Ab/Bb Ab Bb Ab/C Bb/D Am G/B C C/D
still pre - tend - ing. Who's
G F Am C C/D G F Am G/B C C/D
John - ny? Who's John - ny? Who's John - ny? Who's John - ny? "Who's
G F Am C C/D Ab Bb Ab/C Bb/D Abmaj7
John - ny?" she said, and tried to look the oth - er way. Her eyes gave her a - way. Girls like her
Bb Abmaj7 Bb/C Cm Abmaj7
are ver - y spe - cial girls. Girls like her don't rest un - til you too
Bb Ab/C Bb/D C/E
D.C. al Coda (modulate to key of F)
are a be - liev - er, 'til you too have caught their fe - ver.

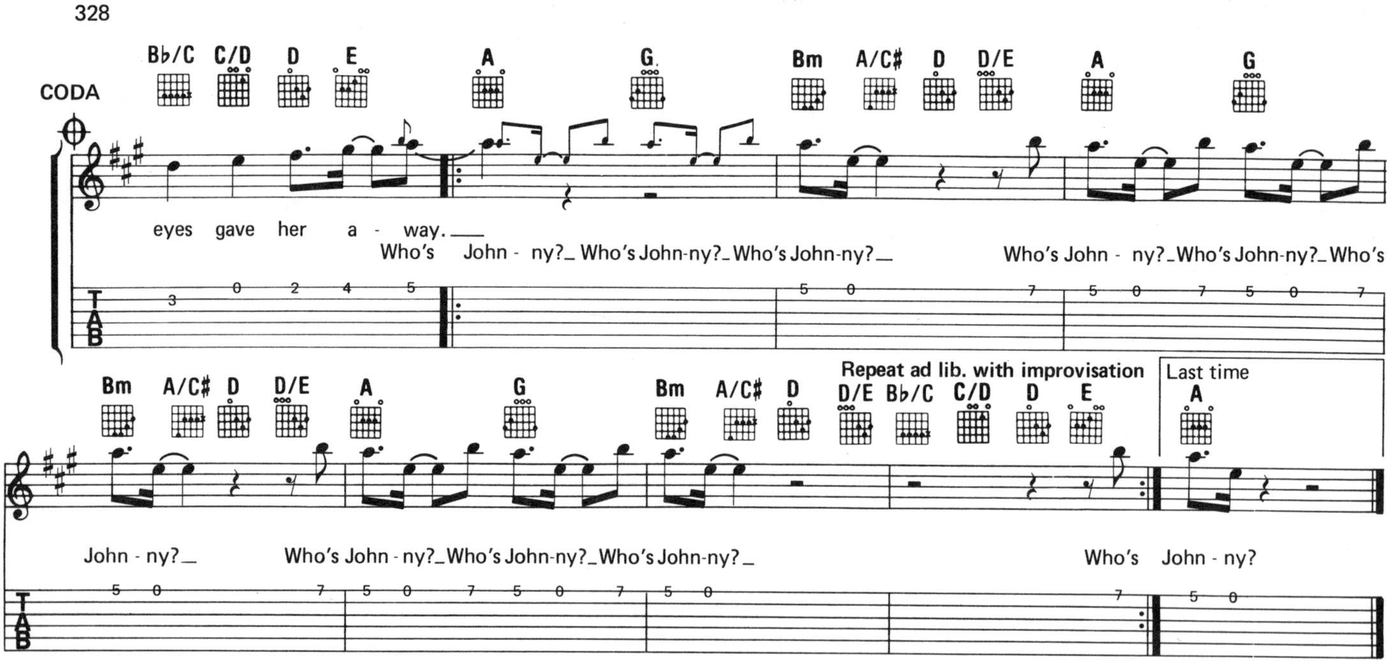

CODA

Bb/C C/D D E A G Bm A/C# D D/E A G

eyes gave her a - way.
Who's John - ny? Who's John-ny? Who's John-ny?
Who's John - ny? Who's John-ny? Who's

Bm A/C# D D/E A G Bm A/C# D

Repeat ad lib. with improvisation D/E Bb/C C/D D E

Last time A

John - ny?
Who's John - ny? Who's John-ny? Who's John-ny?
Who's John - ny?

WILD THING

Words and Music by
CHIP TAYLOR

Moderately Slow Rock/Funk
Strum Pattern: No. 3

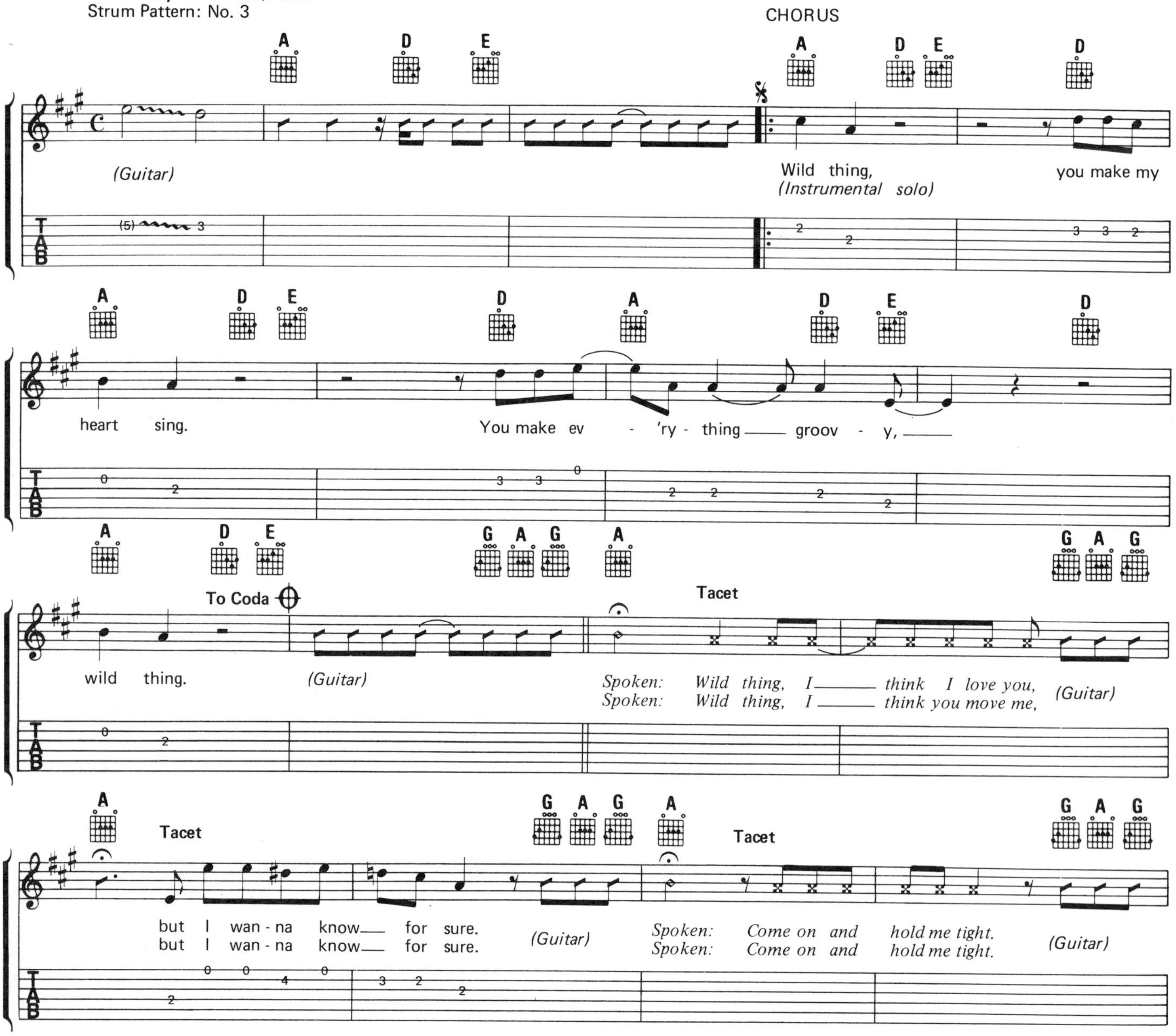

A D E

(Guitar)

CHORUS

A D E D

Wild thing, you make my
(Instrumental solo)

A D E D A D E D

heart sing. You make ev - 'ry - thing groov - y,

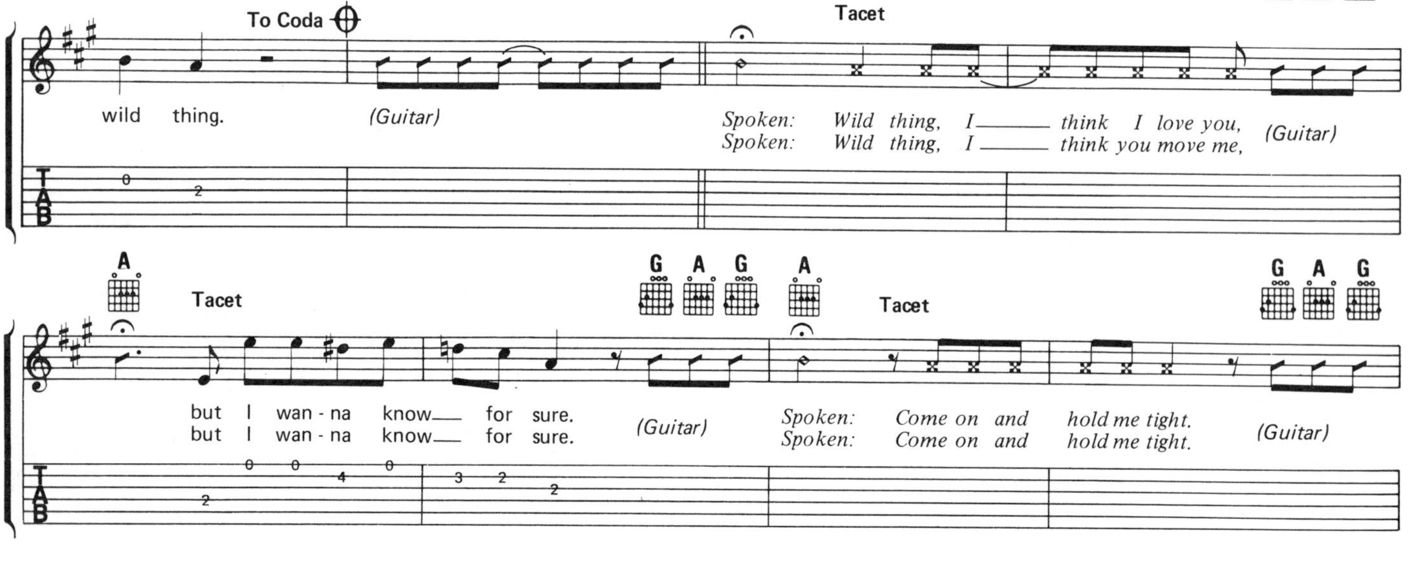

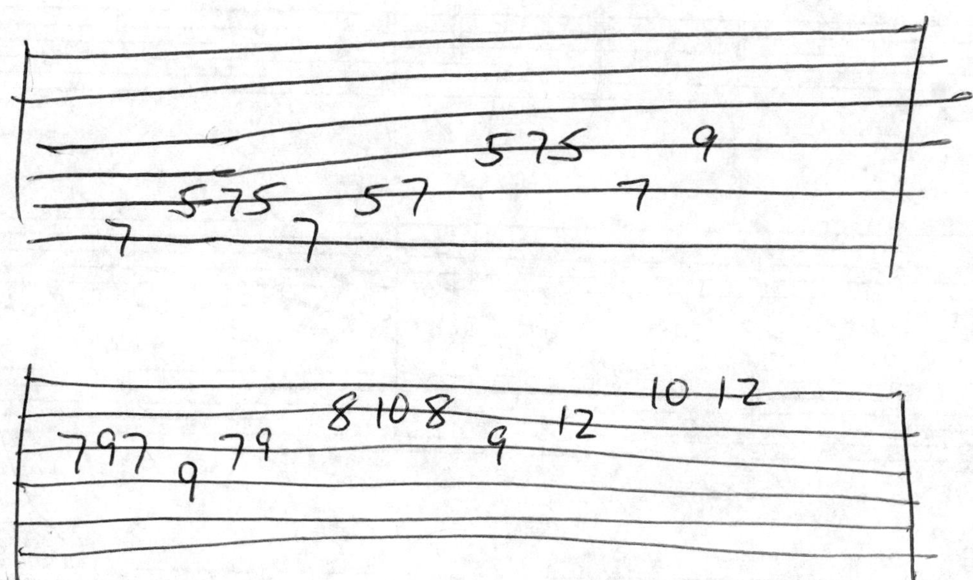

G
G7
C
C7
G
D
C
G
D7

```
--|------0-----|---------------------------|
--|------------|---------------------------|
0-|--0------3--|--0233333320---------------|
--|------------|-2-------------2-----------|
--|------------|-----------------0-0-------|
--|------------|---------------------------|
```

BREAK

Open Strings	1	2	3	4	5	6	7	8	9	10	11	12	13	14	15	16	17	18	19
E	F	F♯ G♭	G	G♯ A♭	A	A♯ B♭	B	C	C♯ D♭	D	D♯ E♭	E	F	F♯ G♭	G	G♯ A♭	A	A♯ B♭	B
B	C	C♯ D♭	D	D♯ E♭	E	F	F♯ G♭	G	G♯ A♭	A	A♯ B♭	B	C	C♯ D♭	D				
G	G♯ A♭	A	A♯ B♭	B	C	C♯ D♭	D	D♯ E♭	E	F	F♯ G♭	G	G♯ A♭	A					
D	D♯ E♭	E	F	F♯ G♭	G	G♯ A♭	A	A♯ B♭	B	C	C♯ D♭	D							
A	A♯ B♭	B	C	C♯ D♭	D	D♯ E♭	E	F	F♯ G♭	G	G♯ A♭	A	etc						
E	F	F♯ G♭	G	G♯ A♭	A	A♯ B♭	B	C	C♯ D♭	D	D♯ E♭	E							

Open

1st String

2nd String

3rd String

4th String

5th String

6th String

The House of the Rising Sun

A
Tacet
A
D
E
D
I love you.
You move me.
(Guitar)
1
CHORUS
Wild thing,
you make my
heart sing.
You make ev - 'ry - thing groov - y,
wild thing.
(Guitar)
2
(Guitar)
D.S. al Coda
CODA
Repeat with vocal ad lib. and Fade
C'm' - on, c'm' - on, wild thing.
(Guitar)

WITH OR WITHOUT YOU

Music by U2
Words by BONO

G D A7sus Bm7 G D
And you give your-self a - way. And you give your-self a - way. And you give, and you give,
A7sus Bm7 G D A7sus Bm7
To Coda
and you give your-self a - way. My hands are tied, the bod- y bruised.
G D A7sus Bm7 G
D.S. al Coda
You got me with noth-ing to win and noth-ing left to lose. And you
CODA
G D A7sus Bm7 G
with or with-out you, with or with - out you, oh. I can't live
D A7sus Bm7 G D
Play 3 times with vocal ad lib.
with or with - out you. with or with - out you.
D Asus Bm G
Repeat and Fade
(Guitar)

WHO DO YOU LOVE?

By ELLAS MCDANIEL

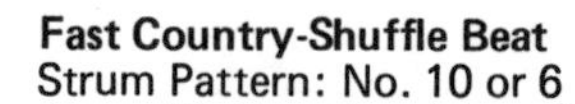

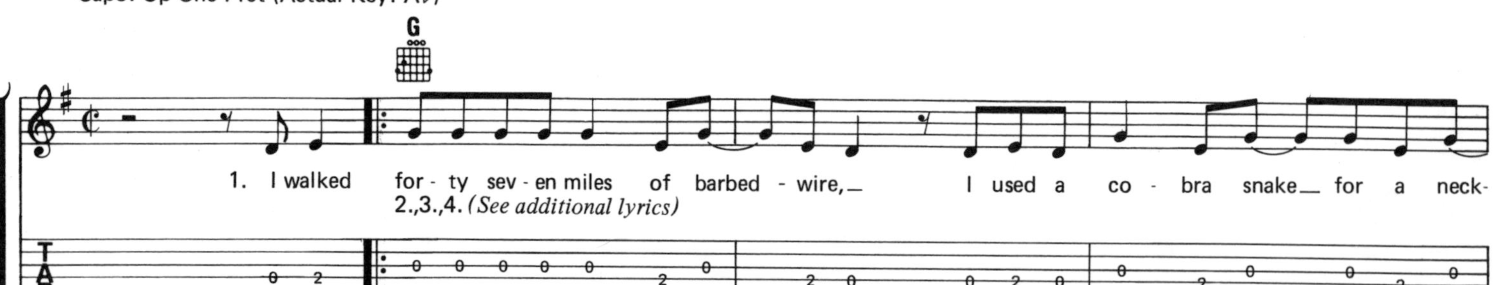

(After last verse, continue rhythm and Fade)

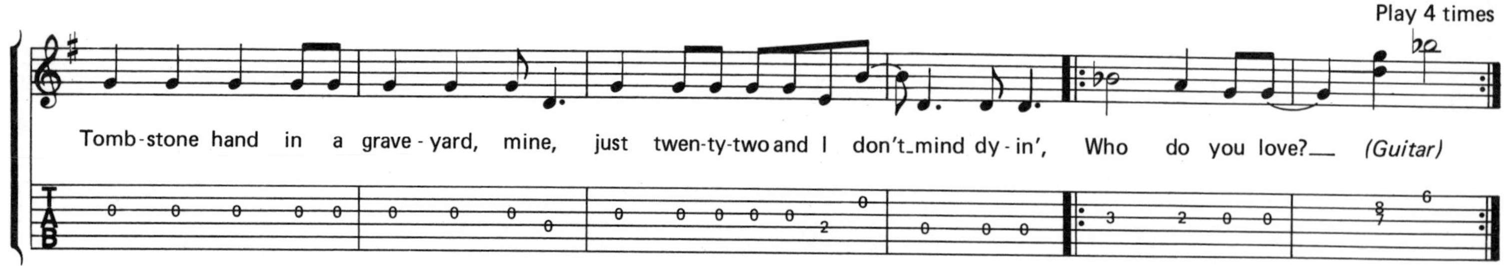

2. I rode a lion to town, used a rattlesnake whip.
   Take it easy, Arlene, don't give me no lip.
   Who do you love? *(4 times)*

3. Night was dark when the sky was blue,
   down the alley a ice-wagon flew.
   Hit a bump and somebody screamed.
   You shoulda heard just what I seen.
   Who do you love? *(4 times)*

4. Arlene took me by my hand,
   she says, "Oo-wee, Bo, you know I understand."
   Who do you love? *(4 times)*

WOOLY BULLY

Words and Music by
DOMINGO SAMUDIO

2. Hatty told Matty, "Let's don't take no chance.
Let's not be L-seven, come and learn to dance."
Wooly bully, wooly bully, wooly bully, wooly bully, wooly bully.

3. Matty told Hatty," That's the thing to do.
Get you someone really to pull the wool with you."
Wooly bully, wooly bully, wooly bully, wooly bully, wooly bully.

WORDS OF LOVE

Words and Music by
BUDDY HOLLY

A
D
E
(Guitar)
D.S. al Coda
(2nd verse)
CODA
Repeat and Fade
Mm.
Mm.

YEAR OF THE CAT

Words and Music by
AL STEWART and PETER WOOD

Cmaj7
D
Em
Cmaj7
D
Em
(Instrumental)
Cmaj7
Em
Am7
D7
D
She
Well, she
B
C
G
D
B
looks at you so cool - ly, and her eyes shine like the moon in the sea. She comes in in-cense and patch -
C
G
F
C/E
D
Tacet
ou - li, so you take her to find what's wait - ing in - side the year of the
Cmaj7
D
Em
Cmaj7
D
Em
cat. (Instrumental)
Cmaj7
D
Em
Am7
D7
D.S. (3rd verse), Fade on instrumental
Well,

YAKETY YAK

Words and Music by
JERRY LEIBER and MIKE STOLLER

2. Just finish cleaning up your room.
Let's see that dust fly with that broom.
Get all that garbage out of sight,
Or you don't go out Friday night.
Yakety yak! (Don't talk back!)

3. You just put on your coat and hat,
And walk yourself to the laundrymat.
And when you finish doing that,
Bring in the dog and put out the cat.
Yakety yak! (Don't talk back!)

4. Don't you give me no dirty looks,
Your father's hip, he knows what cooks.
Just tell your hoodlum friends outside,
You ain't got time to take a ride.
Yakety yak! (Don't talk back!)
Yakety yak, yakety yak! (Repeat and Fade)

YOU REALLY GOT ME

Words and Music by
RAY DAVIES

YOU GIVE LOVE A BAD NAME

Words and Music by DESMOND CHILD,
JON BON JOVI and RICHIE SAMBORRA

Medium Rock
Strum Pattern: No. 1
Capo: Up Three Frets (Actual Key: Cm)

D Am G
Oh, you're a load - ed gun.
Oh, there's no - where to run,
D E Am F G Am F G
no one can save me, the dam - age is done.
Shot through the heart and you're to blame.
You give love a
C(no3rd) Am F G Am F G C(no3rd) Am
bad name, bad name. I play my part and you play your game.
You give love a bad name, bad name. Oh,
F G
you give love,
1
a bad name.
2
Am F G Am
Shot through the heart and you're to blame.
F G C(no3rd) Am F G Am F G
You give love a bad name, bad name. I play my part and you play your game.
You give love a
C(no3rd) Am F G C(no3rd) Am F G C(no3rd) Am
bad name, bad name.
You give love,
you give love
a bad name.
Repeat and Fade
TAB

YOU'RE NO GOOD

Words and Music by
CLINT BALLARD, JR.

Medium Rock
Strum Pattern: No. 1 or 2
Capo: Up One Fret (Actual Key: B m)

Am7 D Am7 D | Am D Am D

Feel-in' bet - ter, now that we're through.
broke a heart that's gen - tle and true. Well, I

Am D Am D F G C

Feel-in' bet - ter 'cause I'm o - ver you. I learned my les - son; it left a scar.
broke a heart o - ver some-one like you. I'll beg his for - give - ness on bend - ed knee.

Am D E Am D Am D

Now I see how you real - ly are, you're no good, you're no good, you're no good, ba - by, you're no good.
I would-n't blame him if he said to me,

Am D Am D Am D Am D

I'm gon-na say it a - gain. You're no good, you're no good, you're no good, ba - by, you're no good.

To Coda

1. Am D Am D | 2. Am

I

Tacet

Am D F7 Am D F7

(Guitar solo continues through next section)

Am
D
F7
F
G
Csus
E7
I'm tell - in' you, don't blame me and I'm
(put-ting you down, ba - by)
go - in' my way.__ For - get a - bout you ba - by, 'cause I'm leav - in' to stay,__ you're no good,
D.S. al Coda
CODA
Tacet
Oh,__ oh,__ no,__ you're no good,__ you're no good,__ you're no good,__ ba - by, you're no__ good.
C
(Guitar solo continues through next section)
C/G
Repeat and Fade

YOU TURN ME ON

By IAN WHITCOMB

Steady, Moderate Shuffle Beat
Strum Pattern: No. 11
Capo: Up One Fret (Actual Key: F)